Introduction to
Feminist Therapy
Strategies for Social and Individual Change

Kathy M. Evans
University of South Carolina

Elizabeth Ann Kincade
Indiana University of Pennsylvania

Susan Rachael Seem
The College at Brockport, State University of New York

In keeping with the egalitarian stance of feminist therapy, all authors of this text equally contributed to the text. The order of the authors' names was determined alphabetically.

Los Angeles | London | New Delhi
Singapore | Washington DC

For information:

SAGE Publications, Inc.
2455 Teller Road
Thousand Oaks,
    California 91320
E-mail: order@sagepub.com

SAGE Publications Ltd.
1 Oliver's Yard
55 City Road
London EC1Y 1SP
United Kingdom

SAGE Publications India Pvt. Ltd.
B 1/I 1 Mohan Cooperative
    Industrial Area
Mathura Road, New Delhi 110 044
India

SAGE Publications Asia-Pacific Pte. Ltd.
33 Pekin Street #02-01
Far East Square
Singapore 048763

Printed in the United States of America.

Library of Congress Cataloging-in-Publication Data

Evans, Kathy M.
Introduction to feminist therapy : strategies for social and individual change / Kathy M. Evans, Elizabeth Ann Kincade, Susan Rachael Seem.
       p. cm.
Includes bibliographical references and index.
ISBN 978-1-4129-1536-6 (cloth) — ISBN 978-1-4129-1537-3 (pbk.)
   1. Feminism. 2. Feminist therapy. 3. Feminist therapy—Moral and ethical aspects. I. Kincade, Elizabeth Ann. II. Seem, Susan R. III. Title.

HQ1155.E93 2011
305.42—dc22   2010015053

This book is printed on acid-free paper.

10   11   12   13   14   10   9   8   7   6   5   4   3   2   1

Acquisitions Editor:	Kassie Graves
Editorial Assistant:	Veronica Novak
Production Editor:	Karen Wiley
Copy Editor:	Sheree Van Vreede
Typesetter:	C&M Digitals (P) Ltd.
Proofreader:	Caryne Brown
Indexer:	Holly Day
Cover Designer:	Candice Harman
Marketing Manager:	Stephanie Adams

CONTENTS

PREFACE

Although feminist therapy is often considered a newcomer to the spectrum of therapeutic modalities, it has a long history. From its inception, feminist therapy has incorporated psychology of women, developmental research, cognitive-behavioral techniques, multicultural awareness, and social action in a coherent, theoretical, and therapeutic package. Although originally conceived as a modality for women only, feminist therapy has evolved to include effective interventions for women, children, and men. In fact, in recent years, standard counseling and psychological theory texts (e.g., Corey, Corsini, & Sharf) have added feminist therapy as a critical theoretical orientation.

Most texts on feminist therapy focus on theoretical issues and on specific clinical issues encountered by women, for example, rape and sexual abuse. Information in these texts is mainly theoretical with skill sets and techniques tacked on at the end of chapters or as addenda. Thus, there is a definite void in the feminist therapy literature on skills and application. This text fills this gap by providing discussions of specific skills and techniques. Additionally, skills and techniques are illustrated in case examples and in critical case studies.

Becoming a feminist therapist is more than thinking about feminist concepts and gender equality while working with clients. It is more than using specific feminist strategies, like gender-role analysis, with clients. It is more than being a woman therapist who works solely with female clients. It is more than being supportive of gender-free behaviors for men and women. Feminist therapy is feminist theory in action in the helping professions. It is about working with our clients so that they can achieve their greatest possible potential as individuals and as members of a world society.

The more conventional counseling and therapy approaches focus primarily on the individual, rather than on the individual as a member of a particular culture at a particular time within a particular sociopolitical context. These conventional approaches rarely consider that the therapeutic enterprise is a part of the larger social–political context and tend to conceptualize and treat clients as encapsulated individuals, separate from the society and its structures. As a result, when the social–political context is not considered, therapeutic approaches unconsciously replicate the dominant culture's beliefs about the way the world should work and the ways in which men and women should be and behave. Feminist therapy seeks to avoid this error and the erroneous thoughts, actions, and feelings that can flow from it. Feminist therapists closely examine the belief systems of their cultures and ask how these deeply embedded beliefs may harm, as well as help, clients achieve what is best for them and their society.

More than any other therapeutic approach, feminist therapy requires us to question and challenge the dominant therapeutic paradigms, especially as they relate to gender and power. We recognize that this is not easy. These paradigms are deeply ingrained in our interactions both in and out of our counseling offices. For instance, most therapeutic modalities view the therapeutic enterprise as having an expert (therapist) and a nonexpert (client). This is not just an assumption of the specific therapeutic work but is a belief embedded in Western culture. Mental health practitioners are the helpers, and clients are the helpees. Clients are in a one-down position from the therapist who is assumed to be more "whole." Therapy often resembles a parental relationship with the client in the child role or as a teacher/learner relationship.

Feminist therapists question where and how this expert, or one-up/one-down model of therapeutic helping, became entrenched in our work. We question whether this and other unconscious oppressive beliefs are part of our own belief system and/or reflect dominant values and beliefs (e.g., definitions of mental health and pathology). We look at our own lives and beliefs as well as the lives and beliefs of our clients. The process of ongoing examination of self and of the dominant culture and its structures is an essential part of effective feminist therapy. Being or becoming a feminist therapist transforms your work with your clients and your life outside the office. Feminist therapy envisions different ways of being in the world and through this perspective envisions societal, as well as individual, transformation.

● BEING A FEMINIST THERAPIST

Being a feminist therapist entails adopting a feminist set of values and assumptions that guide your work. The authors do not believe that it is possible to practice feminist therapy without being a feminist. However, those who do not identify with feminism, or have not yet explored what it means to be a feminist, can certainly use feminist therapeutic techniques and provide nonsexist or gender-free effective therapy. We do believe that learning feminist therapy leads to being a feminist therapist. As you explore more about feminist therapy, you will gain awareness of existing oppressions. You will gain an understanding of power and privilege in cultures, especially the knowledge that the dominant cultures use their power to support and help those like themselves and most often to the detriment of those different from the dominant culture. You will learn that those who are dissimilar from the dominant culture often live in oppressive circumstances that are harmful to their mental health and emotional growth.

Being a feminist therapist is about a way of being in the world, as well as a way of being a mental health practitioner. It is about holding a set of beliefs that helps you make the connections that are necessary in order to live the change you advocate for your clients. It means being a social change agent. Being a feminist therapist means that you cannot be one way as a practitioner and then close the office door and become someone else. It means striving to be consistent in your beliefs in all aspects of your life. Learning to do feminist therapy and/or becoming a feminist therapist is a transformative experience for both the client *and* the mental health practitioner.

ABOUT THIS TEXT ●

This text is a practical manual of feminist therapy. Theory is discussed and informs the techniques taught and presented, but feminist therapy skills are the main focus of the text. Most texts on feminist therapy describe theoretical dilemmas, discuss treatment of women's issues and feminist therapy, or recount therapists' and clients' experiences. This text is a "how-to approach" to feminist therapy. Counseling and psychology students and the participants in our workshops express an interest in feminist therapy but come to us without the knowledge of how to translate theory into practice. This text provides answers to the question, "Yes, but how do I do that?"

The first four chapters cover theory, history, basic tenets of feminist therapy, ethical issues in feminist therapy, and gender-role theory and research.

Chapter 1 covers the origins of feminist therapy starting from the grassroots feminist movement and consciousness-raising groups to the current efforts for greater inclusion of women of color and other oppressed groups.

Chapter 2 presents the basic tenets of feminist therapy and the focus of feminist practice today. It explores the challenges of feminist therapy to mainstream psychology and counseling. It addresses the notion of what it means to be a feminist therapist as opposed to one who uses feminist techniques or gender-fair practices.

Chapter 3 reviews various ethical principles for the mental health professions and specific issues faced by feminist therapists. The Feminist Therapy Institute Code of Ethics is introduced and discussed. Several ethical dilemmas are included for review and discussion. This is a critical chapter in the book as it introduces some of the differences between the practice of feminist therapy and the practice of the more established therapeutic orientations. The concepts of societal good and individual good and the intersection between the two are introduced.

Chapter 4 examines the social construction of gender as a major force in human development. Gender roles are defined as sociocultural learned constructs. Research supporting this view is presented. An understanding of how we "do gender" and learn what it means to be female or male is essential to effective use of the feminist therapy skills identified in Chapters 5–9.

Beginning with Chapter 5, the text focuses on five essential skills that distinguish feminist therapy from other therapeutic modalities. These chapters include case examples, dialogues, and opportunities for readers to apply the skill through skill-specific exercises and case examples.

In Chapter 5, the skill of *mental health diagnosis from a feminist perspective* is presented. The use of the DSM-IV-TR and its predecessors, as well as the history of psychiatric diagnosis, are discussed with reference to gender bias and power. Assessment from a feminist perspective is illustrated. The gender/racial biases of common diagnostic systems are discussed. Information on how to use traditional methods of diagnosis and labeling with the least harm (i.e., abuse of power) to the client are discussed through case example and case studies.

In Chapter 6, readers are coached in the skill of feminist conceptualization. Statistics on women and psychological illness are put into societal perspective with regard to gender roles. Dialogues between client and counselor illustrating the skill are presented. Finally, a case study is included that illustrates the challenges one of the authors experienced in assessment with her client.

Chapter 7 introduces the skill of establishing and maintaining egalitarian relationships. The importance of establishing the relationship and its impact on the success of the clinical endeavor are presented. The specific steps necessary for defining and establishing egalitarian relationships with clients are given. The challenges to these types of relationships, including the inherent power of the therapist and racial and cultural issues that influence power, are presented. The chapter includes client–therapist interactions and how these interactions help or hinder the egalitarian relationship. The therapist's view of challenges experienced in establishing an egalitarian relationship and how these are handled is presented.

Chapter 8 presents the dual skill set of gender-role analysis and power analysis. These two types of analyses are essential to the practice of feminist therapy. It is primarily these interventions that differentiate feminist therapy from other theoretical models. Examples of how mental health practitioners use these to expand client awareness of societal factors and beliefs about gender that hamper the development of mental health are presented and explored. Dialogues between client and counselor serve to illustrate the use of these skills in clinical settings.

Chapter 9 presents two related concepts that are powerful interventions for client change—involvement in social action and client empowerment. Advocating social action as a technique for increasing mental health and preventing future problems is discussed first. The chapter briefly explains the theoretical rationale behind social action as a therapeutic technique (empowerment/self-efficacy). Because social action and social justice are the focus of a new direction in counseling and psychology, we address how feminist therapy has led the way in the helping professions in these areas and meets the guidelines and criteria for a social justice approach to counseling and psychotherapy. Examples of how mental health professionals use this skill to promote and maintain increased client self-esteem/self-efficacy are given. Examples of dialogues between client and counselor illustrating the complementary nature of advocating for social change and client empowerment (individual change) are presented.

Chapters 10 and 11 seek to focus readers on their own practice of counseling and/or therapy. In Chapter 10, we recognize the common factors of theoretical models and discuss strategies for integration of feminist theory and techniques with other therapeutic models. The flexibility of feminist theory and therapy is discussed. The blending of feminist therapy techniques with other theoretical modalities and perspectives is presented (variations of feminist therapy that are based in other perspectives: psychodynamic feminist work, family feminist therapy work, and so on). Additionally, techniques from other modalities that are compatible with feminist therapy theory and practice are discussed. We offer guidelines for mental health practitioners to consider when they are considering combining feminist therapy with other therapies.

In Chapter 11, we present critical cases with clients with difficult issues and how the tenets and skills of feminist therapy were applied to these cases. In addition, this chapter provides readers with a series of vignettes and thought-provoking exercises and questions that will help them consolidate their knowledge of feminist therapy.

Overall, our goals in writing this book are to demystify the feminist therapeutic process and educate students and experienced counselors and therapists in the skills needed to become practitioners of feminist therapy.

Whether or not becoming a feminist therapist is your desire, it is our hope that you will find the information you glean from reading this book useful for your work with a wide diversity of clients regardless of gender.

Please note: In keeping with the egalitarian stance of feminist therapy, all authors equally contributed to the text. The order of authors' names was determined alphabetically.

ACKNOWLEDGMENTS

Kathy M. Evans: My portion of the book could not have been completed without the help, support, and understanding of my two coauthors, Elizabeth and Susan. All of us are dedicated professionals experiencing what it means to be women in this society. My graduate assistants over the years have been invaluable, Matthew Lemberger, Alexanderia Smith, and Tonya Jasinski. I also want to acknowledge the Educational Studies Department at the University of South Carolina who granted my graduate assistants extra hours to work with me on this project. Finally, I want to thank all of my friends who may be happier than I am that this project has been completed. Kassie Graves has been phenomenally patient and supportive of our project and we are truly grateful for her.

Elizabeth Ann Kincade: The support and encouragement of Gary, my significant other, inspired me throughout my portion of this book. My writing partners, Kathy and Susan, have been models of feminist support throughout the writing process. I also want to thank Indiana University of Pennsylvania, which valued the topic enough to grant me a sabbatical leave in support of the project. Kassie Graves and Veronica Novak, at SAGE, stood by all of us when life, work, and political events took control of our time. I want to thank them for their belief in the project and for helping the project become a book.

Susan Rachael Seem: My long-term friendship with Elizabeth Kincade and Kathy Evans provided me with an avenue to expressing my feminist voice and for that I am eternally grateful. Their belief in this book and trust in feminist process were invaluable throughout this writing experience. I want to thank The College at Brockport and the Department of Counselor Education which gave me support throughout this process. I especially want to thank my colleagues, Dr. Tom Hernandez and Dr. Muhyi Shakoor, whose utter belief in who I am and what I do continues to provide me with a safe haven in a sometimes not-so-friendly world. Finally, I want to thank Kassie Graves and the staff at SAGE whose belief in this project and patience with us was unfailingly present.

CHAPTER 1

FEMINIST THERAPY: ROOTS AND BRANCHES

Feminist therapy, like many movements and concerns focused on a revisioning of society, is grounded in history and theory. In the current therapeutic climate of empirically validated treatments and evidence-based practice, we believe it is necessary to understand the roots of feminist therapy theory and practice, the context in which these developed, and the manner in which they continue to flourish.

Contemporary feminist therapy grew out of the Women's Movement of the 1960s. This began as a grassroots movement—a social and political movement that grew out of the dissatisfaction of common women in everyday life. To this day, feminist therapy seeks to remain true to these roots and to be relevant to a wide spectrum of concerns and clients. It is also important to understand that the modern women's movement is well grounded in feminist theory, the philosophical belief system that underlies feminism. Feminist theory is a philosophical point of view with a history reaching back more than 150 years. Feminism as a political-activist movement developed from the experiences of women, in their daily lived experiences in love and work. We acknowledge that because of social, political, and economic factors, the feminist movement was initially based on the experiences of middle-class, majority-culture (e.g., White) women. This is an artifact of the dominant cultural paradigm. Women from lower socioeconomic backgrounds and from oppressed ethnic cultural backgrounds did not have the time or resources to ponder and seek to change their sociopolitical status. They focused on daily survival for themselves and their families. In an ironic twist, it was the male, middle-class domination of the sociopolitical sphere that allowed middle-class, majority-culture women the "privilege" to develop feminist consciousness. Unfortunately, middle-class, majority women did not immediately apply their feminist consciousness of oppression to their sisters who experienced multiple oppressions. We will discuss this in more detail as we examine the history or rather *her-story* of feminist therapy.

The authors view feminist therapy as a therapy focused on eliminating oppressions, both internal and external, for all people—not just for women. Throughout this book we make the case for feminist therapy as transformation on both individual and cultural levels. However, feminist therapy *did* begin as a therapeutic stance for women that privileged women's experience. This stands in direct contrast to previous therapeutic frameworks that privileged men's experience and then attempted to fit women's experience into those frameworks. In understanding the history and context of feminist therapy, it is important to understand feminist philosophy and feminism as privileging women's experience.

● FEMINISM AND FEMINIST PHILOSOPHY

First, it is important to understand the concept of feminism and feminist philosophy because misconceptions about feminism abound. Quite simply, feminism is a social movement to end sexism and sexist oppression (hooks, 1984). Dictionaries agree on a fairly simple definition: "a belief in the social, political, and economic equality of the sexes" (*American Heritage Dictionary,* 2006). An early but still important work on feminism, psychology, and therapy (Mander & Rush, 1974) stated that feminism is about making connections— between feelings and experiences and political context, between personal and economic power, between feelings and theories, between domestic oppression and labor exploitation, and between inner psychological worlds and outside worlds. Feminism provides a lens through which a woman can understand her experience. It allows her to make a connection between what she believes is her individual situation and pain to the larger world in which she lives and which expects her to behave in certain ways regardless of her needs and wants, skills, and abilities.

Feminist philosophy and theory looks closely at power structures in society. For example, all inequities are assumed to be based on institutionalized power. Those who have this power in the United States are generally White, middle-to-upper-class, heterosexual, Christian, able-bodied males.

Discrimination and oppression occur against those without such power, for example, women, racial/ethnic minorities, lower and poor classes, sexual minorities, non-Christian, and non–ablebodied people. The common theme that runs through feminism is the need for social change and the use of power analysis of the dominant culture in order to understand what needs to be done to achieve this change.

WOMEN'S LIBERATION AND ●
THE FEMINIST MOVEMENT

The Women's Liberation Movement emerged during the politically charged 1960s and certainly challenged the gender status quo of that era. However, the seed for what is commonly called the Second Wave of United States Feminism began in the 1940s and 1950s (Sturdivant, 1980). First, World War II led to a shortage of male workers in all fields. Women filled these positions, from factory workers to baseball players to bank administrators. Second, by the end of the 1950s, middle-class White women—many of whom had been professionally employed 15 years earlier or had role models from that era— became disenchanted with the cultural myth of that period that endorsed marriage and children as the only fulfillment of a women's role in life. This was exemplified in the book *The Feminine Mystique* (Friedan, 1963). Finally, the Civil Rights Movement of the 1960s led many to question the United States's value system. Social protest against social inequality began to cut across race and class lines. The Civil Rights Movement called into question the United States's support of a single set of values based on White, middle-class people (Boyd, 1990). This set of values did not acknowledge or support ethnic diversity. Thus, the Civil Rights Movement raised the dominant society's consciousness. Women were strong supporters of, and participants in, the Civil Rights Movement. This participation led women to become aware of their own oppression and to question the gender status quo. In 1966, the National Organization for Women (NOW) was formed to address the legal and economic equality of women. As a result of these social factors, the second wave of feminism began. This second wave of feminism is what most of us are familiar with as the Women's Liberation Movement.

Feminism asks that individuals carefully examine their adherence to dominant cultural assumptions that might be harmful to others. Since the early 1980s, contemporary feminists have examined feminism itself and have asked the following question: What dominant cultural assumptions may be entrenched in feminist theory and practice? Out of this self-reflection grew the awareness that feminism is not a unitary movement, nor does it have to be. To be effective as both a social and an individual change mechanism, feminism must be inclusive. It must recognize that diversity is strength rather than weakness. Current feminist theoreticians embrace multiple points of view under the "feminist" umbrella and talk about feminisms rather than feminism. These feminisms look at a multiplicity of paths leading to a more egalitarian society for all genders. They acknowledge that women are not a monolithic grouping and that power and status inequities exist across women of differing social positions (Brown, 1994; Enns, 1992; Worell & Remer, 2003). Contemporary feminism considers not only the diversity of women's experiences but also the diversity of human experience. This diversity can best be understood by examining the different ways in which feminisms view the cause and cure of oppression.

● FEMINISMS: A DIVERSITY OF POSITIONS

Commonly accepted positions within feminism are as follows: (a) liberal or reformist, (b) radical, (c) socialist, (d) women of color or womanism, and (e) cultural. Each one will be outlined briefly in the following discussion. The annotated bibliography provides more information about the theorists and writers in these areas.

Liberal or reformist feminism (Brown, 1994; Crawford & Unger, 2000; Enns, 1992, 1993; Evans, Kincade, & Seem, 2005; Sturdivant, 1980; Worell & Remer, 2003) views women's oppression as a result of sexism. Sexism involves constraints on individuals with regard to gender-role socialization, culture, laws, and economics. These constraints are primarily focused on women and limit women's opportunities and roles. In liberal feminism, gender is the only important category of political analysis. This perspective tends to exclude other variables, such as class, ability, sexual orientation, and race/ethnicity, all of which could be more important than gender regarding human experiences of power and oppression (Brown, 1994). In liberal or reformist feminism, the solution to women's oppression is to reform the system by changing laws, politics, and educational and employment arrangements to guarantee equal rights for women. This perspective informed the move for an Equal Rights Amendment in the United States. It is the philosophy behind gender equality in sports (Title IX legislation) and nonsexist hiring practices in the workplace.

Radical feminism (Brown, 1994; Crawford & Unger, 2000; Enns, 1992, 1993; Evans, Kincade, & Seem, 2005; Worell & Remer, 2003) views women's oppression as embedded in the patriarchy or the unequal allocation of power to men in our society. Gender-based oppression is perceived as the most basic and pervasive form of oppression and, as such, is common to all women.

Radical feminists believe that the unequal allocation of power leads to institutionalized male domination, heterosexism, and violence. Instead of working within the system to change laws as liberal feminists would do, radical feminists believe that the liberation of women requires the total transformation of patriarchy (male-privileged culture) and advocate altering social institutions and relationships. This perspective has led to women-only movements in therapy (Chesler, 1972/2005) as well as to feminist separatist movements.

In contrast with liberal and radical feminists, *socialist feminists* (Crawford & Unger, 2000; Enns, 1992, 1993; Evans, Kincade, & Seem, 2005; Sturdivant, 1980) believe that oppression is a product of both gender and socioeconomic class. Other categories of inequity, such as race/ethnicity, sexual orientation, ability, and other minority statuses, are also considered important as they are often interwoven into class structures. In fact, multiple oppressions are viewed as inseparable and caused by the impact of gender-role socialization, institutionalized control of reproduction and sexuality (the refusal of insurance to reimburse for birth control prescriptions), the structure of production (gender roles in paid and unpaid employment), and the capitalistic socioeconomic paradigm. Socialist feminists believe that capitalism, the dominant socioeconomic paradigm, upholds a patriarchal system and precludes any lasting change. Restructuring life, both publicly and privately, is the source of liberation. Thus, socialist feminists call for dramatic changes to the dominant socioeconomic paradigm (capitalism) in order to end multiple oppressions and the patriarchal system that benefits from them.

Women of color feminism or womanism (Brown, 1994; Crawford & Unger, 2000; Evans, Kincade, Marbley, & Seem, 2005; Worell & Remer, 2003) challenges other feminists' belief that gender is the only salient category of oppression and insists that the experiences of White women cannot be generalized to the lives of women of color. Womanism identifies institutional racism as a major source of women's oppression and, in general, does not view men of color as sexist oppressors but as co-victims of racism. Womanism focuses its attention on the impact of the combined forces of race/ethnicity and gender not only on women's and men's experiences but also on the entire culture. Liberation occurs through the elimination of White privilege, respect for the values and cultures of people of color, and the elimination of both institutionalized racism and sexism.

Cultural feminism (Enns, 1992, 1993; Evans, Kincade, & Seem, 2005; Sturdivant, 1980; Worell & Remer, 2003) acknowledges differences between women and men and attends to women's unique strengths. Because women's oppression is rooted in the devaluation of women's relational strengths, this perspective seeks to honor women's abilities to be emotionally intuitive, cooperative, altruistic, and communal. The solution to women's oppression lies in the feminization of the culture so that both men and women's ways of being are valued.

Despite the diversity of feminisms, two common themes unite all the feminisms (Crawford & Unger, 2000). All feminisms highly value women's experience and women. All also recognize the need for social change. Because feminisms focus on the social contexts of women's lives, changing social systems and equalizing power are considered necessary to ending all forms of domination, subjugation, and oppression in a patriarchal society. In sum, feminist philosophies focus on the social and political context of women's lives and promote social change, rather than individual adjustment to the status quo, as a way to improve lives and mental health (Rawlings, 1993).

The various forms of feminism as articulated earlier are closely connected to the practice of feminist therapy. Feminist therapy is grounded in two beliefs. First, women's lived experiences and the context of those experiences are important to both women and their therapists and are prioritized in therapy. Second, societal change is necessary for lasting individual change and growth. Contemporary feminist therapists recognize that gender and gender roles are important aspects of the lives of all individuals and underlie the foundations of many contemporary institutions. It is not only women who are impacted. As contemporary feminist therapists, we speak about the focus on the lived experiences of human beings in a society within inflexible and often unconscious gender roles and the need for social change to impact emotional health for both individuals and cultures. Next we turn to the *development of contemporary feminist therapy.*

● PRECURSORS OF FEMINIST THERAPY

Perhaps, the most long-lasting statement from the second wave of feminism of the 1960s and 1970s was the adage that *the personal is the political.* This statement challenged women and men to consider that their personal lives reflected the values and politics of the culture and that the values and politics of the culture also impacted their personal lives. Breaking from traditional ways of thinking about women and men in one's personal life was a political act as well as a personal act. From this mode of thinking arose consciousness-raising (CR) groups.

The Women's Liberation Movement had two major aims (Rosenthal, 1984): (a) to change the social and economic conditions of women and (b) to change individuals. CR groups linked these two goals. Women met in small, leaderless groups to discuss their personal experiences, that is, to bring into their consciousness awareness of problems and issues that had a political as well as a personal context. As women in these groups discovered the similarity of their experiences and concerns, they began to understand that their individual experiences were a result of the condition of women in society and not of their individual failure. Personal experiences were analyzed in political terms (Sturdivant, 1980). The objective of CR groups was to empower women to take social action. Psychological healing was an unintended by-product brought about as members' social isolation decreased and they became aware of their oppression and own internalized sexist beliefs about women's inferiority. This empowered women to think differently about their abilities and their self-worth (Sturdivant, 1980).

On the political level, CR groups developed an analysis of society based on female experience, thus connecting the personal to the political through the sharing of women's stories (Sturdivant, 1980). As a grassroots organization, the Women's Liberation Movement believed that CR groups would create the revolutionary politics necessary for mass, social action (Rosenthal, 1984; Sturdivant, 1980). Women would work together to find solutions to their common problem, oppression.

The norms of CR groups were feminist: a collective structure; the equal sharing of power, responsibility, and resources; the focus on social conditioning and social problems as the roots of women's distress; and women's commonalities (Enns, 1993). Groups were leaderless; each woman was considered an expert about herself and able to help others as much as others aided her. Women's experiences and truths were valued and respected. Although feminists acknowledged that participation in CR groups could be therapeutic, they did not regard CR groups as therapy (Sturdivant, 1980). Therapy meant that the individual was the patient and was sick. Rather, feminists believed that society was the sick patient and that social change was the cure. In sum, feminism and CR groups challenged the traditional assumptions of counseling and psychology and therapy practice and were the precursors of feminist therapy. Both CR groups and feminist therapy were predicated on the belief that women's problems were contextual, not individual, and political, not personal, pathology (Brown, 1994; Collins, 2002; Sturdivant, 1980; Enns, 1992, 1993, 1997; Evans, Kincade, et al., 2005; Worell & Remer, 2003).

FEMINIST CHALLENGES TO ●
TRADITIONAL COUNSELING AND PSYCHOTHERAPY

Freudian theory strongly influenced psychotherapeutic practice during the first 70 years of the last century. Feminists criticized Freudian theory in three major areas (Sturdivant, 1980): (a) its belief in intrapsychic causation of problems, (b) its failure to recognize the impact of sociocultural factors on development, and (c) its sex bias in using male standards as the norm for mental health. Feminist critics of psychotherapeutic practice argued that differing social and gender roles were a result of socialization and institutionalized gender bias, not biology, and that intrapsychic conflict and pain were a result of sexism or the mismatch with socially prescribed gender roles and role conflict, not individual pathology. The feminist critique of Freudian theory focused on its intrapsychic focus, failure to recognize sociopolitical context, and andocentric norms of health.

When the early feminist critics of counseling and psychotherapy looked carefully at the techniques and theories of the time, they focused on the following three areas: (a) the mechanism of control, (b) the failure to acknowledge the impact of context on individual lives, and (c) the androcentrism of psychological theories that underlie psychotherapy. Much research indicates that these failures resulted in a double standard of mental health for women. See Sturdivant (1980) for an excellent review of this research. For our purposes, two critical pieces of research will be discussed.

The Broverman, Broverman, Clarkson, Rosenkrantz, and Vogel study in 1970 was a groundbreaking piece of research. Prior to this time, differential standards of mental health for men and women had not been investigated. These researchers asked mental health workers (i.e., psychologists, psychiatrists, and social workers) to evaluate mental health for men and women on a 122-item questionnaire. They hypothesized that (a) clinical judgments of the characteristics of a healthy, mature individual would differ based on the sex of the person judged and that (b) behavioral characteristics that were regarded as healthy for an adult, sex unspecified, would be more often regarded as healthy for men than for women (i.e., following societal, stereotypic gender-role differences). A high degree of consensus among participants about the qualities characterizing mature, healthy adults (sex unspecified), healthy men, and healthy women was found and did differ as a function of the sex of the person judged. Clinicians' judgments of male mental health did not differ significantly from those held for adults (sex unspecified), whereas judgments of health for women differed significantly from those viewed for healthy males and healthy adults. These differences corresponded with societal gender-role stereotypes for men and women held during that time. For example, mentally healthy women were described as differing from both healthy men and healthy adults in that they were characterized as more emotional, submissive, less independent, and less objective. The authors concluded that a double standard of mental health existed. Men could be perceived as mentally healthy adults, whereas women could not. For a woman to be viewed as mentally healthy by mental health professionals, she needed to be perceived as feminine and not adult-like (i.e., not male-like).

In the mid-1970s, the American Psychological Association (APA), based on input from women psychologists, as well as on concerns for consumers of psychological services, formed the Task Force on Sex Bias and Sex Role Stereotyping in Psychotherapeutic Practice. In 1975 they published their report and recommendations. Three primary areas of sex bias were found: (a) fostering of traditional sex roles, (b) bias in expectations and devaluations of women, and (c) responding to women as sex objects, including seduction of female clients. This task force clearly found that when traditional sex roles were fostered within a psychotherapeutic environment, sociocultural factors in women's problems were not acknowledged and therapy operated as a means of social control. For example, women wishing to explore career options in a traditional male field might be influenced by the counselor's belief system about male and female career roles. Furthermore, psychological interpretations were used to divert attention from the possibilities of social causation. This document marked a significant change in the field of psychology. Prior to this report, feminist critique had not been an accepted part of the mainstream of psychological culture. Guidelines for working with nonsexist psychotherapeutic practice were developed and are still in use (APA, 2007; Fitzgerald & Nutt, 1986).

CHALLENGES TO FEMINIST THERAPY ●

Although feminist theory and philosophy as well as feminist therapy have always prized nondominant realities and values in its vision, early on it was largely a White, middle-class, women's endeavor (Boyd, 1990; Brown, 1991, 1994; Brown & Brodsky, 1992; Worell & Remer, 2003). The consideration of cultural diversity in prevalence, etiology, diagnosis, and treatment was noticeably missing in the early years of feminist therapy (Brown & Brodsky, 1992; Brown & Root, 1990; Evans, Kincade, et al., 2005; Greene, 1994; Sturdivant, 1980; Worell & Remer, 2003). During the 1970s, when feminist therapy was first articulated, gender was viewed as the most salient feature of oppression. Societal privileges enjoyed by White women made it difficult, if not impossible, for them to see how they benefited from the White power structure and thus made them largely insensitive to multiple oppressions (Brown, 1994; Enns, 1993; Espin & Gawelek, 1992; Greene, 1994). Ironically, what feminists charged men with doing—ignoring male privilege—was what White feminists did with women of color—denying White privilege. As a result, most of the first 20 years of feminist therapy ignored the contributions of therapists and theorists of color, the working class, and other oppressed groups (Brown, 1994). In fact, White lesbians have been the only marginalized group that has been consistently included in feminist therapy and theory from the beginning (Brown & Brodsky, 1992).

Marginalized groups challenged feminist therapy in the same manner that White feminist therapists challenged traditional therapy and theory. African American women confronted White feminists who viewed White women's problems as analogous to the African American experience. White feminists were also challenged when they assumed that Black women identified more with White women than with Black men (Boyd, 1990; Evans, Kincade, et al., 2005; Greene, 1992). Historically feminism had ignored the history and contributions of women of color and therefore was not perceived as relevant to their lives (Evans, Kincade, et al., 2005). "Women of color view feminism as yet another system in which they have to define and justify their reality, which makes it (feminism) just as oppressive as the traditional sexist patriarchal system" (Boyd, 1990, p. 162). Thus, feminism and feminist therapy are oppressive if presented as another system that defines reality for all women. To be truly representative, feminist theory must be built on the experiences of all women (Barrett, 1990; Brown, 1994; Worell & Remer, 2003). This means understanding that for many women, gender may not be the most salient feature in their lives. "Although sexism affects all women, the way it affects them varies or can be 'colored' by the lens of race and other parameters" (Greene, 1994, p. 337). The salience of gender may be modified, intensified, or transcended by other variables of a woman's life, such as race/ethnicity, class, and sexual orientation (Espin & Gawelek, 1990; Greene, 1992, 1994).

> It has been a struggle for White and/or middle-class feminist therapists to acknowledge that issues of culture (broadly defined here as those of race, class, ethnicity, linguistic affiliation, age, disability, sexual orientation, spiritual affiliation, and appearance) cannot be of less importance in a feminist analysis than gender and that if our theories are to advance social change and undermine the patriarchy we must include all categories in our analysis. (Brown, 1994, p. 70)

The challenge for feminist therapy in the 1990s was to prize all non-dominant realities in its vision (Evans, Kincade, et al., 2005)). In the last 10 to 15 years, much has been written about the inclusion of diversity in feminist therapy (see, e.g., Boyd, 1990; Brown, 1991, 1994; Brown & Brodsky, 1992; Brown & Root, 1990; Chrisler & Howard, 1992; Espin, 1993; Greene, 1994; Landrine, 1995; Worell & Remer, 2003). The challenge in the early 21st century was to put this new theorizing into action in therapeutic practice—to create a more inclusive form of feminism and feminist therapy (Enns, 1997). The current challenge for feminism is to establish itself as an integral part of the therapeutic landscape without losing its emphasis on egalitarianism, the sociopolitical context, and the use of power.

SUMMARY

This chapter presented an overview of feminist therapy's challenges in its movement toward recognition as an established theoretical orientation. From the early years when there was little distinction between political action and therapy to the more recent emphasis on therapeutic techniques, feminist therapy has embraced the importance of women's reality as situated in the sociocultural context.

REFERENCES

American Psychological Association. (2007). *Guidelines for psychological practice with girls and women.* Washington, DC: Author.

APA Task Force on Sex Bias and Sex Role Stereotyping in Psychotherapeutic Practice. (1975). Report of the task force on sex bias and sex role stereotyping in psychotherapeutic practice. *American Psychologist, 30,* 1169–1175.

Barrett, S. E. (1990). Paths towards diversity: An intrapsychic perspective. In L. S. Brown & M. P. P. Root (Eds.), *Diversity and complexity in feminist therapy* (pp. 41–52). New York: Haworth Press.

Boyd, J. A. (1990). Ethnic and cultural diversity: Keys to power. In L. S. Brown & M. P. P. Root (Eds.), *Diversity and complexity in feminist therapy.* New York: Harrington Park.

Broverman, I. K., Broverman, D. M., Clarkson, F. E., Rosenkrantz, P. S., & Vogel, S. (1970). Sex-role stereotypes and clinical judgments of mental health. *Journal of Consulting and Clinical Psychology, 34,* 1–7.

Brown, L. S. (1991). Antiracism as an ethical imperative: An example from feminist therapy. *Ethics & Behavior, 1,* 113–127.

Brown, L. S. (1994). *Subversive dialogues.* New York: Basic Books.

Brown, L. S., & Brodsky, A. M. (1992). The future of feminist therapy. *Psychotherapy, 29,* 51–57.

Brown, L. S., & Root, M. P. P. (Eds.). (1990). *Diversity and complexity in feminist therapy* (pp. 41–52). New York: Haworth Press.

Chesler, P. (2005). *Woman and madness—revised edition.* New York: Palgrave MacMillan. (Original work published 1972)

Chrisler, J. C., & Howard, D. (1992). *New directions in feminist psychology: Practice, theory and research.* New York: Springer.

Collins, K. A. (2002). An examination of feminist psychotherapy in North America in the 1980s. *Guidance and Counselling, 17,* 105–112.

Crawford, M., & Unger, R. R. (2000). *Women and gender: A feminist psychology* (3rd ed.). Boston: McGraw-Hill.

Enns, C. Z. (1992). Toward integrating feminist psychotherapy and feminist philosophy. *Professional Psychology: Research and Practice, 23,* 453–466.

Enns, C. Z. (1993). Twenty years of feminist counseling and therapy: From naming biases to implementing multifaceted practice. *The Counseling Psychologist, 21,* 3–87.

Enns, C. Z. (1997). *Feminist theories and feminist psychotherapies: Origins, themes and variations.* New York: Haworth Press.

Espin, O. M. (1993). Feminist therapy: Not for White women only. *The Counseling Psychologist, 21,* 103–108.

Espin, O. M., & Gawelek, M. A. (1992). Women's diversity: Ethnicity, race, class, and gender in theories of feminist psychology. In L. S. Brown & M. Ballou (Eds.), *Personality and psychopathology: Feminist reappraisals* (pp. 88–107). New York: Guilford.

Evans, K. M., Kincade, E., Marbley, A., & Seem, S. R. (2005). Feminism and feminist therapy: Lessons from the past and hopes for the future. *Journal of Counseling and Development, 83,* 269–277.

Evans, K. M., & Kincade, E. Seem, S. R., (2005). Case approach to feminist therapy. In G. Corey (Ed.), *Case approach to counseling and psychotherapy* (6th ed.) (pp. 208–241). Belmont, CA: Thompson Brooks/Cole.

Fitzgerald, L. F., & Nutt, R. (1986). The Division 17 principles concerning the counseling/psychotherapy of women: Rationale and implementation. *The Counseling Psychologist, 14*(1), 180-216.

Friedan, B. (1963). *The feminine mystique.* New York: W.W. Norton.

Greene, B. (1992). (1992, Summer). African American women: The burden of racism and sexism. *American Family Therapy Academy Newsletter, 48,* 20–23.

Greene, B. (1994). Diversity and difference: The issue of race in feminist therapy. In M. P. Mirkin (Ed.), *Women in context: Toward a feminist reconstruction of psychotherapy* (pp. 333–351). New York: Guilford.

hooks, b. (1984). *Feminist theory: From margin to center.* Boston: South End Press.

Landrine. H. (1995). *Bringing cultural diversity to feminist psychology: Theory, research and practice.* Washington, DC: American Psychological Association.

Mander, A. V., & Rush, A. K. (1974). *Feminism as therapy.* New York: Random House.

Rawlings, E. (1993). Reflections on "Twenty years of feminist counseling and psychotherapy." *The Counseling Psychologist, 21,* 88–91.

Rosenthal, N. B. (1984). Consciousness raising: From revolution to re-evaluation. *Psychology of Women Quarterly, 8,* 309–326.

Sturdivant, S. (1980). *Therapy with women: A feminist philosophy of treatment.* New York: Springer.

The American heritage dictionary (4th ed.). (2006). Boston: Houghton Mifflin.

Worell, J., & Remer, P. (2003). *Feminist perspectives in therapy: Empowering diverse women* (2nd ed.). Hoboken, NJ: John Wiley & Sons.

CHAPTER 2

FEMINIST THERAPY

A Social and Individual Change Model

In the early 1970s, women gathered at university activities centers, church basements, community centers, and each others' homes for consciousness-raising groups where a facilitator might use a prepared list of questions about gender and power or individual women might come with specific questions for the group. At one such meeting, women were asked: "Do you think that what you do with your day is as important as what your husband does with his day?" (Chicago Women's Liberation Union, 1971). The women in the group discussed this among themselves and realized that they often did not feel that what they did and who they were was important. They talked about feeling invisible. As the discussion continued, some realized that even in this one question, societal assumptions were implicit. The question assumed that they all had husbands, wanted husbands, or needed husbands. Conversation flowed from this about societal assumptions and societal power. These women then asked themselves and each other: How have you come to think what you do? Is this the healthiest way to think for you and for the greater society? If not, then how can we change the society, rather than how can we change ourselves to accept what society dictates? How can we help both ourselves and our society become more mentally healthy? These questions formed the beginning of the practice of feminist therapy. For feminist therapy, then as now, consciousness without action does not produce lasting results.

Feminist therapy differed from other emerging therapies with its focus on the dynamic flow between personal consciousness and political consciousness. Before the emergence of feminist therapy, gender and cultural differences and effects were not considered to have a major role in mental health and the therapeutic process. Consider the following statements and think about what therapy would be like if these statements currently held true:

- Therapists support the assumption that women and men have specific roles in society and that neither should venture outside of these roles.
- Rape is considered an act of sexual attraction and not an act of violence and control.
- Involvement in social change endeavors is not considered healing and empowering.
- The focus of therapy is intrapsychic, and the role of the environment in client distress is ignored.
- Clients' problems are attributed to their own weaknesses and shortcomings rather than to their experiences of oppression.
- Clients who choose careers or have interests in nontraditional arenas for their gender are viewed by psychological theories as maladjusted.
- Couple violence is solely a family problem; the female asked for the violence and could leave if she wanted to.
- The standard for a healthy adult is a healthy male; women are deviants from the norm.
- Conceptualizations of families and couples are based on traditional gender roles and expectations and on heterosexual pairings.
- A therapist's responsibility is only to the client, not to society.
- The therapist is the expert regarding the client's problems and treatment.

If you disagree with *any* of these, you are conceptualizing your clients from a nonsexist, contextual, and feminist point of view. You are on your way to being a feminist therapist.

● FEMINIST THERAPY AS A THEORETICAL ORIENTATION

The development of feminist therapy was spurred by the Women's Movement of the mid-20th century: the recognition that the personal is the political, feminist critiques of psychological theory and practice, male domination of the field, and awareness of social roles as social control. In contrast to traditional therapies, no one individual can be identified as the originator of feminist therapy. Rather, feminist therapy developed from the philosophies and principles of the Women's Movement of the 1960s and 1970s. As in that Movement, collectivity and egalitarianism are valued, and no leader or founding parent is identified. Initially, guidance for feminist therapy conceptualization and technique came from consciousness-raising (CR) groups and informal discussions regarding techniques, style, and experiences as women counselors and therapists attempted to apply feminist political principles to therapeutic practice (Brown, 1994; Brown & Brodsky, 1992). These women found that it was not enough to adjust traditional psychotherapeutic theories and techniques to minimize gender bias. For therapy to be effective, the sociocultural and political context had to be acknowledged and discussed as a cause of women's distress (Faunce, 1985). Another important factor was engaging in social change activities (Brown, 1994; Sturdivant, 1980). Thus, feminist therapy includes the philosophy and values of feminism in its therapeutic values and approaches.

COMMON FACTORS IN FEMINIST THERAPY ●

As there is no identified founder, there is also no one true method of feminist therapy. Varied philosophical and theoretical feminist approaches to feminist therapy practice exist (Brown, 1994; Juntunen, Atkinson, Reyes, & Gutierrez, 1994; Wyche & Rice, 1997). Despite the varied approaches to feminist practice, commonalities have been present since beginning of feminist therapy. In 1977, Rawlings and Carter outlined the following common feminist beliefs, attitudes, and values:

1. A feminist therapist does not value an upper- or middle-class client more than a working-class client.

2. The primary source of women's pathology is social, not personal, external, not internal.

3. The focus on environmental stress as a major source of pathology is not used as an avenue of escape from individual responsibility.

4. Feminist therapy opposes personal adjustment to social conditions; the goal is social and political change.

5. Other women are not the enemy.

6. Men are not the enemy either.

7. Women must be economically and psychologically autonomous.

8. Relationships of friendship, love, and marriage should be equal in personal power.

9. The major difference between "appropriate" sex-role behaviors must disappear.

Two overarching components or essential factors weave the various forms of feminist therapy together. The first one is awareness and acknowledgment of the social and political context in which both therapists and clients exist. The second one is a firm basis in feminist philosophy. It is the integration of these two factors that establishes feminist therapy as a model for both social and individual change. The first establishes a frame for the "house" of feminist therapy, and the second serves as a strong foundation.

Awareness and Acknowledgment of the Social Context

Awareness and acknowledgment of the social and political context are at the core of feminist therapy. This awareness is also referred to as feminist consciousness. Analyses of social and political contexts, in both therapeutic relationships and the world at large, is an essential part of this awareness. Active feminist consciousness includes (a) the valuing of all genders and their experiences and (b) the conceptualization of practice as a means of supporting feminist social action and transformation (Crawford & Unger, 2000; Juntunen et al., 1994). "A feminist belief system affects all treatment dimensions, including the nature of women and mental illness definitions, women's psychological distress etiology, symptom interpretation, therapeutic interventions foci, therapist role, therapist-client relationship, and therapeutic goals" (Faunce, 1985, p. 2). Thus, the belief in sociocultural and political causes of women's distress commits therapists to a model of therapy within which both the personal and the political are examined, and within which both personal and social change are critical therapeutic goals.

Feminist Philosophy

Feminist therapy strives for congruence between what is believed (philosophy) and what is done (action) in therapy and in life (Rosewater, 1988). As such, feminist therapy provides a framework for the translation of philosophy and theory into practice and action. As a result of the multiple sources of feminist therapy, no one approach to feminist therapy exists. Feminist therapy is more akin to a set of values or attitudes, a philosophy of treatment held by the practitioner, than to a set of techniques or a prescription (Brown, 1994; Chester & Bretherton, 2001). Brown (1994) accurately captures this aspect of feminist therapy when discussing the specifics of feminist practice.

> What makes feminist practice is not who the clients are but how the therapist thinks about what she does, her epistemologies and underlying theoretical models rather than her specific techniques, the kinds of problems she addresses, or the demographic makeup of the client population. Feminist therapy requires a continuous and conscious awareness by the therapist that the apparently private transaction between therapist and client occurs within a social and political framework that can inform, transform, or distort the meanings given to individual experience in ways that must be uncovered in the process of the feminist therapeutic relationship. (Brown, 1994, pp. 21–22)

This emphasis on the role that attitude and values play in feminist therapy allows for a variety of therapeutic approaches as long as those approaches reconceptualize the etiology of a client's distress as contextual rather than a individual and call for social action and transformation. In sum, feminist therapy "names the oppression as the cause of most emotional and psychological distress experienced by individuals; focuses on the need for demystification as a necessary step toward freedom from oppression; emphasizes the need for honest and the pursuit of justice in every therapeutic encounter" (McLellan, 1999, p. 327).

If we consider feminist consciousness and feminist philosophy the frame and foundation of feminist therapy's house, then several principles form the "rooms" of this house. Although there is no single founder and feminist therapy is derived from many feminist philosophies, there are several core principles or tenets common to feminist therapy practice. Although various writers have articulated core tenets (see, for example, Brown, 1994; Brown & Brodksy, 1992; Collins, 2002; Enns, 1997; Gilbert, 1980; Morrow & Hawxhurst, 1996; Sturdivant, 1980; Worell & Remer, 2003; Wyche & Rice, 1997), we have identified four tenets that encompass all that have been articulated: (a) the personal is political, (b) egalitarian relationships, (c) privileging of women's experiences, and (d) empowerment.

Personal Is Political. The idea that the personal is the political certainly pre-dates feminism, but this specific adage originated in the late 1960s to address how society impacts women's personal lives. It first appears in print in Carol

Hanisch's essay, "Notes from the Second Year" published in *Sisterhood Is Powerful* (Morgan, 1970). This perspective came from women's participation in consciousness-raising groups of the Women's Movement of the 1960s and 1970s. Remember it was there where women discovered that what they assumed was an individual problem was in reality a universal one grounded in the social and political context of the times. From this lived experience, feminist therapy conceptualized etiology, diagnosis, and treatment of human problems differently than traditional therapy. In terms of etiology, feminist therapy recognized the interrelationship between subjective and objective realities and focused on that interconnection in its understanding of the causality of human behavior. Behavior, therefore, was understood within the broader social context by the use of political analysis (gender and power) that explicated the role of oppression and discrimination as well as the role of intrapsychic issues in the etiology of human distress (Brown & Brodsky, 1992; Enns, 1997; Evans et al., 2005; Hill & Ballou, 1998; Sturdivant, 1980; Worell & Remer, 2003). Personal experience is understood as "the lived version of political reality" (Brown, 1994, p. 50). This does not mean, however, that one can assume universal experiences and causes. Feminist therapy is the one therapeutic modality that balances the tension between subjective and objective views of human behavior and change.

Historically, feminist therapists eschewed diagnosis because one could not diagnose oppression (Rawlings & Carter, 1977; Evans et al., 2005). Intrapsychic interpretations tend to take human distress out of context, support oppression and discrimination, and blame the individual (Enns, 1997). Thus, feminist therapists redefined pathology to include environmental causes. Sturdivant (1980) argued that priority be given to environmental rather than to intrapsychic interpretations of psychopathology.

As with consciousness-raising groups, a major goal of feminist therapy was change, not adjustment to the status quo (Collins, 2002; Enns, 1997; Gilbert, 1980). The focus of treatment, according to Brown and Brodsky (1992), was on empowering the client to change the social, interpersonal, and political environment that has a negative impact on the client's well-being rather than to help the client adjust to an oppressive or discriminatory environment. The ultimate intention of counseling, therefore, was social change (Hill & Ballou, 1998).

Egalitarian Relationship. Like the tenet, the personal is the political, this tenet developed from women's participation in consciousness-raising groups and from women's lived experiences as clients in therapy. The philosophy and practice of CR groups lead to a focus in feminist therapy on client goals rather than on therapist goals. The therapeutic relationship is perceived as a collaborative one in which the therapy process is demystified and therapeutic goals are developed cooperatively (Brown & Brodsky, 1992; Sturdivant, 1980; Worell & Remer, 2003). For example, to foster an egalitarian relationship, some mental health practitioners may use specific therapeutic contracts (Enns, 1997). These contracts may include a description of the counselor's skills, values, attitudes, theoretical orientation, how change is viewed, and any other relevant information. Additional information is provided about the benefits and costs of therapy, client and therapist responsibilities, and what clients can expect from the mental health practitioner. Informed consent is viewed as an ongoing process and discussion, and whenever possible, the issues to be addressed are specified.

Motivated by awareness of the power differential between client and therapist in traditional counseling and therapy as well as by reports of abuse of power by therapists, feminist therapists articulate their awareness of the inherent power in the role of therapist stemming from the therapist's expertise and knowledge (Collins, 2002; Brown & Brodsky, 1992). The challenge for feminist therapists is how to minimize this power differential in the counseling relationship while maintaining the therapeutic frame and boundaries (Brown, 1994). Although acknowledging that the therapeutic relationship cannot be completely egalitarian, feminist therapists work to develop a cooperative relationship with clients in which the client is respected as his or her own best expert on his or her own life. Counselor and client perspectives regarding client concerns are equally valued (Brown & Brodsky, 1992). Because all therapy is value-laden, feminist therapists make explicit their values as these impact work with their clients. This allows clients to make informed decisions about working with a particular therapist.

Privileging of Women's Experiences. Because so much of traditional psychological theory and practice centered on men's experiences and named male experience as the norm, feminist therapy brings female experience from the margins of theory and practice to the center (Brown, 1994; Brown & Brodksy, 1992, Worell & Remer, 2003). Both male and female realities are considered and valued equally. This is what is meant by privileging women's experiences. It is not the intent to value women's experiences more than men's but to take their experiences from being devalued to being valued. In therapy with women, the commonality of women's experience is acknowledged (Sturdivant, 1980). In placing women in the center, feminist therapy normalizes and values women's experiences. Other female ways of being are understood within their cultural context. Brown (1994) speaks of "respecting experience as it is defined by those who live it" (p. 153). This applies to both women and men. Important to feminist therapy is the range of human experiences and the validity of all perspectives (Brown, 1994). In privileging the lived experience of all clients, feminist therapy prizes the complexity of diverse lives and experiences.

Empowerment. Because the etiology of the many problems women brought to therapy resulted from women's subjugation, oppression, and limited power in society (e.g., rape, incest, sexual harassment, and abuse), feminist therapy focused on empowering women to make changes in their lives and in the world. In contrast to traditional psychotherapy, feminist therapy adopted a growth and development approach to treatment rather than an illness and remediation (e.g., medical model of treatment) (Sturdivant, 1980). Client strengths were acknowledged; their ability to survive oppression and discrimination was honored. Morrow and Hawxhurst (1996) define empowerment "as a process of changing the internal and external conditions of people's lives, in the interests of social equity and justice, through individual and collective analyses and action that has at its catalyst a political analysis" (p. 41). Thus, this tenet allows therapists to see client strengths where traditional approaches might focus on client deficits. It further calls for feminist therapists to help clients recognize, value, and use their strengths and abilities to self-nurture and to make changes in themselves and in the world.

● FEMINIST THERAPY, DIVERSITY, AND SOCIAL JUSTICE

A feminist counseling model that incorporates the above tenets and views the experience of oppression as the most salient factor in understanding client concerns is central to this text. Thus, social justice and awareness of culture diversity are essential parts of the model. This approach allows for the complexity of people's lives to be honored and understood. We, the authors, believe that this formulation meets the original purpose of feminist therapy—to help individuals and societies experience change that leads to greater mental health. Our social and individual change approach to feminist therapy assumes that oppression in the United States is complex and that for many individuals reality is constructed and shaped by multiple oppressions. The most common of these oppressions are gender, race/ethnicity, culture, socioeconomic class, sexual orientation, age, and ability. For some, there may be additional or other oppressions. Men and women, clients, and therapists are influenced by these oppressions. It is therapists' responsibility to be aware of their clients' lived experiences of oppression as well as their own lived experiences of oppression.

FEMINIST THERAPY, POWER, AND CULTURE ●

Because of its roots, feminist therapy holds a unique position in the helping professions. It assumes that all therapeutic work (whether feminist or not) takes place in a dominant culture, which reflects androcentric, White, able-bodied, middle- and upper-class, heterosexual, as well as Christian values and beliefs. This culture typically marginalizes, discriminates, and oppresses those who do not fit easily into that culture (Brown, 1994). In addition to helping individuals, feminist therapy seeks to change social structures and institutions that cause and perpetuate discrimination and oppression, thereby eliminating the harmful effect of these forces on mental health (Brown, 1994; Enns, 1997; Hill, 1998).

BEING A FEMINIST THERAPIST: ●
A FEMINIST THERAPIST'S PERSPECTIVE

Being a feminist therapist entails adopting a feminist set of values and assumptions that guide your work. The authors do not believe that it is possible to practice feminist therapy without being a feminist. However, those who do not identify with feminism or have not yet explored what it means to be a feminist can certainly use feminist therapeutic techniques and provide nonsexist or gender-free effective therapy. We do believe that learning feminist therapy leads to being a feminist therapist. As you explore more about feminist therapy, you will gain awareness of existing oppressions. You will gain an understanding of power and privilege in cultures, especially the knowledge that the dominant cultures use their power to support and help those like themselves and most often to the detriment of those different from the dominant culture. You will learn that those who are dissimilar from the dominant culture often live in oppressive circumstances that are harmful to their mental health and emotional growth. Learning to do feminist therapy and/or becoming a feminist therapist is a transformative experience for both the client *and* the mental health practitioner.

Being a feminist therapist means that you believe that causes of psychological distress can be contextual rather than individual. It means personally making those connections between the personal and the political. It means closely and consistently examining your beliefs and values to ensure you have not unconsciously accepted your culture's definitions of what it means to be a man or a woman, about gendered behavior, about relationships, and about power, oppression, and cultural values. This, of course, is no easy task. It requires vigilance. The values and beliefs of the dominant culture are insidiously strong. Being a feminist therapist is about a way of being in the world and, as a mental health practitioner, about a set of beliefs that helps you make those necessary connections in order to live the change you advocate for your clients. It means being a social change agent. Being a feminist therapist means that you cannot be one way as a practitioner and then close the office door and become someone else. It means striving to be consistent in your beliefs in all aspects for your life. Being a feminist therapist means walking your talk on a daily, hourly, minute-by-minute basis the best you can each and every day.

SUMMARY

In conclusion, feminist therapy is unique among psychotherapies, in several ways. It is one of the few theoretical approaches to psychotherapeutic practice whose roots lie outside the profession in a grassroots, sociopolitical movement (Brown & Brodksy, 1992). Its central feature is its recognition of the connection between the internal, psychological world and the external, social world in the range of human problems (Brown, 1994; Chaplin, 1988). Additionally, feminist therapy brings the issue of power into therapy and definitions of mental health (Marecek & Kravitz, 1988. Also distinct to feminist therapy is its focus on both personal and social change (Greene, 1994). The commitment of feminist therapy to change the society that weakens and oppresses its citizens is a testament to the applicability of this therapy for all clients. Feminist therapy is good therapy.

DEFINITIONS ESSENTIAL TO UNDERSTANDING FEMINIST THERAPY

Patriarchy—comes from the Latin word *patri*, which means "rule of the fathers." Patriarchy refers to U.S. culture and social systems rather than being directed at any individual male. The U.S. government, laws, and mores are patriarchal because the people in positions of power within these structures are largely male, and the focus of that power is to maintain the status quo.

Lived experience—means an individual's real day-to-day experiences that leave an indelible mark on his or her psychological well-being.

Grassroots movement—refers to "of or involving the people" and means the ordinary people in a society or an organization. Change comes from the ground up, from ordinary people rather than from the government and its leaders. Change emerges from people coming together to discuss their experiences in order to better their lives and through organizing to change the system.

New psychology of women—refers to the body of work since 1976 that placed women in the center of its understanding of women's psychological development and lived experiences. This body of work sought to understand women not from the male model of mental health but rather brought women and women's experience to the center of their understanding.

Political analysis—involves the identification of those who have power to name, to define, and to control the experience and lives of others. This type of analysis helps an individual to understand how his or her individual experience is shaped by societal structures and laws, and so on.

REFERENCES

Brown, L. S. (1994). *Subversive dialogues.* New York: Basic Books.

Brown, L. S., & Brodsky, A. M. (1992). The future of feminist therapy. *Psychotherapy, 29,* 51–57.

Chaplin, J. (1988). *Feminist counseling in action.* London: Sage.

Chester, A., & Bretherton, P. (2001). What makes feminist counseling feminist? *Feminism and Psychology, 11,* 527–545.

Chicago Women's Liberation Union Herstory Project. Retrieved February 4, 2010, from http://www.cwluherstory.org/how-to-start-your-own-consciousness-raising-group.html

Collins, K. A. (2002). An examination of feminist psychotherapy in North America during the 1980s. *Guidance and Counselling, 17*(4), 105–112.

Crawford, M., & Unger, R. R. (2000). *Women and gender: A feminist psychology* (3rd ed.). Boston: McGraw-Hill.

Enns, C. Z. (1997). *Feminist theories and feminist psychotherapies: Origins, themes, and variations.* New York: Haworth Press.

Evans, K. M., Kincade, E. & Seem, S. R., (2005). Case approach to feminist therapy. In G. Corey (Ed.), *Case approach to counseling and psychotherapy* (6th ed.) (pp. 208–241). Belmont, CA: Thompson Brooks/Cole.

Faunce, P. S. (1985). A feminist philosophy of treatment. In L. B. Rosewater & L. E. A. Walker (Eds.), *Handbook of feminist therapy: Women's issues psychotherapy* (pp. 1-4). New York: Springer.

Gilbert, L. A. (1980). Feminist therapy. In A. M. Brodsky & R. T. Hare-Mustin (Eds.), *Women and psychotherapy: An assessment of research and practice* (pp. 245–265). New York: Guilford.

Greene, B. (1994). Diversity and difference: The issue of race in feminist therapy. In M. P. Mirkin (Ed.), *Women in context: Toward a feminist reconstruction of psychotherapy* (pp. 333–351). New York: Guilford.

Hanisch, C. (1970). Notes from the second year. In R. Morgan (Ed.), *Sisterhood is powerful: An anthology of writings from the Women's Liberation Movement.* Visalia, CA: Vintage.

Hill, M., & Ballou, M. (1998). Making therapy feminist: A practice survey. In M. Hill (Ed.), *Feminist therapy as a political act* (pp. 1–16). New York: Haworth Press.

Juntunen, C. L., Atkinson, D. R., Reyes, C., & Gutierrez, M. (1994). Feminist identity and feminist therapy behaviors of *women psychotherapists. Psychotherapy: Theory/Research/Practice/Training, 31,* 327–333.

Mareck, J., & Kravetz, D. (1998). Putting politics into practice: Feminist therapy as feminist praxis. *Women & Therapy,* 21, 17–36.

McLellan, B. (1999).The prostitution of psychotherapy: A feminist critique. *British Journal of Guidance and Counselling, 27*(3), 325–337.

Morgan, R. (1970). *Sisterhood is powerful: An anthology of writings from the women's liberation movement.* New York: Random House.

Morrow, S. L., & Hawxhurst, D. M. (1996). Feminist therapy: Integrating political analysis in counseling and psychology. In M. Hill (Ed.), *Feminist therapy as a political act* (pp. 37–50). New York: Haworth Press.

Rawlings, E. I., & Carter, D. K. (1977). *Psychotherapy for women: Treatment toward equality.* Springfield, IL: Charles C Thomas.

Rosewater, L. B. (1988). Feminist therapies with women. In M. Dutton-Douglas and L. E. A. Walker (Eds.), *Feminist psychotherapies: Integration of therapeutic and feminist systems* (pp. 137–153). Norwood, NJ: Ablex.

Sturdivant, S. (1980). *Therapy with women: A feminist philosophy of treatment.* New York: Springer.

Worell, J., & Remer, P. (2003). *Feminist perspectives in therapy: Empowering diverse women* (2nd ed.). Hoboken, NJ: John Wiley & Sons.

Wyche, K. F., & Rice, J. K. (1997). Feminist therapy: From dialogue to tents. In J. Worell & N. G. Johnson (Eds.), *Shaping the future of feminist psychology: Education, research, and practice* (pp. 57–71). Washington, DC: American Psychological Association.

CHAPTER 3

ETHICS AND VALUES IN FEMINIST COUNSELING AND PSYCHOTHERAPY

Books, videos, and workshops on ethical concerns and professional standards of behaviors for mental health practitioners abound. Excellent in-depth treatises on feminist and other relevant psychological ethics from philosophical and academic viewpoints exist and are certainly recommended (see Brabeck, 2000; Kitchner, 1996; Meara, Schmidt, & Day, 1996). This chapter, however, focuses on ethics as applied to feminist therapy. Our primary focus is practical as we review and synthesize feminist therapy practice and feminist therapy ethics. Our goal is for you to apply and understand the ethics and professional standards of your profession from a feminist perspective. We want to instill in you the need for self-awareness and self-examination with regard to the values and worldviews you hold about yourself and your profession and how they impact your ethical decision making. Throughout the process of learning about ethics and making ethical decisions, we ask you to remember that adherence to formal ethical principles must be tempered with an active, thoughtful, and even creative approach (Pope & Vasquez, 2007). This is true for all practitioners but takes on enhanced meaning for feminist practitioners because of the additional responsibilities of being an ethical feminist as well as an ethical therapist. In this chapter, you will encounter some differences and similarities between feminist ethics and values and more traditional approaches. You will learn more about distinguishing between ethics and values. You will consider what makes feminist ethics in practice "feminist." You will also learn about feminist ethical decision making. You will have the opportunity to consider ethical dilemmas from a feminist perspective.

● ETHICS AND THE MENTAL HEALTH PROFESSIONS

Selected Organizations and Ethical Codes

Websites for the selected organizations are listed below. Ethical Codes can be found on the websites.

American Association for Marriage and Family Therapy (AAMFT) Code of Ethics (2001)

http://www.aamft.org

American Counseling Association (ACA) Code of Ethics (2005)

http://www.counseling.org

American Mental Health Counselors Association (AHMCA) Code of Ethics (2001)

http://www.amhca.org

American Psychiatric Association (APA) The Principles of Medical Ethics With Annotations Especially Applicable to Psychiatry

http://www.psych.org

American Psychological Association (APA) Ethical Principles of Psychologists and Code of Conduct (2002)

http://www.apa.org

Canadian Psychological Association/Société Canadienne de Psychologie (CPA/SCP) Code of Ethics, 3rd ed. (2005)

http://www.cpa.ca

National Association of Social Workers (NASW) Code of Ethics (1999)

http://www.naswdc.org

Please be aware that website addresses change frequently. However, these organizations do make their ethical codes available to the public online. If you cannot find the codes, please search the associations' websites.

Ethical codes are sets of principles that members of professions are bound by honor to follow. They are not laws or morals. As mental health practitioners, we learned to articulate and honor the ethical codes of our professions. The American Counseling Association (ACA, 2005), The American Psychological Association (APA, 2002a), The Canadian Psychological Association (CPA, 2000), The American Association for Marriage and Family Therapy (2001), and the National Association of Social Workers (NASW, 1999), to name some of the most prominent professional organizations, all have published standards of behavior for members of their professions. When you become a member of a professional organization, you agree to abide by the ethical and professional standards of that organization (Fisher, 2003).

These ethical codes serve the following three functions: (a) education into the worldview of the profession, (b) professional accountability to ourselves and others, and (c) ongoing critical thinking about various issues in the field (Herlihy & Corey, 2006).

If you approach professional organizations looking for answers to specific ethical questions, you will most likely be frustrated. With only a few exceptions, the ethical codes tend toward broad generalities rather than toward specific prohibitions. Ethical codes represent a profession's aspirations in terms of practitioners' conduct with clients. For instance, the APA, CPA, and ACA codes explicitly prohibit sexual or romantic relationships with clients. Guidelines for this concern are very specific (see APA Ethics Standard 10.08, 2002a, and ACA Ethics Standard A.5.a and A.5.b, 2005). With regard to other ethical quandaries, the codes do not always tell practitioners specifically what to do or how to behave. Judgment, or ethical decision making, is left up to practitioners. For instance, the ACA Code of Ethics (2005) states that counselors may have a nonsexual or nonromantic relationship with a client or former client if the "nonprofessional interaction . . . may be potentially beneficial to the client." The decision about what is potentially beneficial is left up to the counselor. Recognizing that applying ethical codes or professional standards of behavior involves good judgment and decision making, many codes emphasize the importance of sound ethical decision making. The Canadian Psychological Association (2005) goes beyond stating the necessity for ethical decision making and outlines the steps for ethical decision making as part of its code (see sidebar). The American Counseling Association endorses the following principles of decision making (Forester-Miller & Davis, 1996):

1. Identify the problem.

2. Apply the ACA Code of Ethics.

3. Determine the nature and dimensions of the dilemma.

4. Generate potential courses of action.

5. Consider the potential consequences of all options, choose a course of action.

6. Evaluate the selected course of action.

7. Implement the course of action.

ETHICAL DECISION MAKING

Canadian Code of Ethics for Psychologists (CPA, 2000)

The following basic steps typify approaches to ethical decision making:

1. Identification of the individuals and groups potentially affected by the decision.

2. Identification of ethically relevant issues and practices, including the interests, rights, and any relevant characteristics of the individuals

(Continued)

(Continued)

    and groups involved and of the system or circumstances in which the ethical problem arose.

3. Consideration of how personal biases, stresses, or self-interests might influence the development of or choice between courses of action.

4. Development of alternative courses of action.

5. Analysis of likely short-term, ongoing, and long-term risks and benefits of each course of action on the individual(s)/group(s) involved or likely to be affected (e.g., client, client's family or employees, employing institution, students, research participants, colleagues, the discipline, society, or self).

6. Choice of course of action after conscientious application of existing principles, values, and standards.

7. Action, with a commitment to assume responsibility for the consequences of the action.

8. Evaluation of the results of the course of action.

9. Assumption of responsibility for consequences of action, including correction of negative consequences, if any, or re-engaging in the decision-making process if the ethical issue is not resolved.

10. Appropriate action, as warranted and feasible, to prevent future occurrences of the dilemma (e.g., communication and problem solving with colleagues or changes in procedures and practices).

Both of these are excellent models for ethical decision making. They ask practitioners to identify the ethical issue or concern, to consider who will be impacted by any resolution of the issue, to read carefully and apply ethical codes of behavior, to think about alternatives before deciding on a course of action, and to evaluate their course of action before implementing it. However, they do not address the basic tenets of feminist therapy. They do not address political or cultural concerns, and they do not address striving for equality within the therapeutic relationship and engaging clients in the ethical decision-making process. The traditional models of ethical decision making make the assumptions that "there is some agreed upon sense of what constitutes harm and human welfare and . . . that one's judgment about these principles is unaffected by one's personal and social context" (Hill, Glaser, & Hardin, 1998, p. 104). For feminist therapists, ethical decision making is more complex. For example, we strive for equality of power in the relationship with our clients and engage them in the decision-making process while recognizing that power is not equal and understanding that we must take responsibility when ethical decisions are made. Later in the chapter, in Table 3.2, we will present a model of feminist ethical decision making (Hill et al., 1998).

VALUES AND FEMINIST ETHICS ●

As practitioners, we strive for the least error in our ethical behavior. Common factors among the ethics codes ensure that mental health practitioners support the ethical principles of nonmalfeasance (first, do no harm) and beneficence (strive for the greatest good). These are the bases of the ethics codes of our professions. As *feminist* practitioners, we have additional ethical responsibilities. We strive to facilitate clients' growth in ways that recognize clients' strengths, encourage empowerment, work toward egalitarianism, value diversity, and create a more just world. These feminist values are reflected in ethical feminist counseling and therapy.

Values are ideals in which we have an emotional investment. They are beliefs that we deem to be beneficial, and they help guide our behavior both professionally and personally. We strive to live up to the values and beliefs of our professions while honoring our personal belief systems. As mentioned, the ethical codes and standards of behaviors are interpreted through individuals' values and decision-making processes.

Professional Values and Beliefs

Differences exist in how ethical codes are enacted and decisions are made based on individual mental health practitioners' professional value systems. For instance, on the one hand, classically trained psychoanalytic therapists might deem it harmful to interact directly with their patients to instruct them on how to be more active and less depressed. On the other hand, therapists who adhere to a social learning model of human behavior and cognitive behavioral principles of change might deem it harmful to not instruct and impart information about depression and techniques for improving and changing moods. Thus, the APA's ethical principle of beneficence and nonmalfeasance (APA, 2002a) and the ACA's ethical guidelines for avoiding harm and imposing values (ACA, 2005), which are concepts that are referred to colloquially as "first, do no harm," may be interpreted differently by different practitioners based on the counseling theory used by the individual.

Ethical principles are codes of conduct set forth by organizations. They are based on various philosophical assumptions (like beneficence and multi-cultural sensitivity) to which we aspire. How ethical principles are interpreted is dependent on individuals' training, culture, and background. Some may argue that this perspective endorses a relativistic view of ethical principles and is not in keeping with the philosophies from which ethical principles and standards are developed. However, as feminist therapists, we would argue that this is not relativism but rather a deep understanding of how training, culture, and background influence the philosophical assumptions of therapists.

Personal Values and Beliefs

In addition to practitioners' theoretical orientations impacting the interpretation of ethical principles, as discussed, personal value systems impact ethical stance. This is observed in situations where clinicians differ in personal value systems that are an outgrowth of their cultures and backgrounds. When discussing ethics and values, we need to remember that the APA Ethical Principles of Psychologists and Code of Conduct (2002a) and the ACA Code of Ethics (2005) reflect the values of these mental health professions. Our professions' foundational values are informed by and grow out of rich and established Western Europe philosophical thought; however, we must pay attention to other equally rich and established cultural values. We bring our professional and personal cultural and subcultural understanding and values into our relationship with our clients, just as they bring their culture and subcultures into the therapeutic relationship. This is an essential component of feminist therapy ethical principles. As an example of differing value systems, consider marriage. Marriage carries cultural connotations. For some, it is a lasting, spiritual, or religious commitment; for others, it is a social contract. Also, for some, it is mainly for companionship or economic reasons; for others, marriage exists to legitimatize sexual relationships and to reproduce. Marriage values differ among individuals, cultures, and countries. A clinician who holds a strong personal belief that marriage is a sacred commitment between a man and a woman that is irrevocable will approach marital therapy from a different perspective than a clinician who views marriage as a social or legal agreement between two people that can be renegotiated or terminated if either party is unhappy with the agreement. It is essential for feminist therapists to find balance and integration between their values and beliefs and the ethics of their mental health profession.

Feminist Therapy Values and Beliefs

As mentioned in Chapter 1, feminist therapy grew out of feminist philosophy and a political stance that privileges women's experiences. This genealogy grants feminist therapy a unique ethical perspective in the mental health professions. This philosophy espouses such concepts as egalitarian relationships and mandates for sociopolitical action. These values and beliefs may conflict with mainstream or traditional viewpoints about what is therapy and what is therapeutic. For instance, is it therapeutic to share your personal experiences with a client? Is therapy an enterprise that is culture free? We recognize that many emerging theoretical perspectives also consider these issues (for instance, social justice perspectives) and that recent changes in professional ethics codes address these changes (see ACA, 2005; APA, 2002a; NASW, 1999). Therefore, we must also consider what makes ethical decision making from a feminist therapy stance distinct. What makes feminist therapy ethics *feminist?*

A FEMINIST ETHICAL STANCE: ●
THE FEMINIST THERAPY INSTITUTE CODE OF ETHICS

The Feminist Therapy Institute (FTI) was a North American (Canada and the United States) organization and professional association established in 1983 with the goal of supporting advanced feminist therapists and to provide education and training in feminist therapy (FTI, 2008). For more than 25 years, the FTI provided advanced training in feminist therapy for feminist practitioners, as well as a large body of literature on feminist therapy. One of the first tasks of the FTI was to develop a Feminist Therapy Code of Ethics. This code was published originally in the late 1980s and was revised in 1999. The Feminist Therapy Code of Ethics (FTI, 1999) was intended to *add* depth and substance to the professions in which feminist therapists practice (Hawxhurst, 2009). In late 2009, the steering committee and membership of The Feminist Therapy Institute made the decision to become part of The Association for Women in Psychology (AWP). AWP, which is a sister organization of FTI, "is a not-for-profit scientific and educational organization committed to encouraging feminist psychological research, theory, and activism . . . [it is] an organization with a history of affirming and celebrating differences, deepening challenges, and experiencing growth as feminists" (AWP, 2009, Home section, para 1). The work of the FTI will now be part of AWP's Feminist Therapy Practice and Issues Committee. The Feminist Therapy Code of Ethics can be found on the FTI website (www.feminist-therapy-institute.org). The Code of Ethics will soon be on the AWP website (www.awpsych.org).

The Feminist Therapy Code of Ethics (FTI, 1999) identified five areas of ethical consideration distinct to feminist therapy. These areas do not replace the ethical codes of the feminist practitioner but, rather, are viewed as additive. As mentioned, they add feminist depth and substance to our ethical stance. (See Table 3.1: Feminist Therapy Code of Ethics.) The five areas are as follows (FTI, 1999):

1. Cultural Diversity and Oppressions

2. Power Differentials

3. Overlapping Relationships

4. Therapist Accountability

5. Social Change

These areas reflect identified ethical concerns or areas of ethical responsibility in the codes of the major mental health associations, as follows:

American Psychological Association (2002a) General Principles

Principle A: Beneficence and Nonmalfeasance

Principle B: Fidelity and Responsibility

Principle C: Integrity

Principle D: Justice

Principle E: Respect for People's Rights and Dignity

American Counseling Association (2005) Sections A–H

Section A: The Counseling Relationship

Section B: Confidentiality, Privileged Communication, and Privacy

Section C: Professional Responsibility

Section D: Relationships With Other Professionals

Section E: Evaluation, Assessment, and Interpretation

Section F: Supervision, Training, and Teaching

Section G: Research and Publication

Section H: Resolving Ethical Issues

National Association of Social Workers (1999) Core Values:

- Service
- Social Justice
- Dignity and Worth of the Person
- Importance of Human Relationships
- Integrity
- Competence

When we compare these principles, we recognize the differences and similarities between an ethical code that grows out of feminist philosophy and ethical codes that do not. Take a moment to think about your major professional association and how it prioritizes its values or general statements. You will notice the FTI emphasis on the feminist principle that the personal is the political. Unlike other codes, there is an *explicit,* rather than an *implicit,* emphasis on awareness of power and oppression and involvement in social action. Also, remember that the FTI Code of Ethics (1999) is meant to be additive. As you read the next section, think about how the principles and values of the FTI Code (see Table 3.1) will integrate with the code of ethics of your primary association.

Table 3.1   Feminist Therapy Code of Ethics (FTI, 1999)

Preamble

Feminist therapy evolved from feminist philosophy, psychological theory and practice, and political theory. In particular feminists recognize the impact of society in creating and maintaining the problems and issues brought into therapy.

Briefly, feminists believe the personal is political. Basic tenets of feminism include a belief in the equal worth of all human beings, a recognition that each individual's personal experiences and situations are reflective of and an influence on society's institutionalized attitudes and values, and a commitment to political and social change that equalizes power among people. Feminists are committed to recognizing and reducing the pervasive influences and insidious effects of oppressive societal attitudes and society.

Thus, a feminist analysis addresses the understanding of power and its interconnections among gender, race, culture, class, physical ability, sexual orientation, age, and anti-Semitism as well as all forms of oppression based on religion, ethnicity, and heritage. Feminist therapists also live in and are subject to those same influences and effects and consistently monitor their beliefs and behaviors as a result of those influences.

(Continued)

Table 3.1 (Continued)

Feminist therapists adhere to and integrate feminist analyses in all spheres of their work as therapists, educators, consultants, administrators, writers, editors, and/or researchers. Feminist therapists are accountable for the management of the power differential within these roles and accept responsibility for that power. Because of the limitations of a purely intrapsychic model of human functioning, feminist therapists facilitate the understanding of the interactive effects of the client's internal and external worlds. Feminist therapists possess knowledge about the psychology of women and girls and utilize feminist scholarship to revise theories and practices, incorporating new knowledge as it is generated.

Feminist therapists are trained in a variety of disciplines, theoretical orientations, and degrees of structure. They come from different cultural, economic, ethnic, and racial backgrounds. They work in many types of settings with a diversity of clients and practice different modalities of therapy, training, and research. Feminist therapy theory integrates feminist principles into other theories of human development and change.

The ethical guidelines that follow are additive to, rather than a replacement for, the ethical principles of the profession in which a feminist therapist practices. Amid this diversity, feminist therapists are joined together by their feminist analyses and perspectives. Additionally, they work toward incorporating feminist principles into existing professional standards when appropriate.

Feminist therapists live with and practice in competing forces and complex controlling interests. When mental health care involves third-party payers, it is feminist therapists' responsibility to advocate for the best possible therapeutic process for the client, including short- or long-term therapy. Care and compassion for clients include protection of confidentiality and awareness of the impacts of economic and political considerations, including the increasing disparity between the quality of therapeutic care available for those with or without third-party payers.

Feminist therapists assume a proactive stance toward the eradication of oppression in their lives and work toward empowering women and girls. They are respectful of individual differences, examining oppressive aspects of both their own and clients' value systems. Feminist therapists engage in social change activities, broadly defined, outside of and apart from their work in their professions. Such activities may vary in scope and content but are an essential aspect of a feminist perspective.

This code is a series of positive statements that provide guidelines for feminist therapy practice, training, and research. Feminist therapists who are members of other professional organizations adhere to the ethical codes of those organizations. Feminist therapists who are not members of such organizations are guided by the ethical standards of the organization closest to their mode of practice.

These statements provide more specific guidelines within the context of and as an extension of most ethical codes. When ethical guidelines are in conflict, the feminist therapist is accountable for how she prioritizes her choices.

These ethical guidelines, then, are focused on the issues feminist therapists, educators, and researchers have found especially important in their professional settings. As with any code of therapy ethics, the well-being of clients is the guiding principle underlying this code. The feminist therapy issues that relate directly to the client's well-being include cultural diversities and oppressions, power differentials, overlapping relationships, therapist accountability, and social change. Even though the principles are stated separately, each interfaces with the others to form an interdependent whole. In addition, the code is a living document and thus is continually in the process of change.

The Feminist Therapy Institute's Code of Ethics is shaped by economic and cultural forces in North America and by the experiences of its members. Members encourage an ongoing international dialogue about feminist and ethical issues. It recognizes that ethical codes are aspirational and that ethical behaviors are on a continuum rather than reflecting dichotomies. Additionally, ethical guidelines and legal requirements may differ. The Feminist Therapy Institute provides educational interventions for its members rather than disciplinary activity.

Ethical Guidelines for Feminist Therapists

I. Cultural Diversities and Oppressions

A. A feminist therapist increases her accessibility to and for a wide range of clients from her own and other identified groups through flexible delivery of services. When appropriate, the feminist therapist assists clients in accessing other services and intervenes when a client's rights are violated.

B. A feminist therapist is aware of the meaning and impact of her own ethnic and cultural background, gender, class, age, and sexual orientation, and actively attempts to become knowledgeable about alternatives from sources other than her clients. She is actively engaged in broadening her knowledge of ethnic and cultural experiences, nondominant and dominant.

C. Recognizing that the dominant culture determines the norm, the therapist's goal is to uncover and respect cultural and experiential differences, including those based on long-term or recent immigration and/or refugee status.

D. A feminist therapist evaluates her ongoing interactions with her clientele for any evidence of her biases or discriminatory attitudes and practices. She also monitors her other interactions, including service delivery, teaching, writing, and all professional activities. The feminist therapist accepts responsibility for taking action to confront and change any interfering, oppressing, or devaluing biases she has.

(Continued)

Table 3.1 (Continued)

II. Power Differentials

   A. A feminist therapist acknowledges the inherent power differentials between client and therapist and models effective use of personal, structural, or institutional power. In using the power differential to the benefit of the client, she does not take control or power which rightfully belongs to her client.

   B. A feminist therapist discloses information to the client which facilitates the therapeutic process, including information communicated to others. The therapist is responsible for using self-disclosure only with purpose and discretion and in the interest of the client.

   C. A feminist therapist negotiates and renegotiates formal and/or informal contacts with clients in an ongoing mutual process. As part of the decision-making process, she makes explicit the therapeutic issues involved.

   D. A feminist therapist educates her clients regarding power relationships. She informs clients of their rights as consumers of therapy, including procedures for resolving differences and filing grievances. She clarifies power in its various forms as it exists within other areas of her life, including professional roles, social/governmental structures, and interpersonal relationships. She assists her clients in finding ways to protect themselves and, if requested, to seek redress.

III. Overlapping Relationships

   A. A feminist therapist recognizes the complexity and conflicting priorities inherent in multiple or overlapping relationships. The therapist accepts responsibility for monitoring such relationships to prevent potential abuse of or harm to the client.

   B. A feminist therapist is actively involved in her community. As a result, she is aware of the need for confidentiality in all settings. Recognizing that her client's concerns and general well-being are primary, she self-monitors both public and private statements and comments. Situations may develop through community involvement where power dynamics shift, including a client's having equal or more authority than the therapist. In all such situations a feminist therapist maintains accountability.

   C. When accepting third-party payments, a feminist therapist is especially cognizant of and clearly communicates to her client the multiple obligations, roles, and responsibilities of the therapist. When working in institutional settings, she clarifies to all involved parties where her allegiances lie. She also monitors multiple and conflicting expectations between clients and caregivers, especially when working with children and elders.

   D. A feminist therapist does not engage in sexual intimacies nor any overtly or covertly sexualized behaviors with a client or former client.

IV. Therapist Accountability

   A. A feminist therapist is accountable to herself, to colleagues, and especially to her clients.

   B. A feminist therapist will contract to work with clients and issues within the realm of her competencies. If problems beyond her competencies surface, the feminist therapist utilizes consultation and available resources. She respects the integrity of the relationship by stating the limits of her training and providing the client with the possibilities of continuing with her or changing therapists.

   C. A feminist therapist recognizes her personal and professional needs and utilizes ongoing self-evaluation, peer support, consultation, supervision, continuing education, and/or personal therapy. She evaluates, maintains, and seeks to improve her competencies, as well as her emotional, physical, mental, and spiritual well-being. When the feminist therapist has experienced a similar stressful or damaging event as her client, she seeks consultation.

   D. A feminist therapist continually re-evaluates her training, theoretical background, and research to include developments in feminist knowledge. She integrates feminism into psychological theory, receives ongoing therapy training, and acknowledges the limits of her competencies.

   E. A feminist therapist engages in self-care activities in an ongoing manner outside the work setting. She recognizes her own needs and vulnerabilities as well as the unique stresses inherent in this work. She demonstrates an ability to establish boundaries with the client that are healthy for both of them. She also is willing to self-nurture in appropriate and self-empowering ways.

V. Social Change

   A. A feminist therapist seeks multiple avenues for impacting change, including public education and advocacy within professional organizations, lobbying for legislative actions, and other appropriate activities.

   B. A feminist therapist actively questions practices in her community that appear harmful to clients or therapists. She assists clients in intervening on their own behalf. As appropriate, the feminist therapist herself intervenes, especially when other practitioners appear to be engaging in harmful, unethical, or illegal behaviors.

   C. When appropriate, a feminist therapist encourages a client's recognition of criminal behaviors and also facilitates the client's navigation of the criminal justice system.

(Continued)

Table 3.1	(Continued)

> D. A feminist therapist, teacher, or researcher is alert to the control of information dissemination and questions pressures to conform to and use dominant main-stream standards. As technological methods of communication change and increase, the feminist therapist recognizes the socioeconomic aspects of these developments and communicates according to clients' access to technology.
>
> E. A feminist therapist, teacher, or researcher recognizes the political is personal in a world where social change is a constant.

Source: From *Feminist Therapy Code of Ethics*, by the Feminist Therapy Institute, 1999, www.feminist-therapy-institute.org. Copyright 2000 by the Feminist Therapy Institute, Inc.

The Feminist Therapy Code of Ethics (FTI, 1999) begins with a preamble, which is similar to those of the major mental health professional associations, and proceeds to a set of ethical guidelines organized by a series of principles or concerns (see Table 3.1). The Feminist Therapy Code of Ethics preamble, like most of the ethics codes, states a basic belief in the concepts of nonmalfeasance and beneficence. The code states that "the well-being of the client is the guiding principle." However, commitment to the feminist concept that the personal is the political is woven into the preamble. The well-being of the client (the personal) and consideration of the sociopolitical context (the political) inform the FTI Code of Ethics. The major differences between the FTI Code and other codes are the (a) emphasis by the FTI on the client in the sociopolitical context, (b) use of power analyses, and (c) importance of continuing therapist self-examination of biases and oppressions as they impact the counseling relationship. In keeping with the belief that the sociopolitical context is important, the preamble specifies that the Feminist Therapy Code of Ethics was shaped by North American sociopolitical forces and that these should be taken into account when dealing with biases and oppressions.

The first guideline or area of ethical practice addressed in the Feminist Therapy Code of Ethics (FTI, 1999) deals with *cultural diversity and oppressions.* This refers to feminist therapists' awareness of biases in their culture. Feminist therapists have an ethical responsibility to take into account all forms of oppression and how these might affect the well-being of clients, as well as how therapists themselves are impacted by oppression. The guideline states that therapists should constantly reexamine their own biases, awareness of oppressions, and uses of power as they engage in therapeutic work.

In addition, this guideline acknowledges that mental health is not a stand-alone issue but is tied to the sociopolitical position of the client. Clients come from different ethnic and cultural backgrounds. They vary with regard to sexuality and sexual orientation, physical ability and attributes, socioeconomic status, religion and spiritual perspectives, and so on. It is the responsibility of the feminist therapist to be aware of how these diversities are positioned in the culture and to ascertain level of oppression and how this impacts clients' well-being and mental health. Mental health is not viewed as primarily centered within individuals but rather as a consequence of how individuals are positioned in society.

The next FTI ethical guideline concerns *power differentials*. This guideline addresses how power and power relationships in the world outside therapists' offices impact therapists, clients, and the process of therapy. Therapists are instructed not to take control of power that belongs to clients, to disclose information to clients that is communicated to others, to use self-disclosure only in the interest of the client, and to engage clients in therapy as an ongoing mutual process. It is important for therapists to realize that clients are consumers of therapy. Feminist therapists educate clients in the legality, ethics, and power of therapy as a healing process but also as a business agreement. Feminist therapists are aware of their own power in the session as well as of their power relationships with others. For example, feminist therapists discuss with clients their relationships with insurance companies, payment, and how diagnosis may or may not be in the best interest of their client. We will discuss diagnosis and conceptualization from a feminist stance in Chapters 4 and 5.

The emphasis of the FTI Code of Ethics (FTI, 2008) on *overlapping relationships* is somewhat different from the traditional conceptualization of dual or multiple relationships. Dual or multiple relationships occur when therapists have at least one other role with an individual beyond that of the client–counselor relationship. In small communities, nonsexual, nonromantic multiple roles are not uncommon. Your client may serve you breakfast at the local diner, be a teacher at your children's school, work out at the same gym, work for the electrician you hire, or be related to your neighbor. Mental health trainees are often told simply to avoid these multiple relationships. APA Standard 3.05 (2002a) addresses multiple relationships and gives therapists leeway in deciding what may or may not be expected to cause harm or exploitation to the clients. ACA Standard A.5 (2005) does not speak explicitly to the multiple relationship dilemma but instead discusses behaviors and directs practitioners to avoid relationships outside of therapy that are not potentially beneficial to clients. The problem with how major mental health professional organizations approach overlapping relationships is that they do not consider the position of therapists and clients in the greater sociopoliti-cal context and how that position impacts change and healing. The Feminist Therapy Code of Ethics recognizes the complexity of the world in which we live and speaks about overlapping relationships. Some of these cannot be avoided, and others should not be avoided.

Clients who choose a feminist therapist often belong to similar organi-zations and are involved in activities similar to those of their therapists. Additionally, in the course of therapy, feminist therapists may use involve-ment in social action as a therapeutic and healing technique. Feminist thera-pists, therefore, might find themselves in more complex, overlapping relationships than other therapists. This is a result of feminist therapy's stance that individual therapy cannot achieve lasting psychological change for clients as long as the sociopolitical environment is harmful to individuals and power is distributed unequally. Thus, there is an ethical mandate for fem-inist therapists to participate in social change for the good of all clients. Feminist therapists might find themselves volunteering at the local women's shelter or on a political campaign where a client is leading an initiative or in a supervisory position. The FTI Code of Ethics recognizes this and stipulates that, "In all such situations a feminist therapist maintains accountability" (FTI, 1999). In short, this means that feminist therapists are always aware of their therapeutic relationship with clients even when interacting with clients outside the therapy office. They do not avoid these relationships or curtail their activism; rather, they remain responsible for acting in the best interest of the client when interacting with them outside the office. Feminist thera-pists are aware of the therapeutic power of confidentiality and "self-monitor both public and private statements and comments" (FTI, 1999).

The FTI Code of Ethics (FTI, 2008) also addresses institutional and struc-tural overlapping relationships. Therapists' relationships with third-party payers, therapists' employers, state agencies, and other relevant institutions are defined as overlapping relationships. In these relationships, therapists must communicate clearly to client therapists' "multiple . . . roles and responsibilities." Consider a feminist therapist who works for a local, pri-marily state-funded, community mental health agency. The therapist was told recently that because of budget cuts, clients will have only six individual ther-apy sessions in a six-month period. All clients will be seen in group therapy. The therapist has already gone over the limit with two clients. She received an official warning from the clinic's business director. What is the feminist therapist's responsibility to the agency? To the client? To the state? To herself/himself? To other clients? To agency clients who are in group therapy with his/her client? These are complex questions that are part of feminist ethical decision making.

Feminist therapists have long been in the forefront of the movement to stop therapist sexual use and abuse of clients. The FTI Code (FTI, 1999) clearly states that feminist therapists do not engage in sexual behavior or sexualization of the therapeutic relationship with a client or former client. When compared with other ethical codes, this is strong and unequivocal. APA Standard 10.08 (2002a) stipulates that therapists do not have sexual contact with current clients under any circumstances; however, therapists may consider a sexual relationship with former clients 2 or more years after termination if certain requirements are met. ACA Standards A.5.a and A.5.b (2005) address these issues. Sexual relationships with current clients and their families are prohibited. Sexual relationships can be considered 5 years after termination if certain requirements are met (ACA, 2005). The FTI Code of Ethics recognizes that the therapeutic relationship is a particularly strong and deep type of relationship. Even when individuals end their course of therapy, the therapeutic relationship remains, and therapists should remain aware of this and the continuing possibility of power imbalances.

The fourth ethical guideline addresses *therapist accountability.* This is essentially feminist therapy professionalism. Feminist therapists work, like all mental health professionals, within their areas of competency; they seek to remain knowledgeable in the profession and seek continuing education opportunities. A feminist therapist does not merely recognize therapeutic limitations but, rather, "respects the integrity of the relationship by stating the limits of her training" (FTI, 1999). The relationship and the well-being of clients remain foremost, although there is an emphasis on mutuality within the relationship.

As accountable, feminist professionals, feminist therapists regularly monitor their awareness of feminism, feminist theory, and new developments in feminist therapy and seek to integrate these into their practice. Although no formal training programs exist for feminist therapy, it is essential for feminist therapists to have training in both the theory and practice of feminist therapy. Feminist therapists are both feminists and therapists. It is essential for us to keep abreast of new knowledge and application of knowledge in both areas.

The FTI's articulation of therapist accountability is distinguished from more traditional ethics codes in two ways. First is the emphasis on consultation and peer support. Although other ethics codes address the need for supervision and consultation, the FTI acknowledges that therapists (feminist or not) do not work in a vacuum and are impacted by the work that they do. It is often difficult work that can affect our "emotional, physical, mental and spiritual well being" (FTI, 1999, Section IV, Point C). A central component of feminism is the concept of community. Feminist therapists are urged to use their community for consultation, supervision and support. Furthermore, the FTI Code of Ethics (FTI, 1999) prioritizes feminist therapist self-care. Feminist therapists are "willing to self-nurture in appropriate and self-empowering ways" (FTI, 1999). This speaks to the mutuality of the counseling relationship. Therapists and clients are mutual partners in the therapeutic encounter. Therapists are no less likely to have problems in living than their clients and should be aware of their own health and well-being. Therapists' problems may impact clients. This principle of self-care can be observed in such things as therapists' supervision groups, but it is also evident when therapists take time to have lunch, go for a walk, read a novel, engage in an avocation, enjoy an afternoon with friends and family, and so on. Feminist therapists are human beings and, as such, need to take their own advice and treat themselves at least as well as they treat their clients.

The last guiding principle for the FTI Code of Ethics (FTI, 1999) is *social change*. Although other ethics codes (see ACA, 2005; APA, 2002a; NSWA, 1999) speak to social justice issues, the FTI Code is unique in its focus on social action. There are five elements to this guideline.

First, therapists do not view therapy as the only mechanism for social change. Feminist therapists are bound by honor to seek other ways of impacting change, for instance, leadership within professional organizations or serving as a lobbyist for mental health issues. Feminist therapists are not silent participants in injustices. This goes beyond counselors' offices. On the one hand, it is clear to most of us that if we know a professional colleague is abusing or having sexual intimacies with a client, then it is our ethical duty to protect the client and appropriately confront or report our colleague. On the other hand, if we know a local retailer is specifically not paying a large immigrant population in our community wages and benefits equal to other members of the community, then this too is harmful to our clients and our community, and it is our responsibility to do something about it. It is oppression and encourages second-class citizenship and poverty. It disempowers, rather than empowers, and thus creates a sociopolitical climate that is unjust and encourages unhealthy ways of feeling and being. Disenfrachisment and despair for the future are causes of depression.

Second, feminist therapists actively intervene when they are aware of therapist abuses of power. This intervention may focus on helping clients to confront practitioners engaging in unethical and/or illegal practices and solve issues on their own, or it may be appropriate for a feminist therapist to intervene herself appropriately and model assertive behavior. Feminist therapists are active role models for their clients.

Third, when clients are involved in the legal or justice system, feminist therapists help clients to understand criminal behaviors from a sociopolitical context, particularly with regard to power. Feminist therapists, for example, will have information about the criminal justice system from a feminist perspective that includes various analyses of power within that system. Feminist therapists can make referrals to and seek information from feminist criminal justice advocates and professionals, which include attorneys, advocates, and civil servants. Thus, feminist therapists can advise and inform their clients accurately with respect to sociopolitical power but also make informed referrals to appropriate feminist professionals.

Fourth, feminist therapists engaged in therapy, teaching, or research are aware of the power dynamics in the dissemination of information. Feminist therapists ask themselves and others if the dominant paradigm of how knowledge is obtained is both accurate and complete. For instance, it is reported commonly in popular media that men are better at math than women. Feminist therapists are aware of research that contradicts this popular belief (Hyde & McKinley, 1997; Spelke, 2005). They speak up and help others to resist the dominant paradigm, but beyond this they understand the power roles inherent in the dominant paradigm. They understand why it is important for the dominant culture to cultivate and maintain the belief that men are better at science and math than women are. They are aware of the sociopolitical and economic context of this belief. Finally, above all else, the feminist therapist bears in mind that "the political is the personal in a world where social change is constant" (FTI, 1999).

The FTI Code of Ethics (FTI, 1999) is an addition to professional ethical codes. It does not supplant the ethics code of your profession. For example, as a feminist social worker, you would abide by the National Association of Social Workers ethical code, but you would also consider the five areas of feminist ethical practice. Those whose major professional affiliation is with The American Counseling Association would take those into consideration. The same holds true for those working under the auspices of the American Psychological Association. If therapists do not belong to a professional organization, then they are guided by the ethical codes of the organization closest to their "mode of practice" (FTI, 1999).

SOCIAL JUSTICE PERSPECTIVES ●

The FTI Code (FTI, 1999) is a product of the Feminist Therapy Institute and reflects the values of the FTI. Other authors have addressed ethics from feminist and social justice perspectives. Drs. Kenneth Pope and Melba Vasquez identify seven assumptions about ethics. These assumptions address the impact of counseling/therapy on the practitioner, client, and culture at large. These assumptions parallel basic tenets of feminist therapy and urge ethical practitioners to be self-aware, consider power relationships, be competent within their area of practice, and understand cultural influences on themselves and their clients. The assumptions are as follows (Pope & Vasquez, 2007, pp. xii–xv):

1. Ethical awareness is a continuous, active process that involves constant questioning and personal responsibility.

2. Awareness of ethical codes and legal standards is important, but formal codes and standards cannot take the place of an active, thoughtful, creative approach to our ethical responsibilities.

3. Awareness of the evolving research and theory in the scientific and professional literature is another important aspect of ethical competence, but the claims and conclusions that emerge in the literature can never be passively accepted or reflexively applied no matter how popular, authoritative, or seemingly obvious.

4. We believe that most therapists and counselors are conscientious, dedicated, caring individuals who are committed to ethical behavior. But none of us is infallible.

5. Many of us find it easier to question the ethics of others than to question our own beliefs, assumptions, and actions. It is worth noticing if we find ourselves preoccupied with how wrong others are in some area of ethics and certain that we are the ones to set them right, or at least to point out repeatedly how wrong they are.

6. Many of us find it easier and more natural to question ourselves in areas where we are uncertain. It tends to be much harder—but often much more productive—to question ourselves about what we are most sure of, what seems beyond doubt or question. Nothing can be placed off- limits for this questioning.

7. As psychologists (and other mental health practitioners), we often encounter ethical dilemmas without clear and easy answers. There is no legitimate way to avoid these ethical struggles. They are part of our work.

These assumptions are an excellent complement to both the FTI ethical guidelines and the ethical codes of the major mental health professional associations.

Many professional associations recognize that not all clients are alike and that a generic therapeutic model is rarely the most effective. In contemporary societies, ethical mental health practitioners from a variety of orientations view clients as human beings who exist within the framework of their lives. For example, the American Psychological Association has developed several guidelines that are pertinent to ethical feminist therapy, as follows:

1. Guidelines for Psychological Practice with Girls and Women (APA, 2007).

   http://www.apa.org/about/division/girlsandwomen.pdf

2. Guidelines for Psychotherapy with Lesbian, Gay, and Bisexual Clients (APA, 2000).

   http://www.apa.org/pi/lgbc/guidelines.html

3. Guidelines on Multicultural Education, Training, Research, Practice, and Organizational Change for Psychologists (APA, 2002b).

   http://www.apa.org/pi/multiculturalguidelines/formats.html

These are excellent guidelines for all feminist therapists (and therapists in general), but you should also explore your specific professional organization for its recommendations.

Shauna and Maria are both feminist therapists who primarily work with women with abuse issues.

Shauna is a feminist family therapist who values marriage as an important social institution and a commitment between two people. She is active in various organizations that combat violence against women. She strongly believes (values) that marriage laws provide women greater protection from partner abuse. Her reading and research indicate that the police in her area are more apt to prosecute husbands than they are boyfriends. Marriage, she says to her colleagues, also brings with it divorce rather than informal breaking up. Divorce is a legal decree that can impose restrictions on the abusive partner. Marriage and divorce together provide stronger legal protections for women. She often advises abused women in her practice to leave and initiate divorce proceedings immediately for maximum safety.

However, Maria, a feminist social worker who works mainly with individual women, believes that marriage constricts women's rights to manage and control their lives. Marriage limits their rights over their children and their finances. She believes that marriage is not essential to society and that the individual commitment partners make to each other is more important. Her reading and research indicate that married women are more apt to stay with abusive partners and, even once they have left, to have more contact with those partners because of legal issues. Maria often advises abused women in her practice to not marry and when leaving to have no additional contact with the abuser and to move away.

Mindy is a 35-year-old woman who is seeking therapy. Her fiancée is emotionally abusive, however, and on one occasion he slapped her hard enough to leave a bruise on her face.

How might Shauna and Maria approach therapy differently with Mindy? What interventions might each use in therapy? What values would inform their clinical work? What ethical dilemmas might each have to work through given the ethical codes of their professions and the FTI Code of Ethics?

● SPECIAL ISSUES FOR ETHICAL FEMINIST THERAPISTS

Two areas are particularly relevant to feminist therapy and the practice of feminist therapy ethics: power and values. It is in these areas that you may experience the greatest discrepancy between feminist therapy ethics and your primary code of ethics and standards of professional behavior. This does not mean that feminist therapists apply ethics differently from other therapists when considering power and value issues. It means that after looking at your own beliefs about the personal and political in your life, you might choose an alternative course of action to the one you would choose if you did not also apply your feminist view of ethical behavior. Because our concepts of power and values lie at the crossroads of our personal and professional lives and feminist therapy asks for an integration of personal and professional beliefs and principles, it will help us to take a closer look at these two issues.

Power

The codes of ethics for mental health professions ensure that mental health practitioners share broad professional worldviews to protect clients from gross negligence or even harm by practitioners who might be unaware of the power held by therapists and either purposefully or inadvertently abuse that power. Boundary violations are the most common power abuses in therapy. Boundaries are those therapist and client beliefs and values that set the framework for therapeutic mental health work. In feminist therapy, boundaries are set through discussion with clients and mutual agreement about limits and the relationship. This is done with an understanding of how power is and is not used in the therapeutic relationship. As therapists and, therefore, the experts in mental health work, we take the initiative and discuss power and boundary issues with our clients. We recognize that clients' lived experience gives them expertise in their own lives. When counselors and clients either deny their power in the relationship or abuse it, boundary violations occur. For instance, we can mistake our therapy relationships with clients for friendship. One of the authors' friends once had a therapist who read his poetry to her and asked her to critique it. He did not understand the nuances of power in their therapeutic relationship. We can take advantage of our clients' strengths. Perhaps they have some business expertise, and we come to rely on them for financial advice. We can slide from consultative, supervisory discussions with our colleagues into gossip about clients. These are abuses of power and boundary violations.

When mental health practitioners do not pay attention to or seek to understand power dynamics both in and out of the consultation space, they can mistake clients' attention and pleasure in the therapeutic process for sexual or romantic attraction and then act on this mistaken assumption. This is, perhaps, the most prominent and harmful boundary violation and abuse of power. It is an abuse of power that feminist therapy has long sought to stop (Remer & Worell, 2003). It is important to note that most cases of therapist–client sexual relationships are between male therapists and female clients (Kirkland, Kirkland, & Reaves, 2004; Lamb, Catanzaro, & Moorman, 2003). Thus, sexualization of clients is most frequently an abuse of male power over women as well as an abuse of therapeutic power. Recently, therapist sexual use and abuse of clients have become more visible. Clients are more willing to speak out. Because of the strong prohibitions in the current ethics codes, therapists recognize that sexual relationships with clients are an ethical violation and abuse of power. Feminist therapy can take a great deal of credit for this change; however, this breach of ethics is still commonly reported (Lamb et al., 2003; Pope & Tabachink, 1993). In a recent case, a well-regarded, well-known psychologist surrendered his license when a female client reported a sexual relationship with him (McKinnon, 2008). This case exemplifies an important piece of information about therapists' sexual use and abuse of clients—it continues to be a problem for the mental health professions despite ethical prohibitions (ACA, 2005; APA, 2002a; CPA, 2000).

Other kinds of power exist as well and pose additional ethical concerns. In Chapter 5, we discuss the power to diagnose and how that impacts our clients.

As therapists, we also hold influence power over our clients. We have the power to influence their opinions and beliefs. As we will discuss in the next section, this is one of the criticisms of feminist therapy—that feminist therapy seeks to influence clients to become feminist and to adopt feminist values. Power and awareness of power of others, whether in therapy sessions or our ongoing lives and those of our clients, is a central concept in feminist therapeutic work.

Values

A critique of feminist therapy is that as a modality based in feminism, it has a political agenda. Feminism advocates equality between genders, and so does feminist therapy. In Chapter 2, we discussed the basic tenets of feminist therapy as follows: (a) the personal is political, (b) egalitarian relationships, (c) privileging of women's experiences, and (d) empowerment. A core tenet of feminist therapy is that the personal is the political. In other words, for lasting individual change, there must be societal change. Feminist therapists now recognize that in many cases, culture is inimical to mental health. Oppression and power differences exist and are causes of psychological distress and illness. To be maximally effective with clients, feminist therapists analyze societal influences that negatively impact mental health and are active in bringing about social change. Feminist therapists are often vocal about political issues and have strongly held beliefs about sociopolitical concerns. Feminists take a larger, cultural view of mental health and mental illness. This is discussed further in Chapters 5 and 6, which discuss conceptualization and diagnosis from a feminist perspective.

Feminist therapy is unique in that feminist therapists talk with their clients about their values and beliefs and how these influence their work as therapists. As a result, the client is an informed consumer—the client can make a decision about whether to work with this particular therapist who holds feminist values and beliefs. Other therapeutic modalities do not require that as a practice. Thus, rather than imposing values on clients, feminist therapists articulate those values so that clients can make an informed decision. We argue that therapists who use other therapeutic modalities are more at risk for imposing their values on their clients because the mandate to articulate values and beliefs is missing.

Therapy is always in service to the client. Therapy is not for therapists. If we cannot work with clients because they are different from us, we do not try to change them into us. This would be neither moral nor ethical. We do not "force-feed" our values to our clients. Clients enter therapy with feminist therapists knowing and understanding that their therapist is a feminist therapist. Clients should have choice about the mode and type of therapy. We keep our clients informed of our methods of working and our beliefs about the efficacy of therapy—why therapy works. We also share with our clients our values about health and illness and our beliefs about the change process.

● FEMINIST THERAPY ETHICAL DECISION-MAKING MODELS

What makes ethical decision making a feminist endeavor? We present two models. First is a feminist model for ethical decision making developed by Marcia Hill, Kristin Glaser, and Judy Harden (1998). Next, we will discuss integrating feminist theory and perspective into standard models of ethical decision making.

A Feminist Model for Ethical Decision Making

Hill et al.'s (1998) model assumes that using two processes for decision making is better than one (See Table 3.2). It integrates a rational–evaluative process with a feeling–intuitive process. Simply put, the rational–evaluative process is information from ethics codes, legal codes, learned professional

Table 3.2 Feminist Ethical Decision-Making Model

Rational–Emotive Process	Feeling–Intuitive Process
Step #1: Recognizing a Problem	
Information from therapist's knowledge.	Uncertainty about how to proceed.
Advice from supervisor or colleague.	Identify what stands in the way of working through the problem, feelings about the nature of the issue, feelings about the consultant or about asking for help (decision to consult may occur here).
Step #2: Defining the Problem	
What is the conflict? Who are the players?	What else is my discomfort about?
What are the relevant standards (rules, codes, or principles)?	What do my feelings tell me about the situation? What am I worried about?
What personal characteristics and cultural values do I bring to this decision? How do these factors influence my definition of the problem?	
How does the client define the problem? (decision to consult may occur here)	What are the client's feelings about the dilemma?
What personal characteristics, values does the consultant bring to this process?	How do the consultant's characteristics affect me?
Step #3: Developing Solutions	
Brainstorm possibilities; perform a cost-benefit analysis and prioritize values.	What do my reactions to each choice tell me?
Step #4: Choosing a Solution	
What is the best fit emotionally and rationally?	Does this solution meet everyone's needs, including mine? Can I implement and live with the effects?

(Continued)

Table 3.2 (Continued)

Rational–Emotive Process	Feeling–Intuitive Process
Step #5: Reviewing the Process	
Would I want to be treated this way?	Does this decision feel right?
Is the decision universalizable? Would this decision withstand the scrutiny of others?	Have I given myself time to let reservations emerge?
How are my values, personal characteristics influencing my choices? How am I using my power?	Does the manner in which I carry out this decision fit my style?
Have I taken the client's perspective into account?	
Step #6: Implementing and Evaluating the Decision	
Carry out the decision.	Is this solution the best I can do?
Observe the consequences.	Does this outcome continue to feel right?
Reassess the decision.	How has this decision affected the therapeutic process?
Step #7: Continuing Reflection	
What did I learn?	Have I changed as a result of this process? How?
What would I do differently?	How might this experience affect me in the future?

Source: From "A Feminist Model for Ethical Decision Making" by M. Hill, K. Glaser, and J. Harden, 1998, *Women & Therapy, 21,* pp. 116–118. Copyright 1998, Routledge.

information, informed consultation from supervisors or colleagues, and so on. This process is advocated by most ethical decision-making models, including the ones we have discussed previously. However, this model goes further and, true to feminist therapy principles, assumes that ethical decision making is a solid integration of who we are as people, as well as who we are as professionals. It addresses many levels of clients' identities as well as how clients are involved in the ethical decision-making process. The feeling–intuitive process asks us as therapists to examine our feelings about making these decisions. We are asked to examine any values or beliefs we may hold about the issues involved, to know our own level of comfort when dealing with our clients and these issues at this time, and so on. At each step in the process, we need to assess our own feelings and values about the issues and the decisions being made.

As the model in Table 3.2 illustrates, feminist therapists must also view their work through the feminist lens. As feminist therapists, we hold as one of our core beliefs that feminism is in the best interest of the client, and furthermore, it is in the best of interest of humankind. One does not simply apply ethical codes; one uses an ethical decision-making model to reach the best possible solution for one's clients. The model presented in Table 3.2, although excellent, is only one way to view clients through feminist ethics. It may or may not fit comfortably with your primary profession. We ask that as you read over the ethics code for your primary profession, keep the FTI Code of Ethics (FTI, 1999) nearby and ask yourself the following questions at each step of the process of ethical decision making:

What outside influences (societal/cultural) are at work in this situation and influencing this dilemma? [FTI: Cultural Diversities and Oppression]

What power inequities (gender, race, culture, physical ability, socioeconomic status, etc.) are there in this dilemma? How am I a part of the power inequities? [FTI: Power Differentials]

Which parts of the ethical process respect clients? Which parts of the process might be oppressive? [FTI: Power Differentials]

How am I involving the client in solving this dilemma? [FTI: Power Differentials]

Do I have enough knowledge about the psychology of gender, race, and other oppressions to solve this dilemma effectively at this time? [FTI: Therapist Accountability]

What are the complexities inherent in my relationship with this client? What is most helpful to this client? [FTI: Overlapping Relationships]

Are there political and/or social aspects of this dilemma that I am not considering? Are there political social resources that might help me to solve this dilemma? [FTI: Social Change]

The most important message to take away from a discussion on ethical decision making is that the use of ethics is not prescriptive. Behaving as an ethical professional is not simply adhering to a list of what not to do. It is a way of thinking about your work that places your clients at the forefront of your decision making process. It demands that the needs and well-being of your clients be paramount. An ethical perspective ensures that your work is always in the interest of the client, not your self-interest. The important thing to remember is to *think ethically*—that is, to use an ethical decision-making model. All ethical decision-making models are only starting points for the process. As a feminist therapist you are part of a feminist community. One of the best pieces of ethical advice is to consult with others feminist therapists as you go through the decision-making, dilemma-solving process.

SUMMARY

Ethics codes and standards of professional behavior primarily exist to safeguard the client. However, they also safeguard the profession and the role of the profession in its culture. Professional ethics are not laws or rules. They are principles to which we aspire. Ethical concerns and dilemmas rarely have simple answers. Solutions to ethical dilemmas and concerns can vary somewhat. To determine the appropriate answers to ethical dilemmas and concerns, one needs to be well versed in one's own values as well as the ethical standards of behavior within one's profession. Feminists add feminist therapy ethics to their practice and integrate their personal and professional values with the feminist values of egalitarianism, awareness of power differentials, and centering women's lived experiences.

FOR FURTHER DISCUSSION

These situations are not specific to feminist therapy but are situations that feminist therapists might view with more complexity than therapists who do not add the FTI Code of Ethics (FTI, 1999) to their ethical practice.

1. Read and discuss the following situations. Each incorporates at least two ethical concerns. First, identify areas of concern, and then identify the sections of your professional ethical codes that address these issues. Finally, look carefully at the FTI and identify and discuss how the Feminist Therapy Institute Code of Ethics approaches these ethical concerns. Discuss any discernible differences between the ethical codes of your professional organization and the FTI ethical code.

2. Using both feminist awareness and one of the ethical decision-making models discussed in the chapter, apply the various steps to each of the ethical dilemmas.

Ethical dilemmas

1. You live in a small town and frequently patronize the same coffee shop as one of your clients. He asks you to sit with him and have coffee. She asks you to sit with her and have coffee.

2. A friend refers a family member to you. The potential client asserts that he or she is interested in therapy with you because you are the only feminist therapist in the area.

3. While working with a client, the client asks if you are married.

4. Your client asks if you have ever been raped.

5. You meet a client at a social action event and are assigned to the same work group.

6. A male client is threatening suicide but will not consent to hospitalization.

7. A female client is threatening suicide but will not consent to hospitalization.

8. You are a counselor in private practice. The local "Y" has asked you to do a workshop on stress reduction for women. A previous client who had terminated therapy abruptly is at the workshop. She self-discloses about her therapy with you.

9. Your client is a professional woman in a stable, same-sex relationship. Her ex-husband is demanding full custody of their 12-year-old son.

10. Your client is an immigrant and has asked you to attend a meeting with his mortgage lender as he (a) is not a native speaker of English, (b) does not understand North American lending laws, and (c) believes that the potential lender is taking advantage of him based on the first two facts. He wants your opinion on the whether the mortgage lender is honest.

11. Your 14-year-old male client hugs you and touches you inappropriately.

Ethics and Values: Self-Exploration Exercise

The following concepts and ideas are ones that are influenced by our personal and professional values. These particular concepts focus on power, gender, or both and are, therefore, particularly important to explore for feminist therapists. In the space provided jot down your ideas about:

1. What ethical dilemmas might arise around this concept.

2. What your personal values are about the concept.

3. What your professional values are about the concept.

4. How feminist values might impact your decision making about the concept.

Values and Beliefs	Ethical Dilemmas	Personal Values	Professional Values	Feminist Values
Marriage				
Abortion				
Adoption				
Parenting skills				
Sexuality				
Class/socioeconomic status				
Race/culture/ethnicity				
Science and religion				
Family				
Gender roles				
Authority				
Emotions				
Tolerance				
Education				
Age				
Physical ability				
Spirituality/religion				

DEFINITIONS

Value—a belief about what is right, beneficial, or commendable. Values are based on one's choice and are considered important in guiding one's conduct.

Personal values—for example, valuing safety, harmony, and so on.

Cultural values—for example, valuing individual autonomy, importance of extended family, and so on.

Value system—a set of values adopted by an individual or society that governs the behavior of the individual or the members of the society, often without the conscious awareness of the individual or the members of the society.

Morals—morality is an evaluation of one's conduct on the basis of some broad cultural context or religious standard.

REFERENCES

American Association of Marriage and Family Therapy. (2001*). AAMFT code of ethics.* Washington, DC: Author.

American Counseling Association. (2005). *ACA code of ethics.* Alexandria, VA: Author.

American Mental Health Counselors Association. (2010). *AMHCA code of ethics.* Washington, DC: Author.

American Psychiatric Association. (2008). *The principles of medical ethics with annotations especially applicable to psychiatry.* Washington, DC: Author.

American Psychological Association. (2000). *Guidelines for psychotherapy with lesbian, gay, and bisexual clients.* Washington, DC: Author.

American Psychological Association. (2002a). *Ethical principles of psychologists and code of conduct.* Washington, DC: Author.

American Psychological Association. (2002b). *Guidelines on multicultural education, training, research, practice, and organizational change for psychologists.* Retrieved April 13, 2010, from http://www.apa.org/pi/multiculturalguidelines/formats.html

American Psychological Association. (2007). *Guidelines for psychological practice with girls and women.* Washington, DC: Author.

Brabeck, M. M. (Ed.). (2000). *Practicing feminist ethics in psychology.* Washington, DC: American Psychological Association.

Canadian Psychological Association/Société Canadienne de Psychologie. (2005). *Canadian code of ethics for psychologists* (3rd ed.). Ottawa, Ontario, Canada: Author.

Feminist Therapy Institute. (1999). *Feminist therapy code of ethics* (revised). Retrieved November 13, 2009, from http://www.feminist-therapy-institute.org/ethics.htm

Feminist Therapy Institute. (2008). Home page. Retrieved October 2009, http://www.feminist-therapy-institute.org

Fisher, C. (2003). *Decoding the ethics code: A practical guide for psychologists.* Thousand Oaks, CA: Sage.

Forester-Miller, H., & Davis, T. (1996). *A practitioner's guide to ethical decision making.* Washington, DC: American Counseling Association.

Hawxhurst, D. (2009, Fall). CoCo's corner 9–09. *The Association for Women in Psychology Newsletter,* 7.

Herlihy, B., & Corey, G. (Eds.). (2006). *ACA ethical standards casebook* (6th ed.). Alexandria, VA: American Counseling Association.

Hill, M., Glaser, K., & Harden, J. (1998). A feminist model for ethical decision making. *Women & Therapy, 21,* 101–121.

Hyde, J. S., & McKinley, N. (1997). Gender difference in cognition: Results from meta-analyses. In P. J. Caplan, M. Crawford, J. S. Hyde, & J. T. E. Richardson (Eds.), *Gender differences in human cognition* (pp. 30–51). New York: Oxford University.

Kirkland, K., Kirkland, K. L., & Reaves, R. (2004). On the professional use of disciplinary data. *Professional Psychology: Research and Practice, 35,* 179–184.

Kitchner, K. S. (1996). There is more to ethics than principles. *The Counseling Psychologist, 24,* 92–97.

Lamb, D., Catanzaro, S., & Moorman, A. (2003). Psychologists reflect on their sexual relationships with clients, supervisees, and students: Occurrence, impact, rationales, and collegial intervention. *Professional Psychology: Research and Practice, 34,* 102–107.

McKinnon, J. M. (2008). Sylvania psychologist cedes license in sex charge: Female patient complained. Retrieved October 22, 2008, from http://www.toledoblade.com/apps/pbcs.dll/article?AID=/20081022/NEWS02/810220368

Meara, N. M., Schmidt, L. D., & Day, J. D. (1996). Principles and virtues: A foundation for ethical decisions, policies, and character. *The Counseling Psychologist, 24,* 4–77.

National Association of Social Workers. (1999). *Code of ethics.* Washington, DC: Author.

Pope, K. S., & Tabachink, B. G. (1993). Therapists' anger, hate, fear, and sexual feelings: National survey of therapist responses, client characteristics, critical events, formal complaints, and training. *Professional Psychology: Research and Practice, 24,* 142–152.

Pope, K. S., & Vasquez, M. J. T. (2007). *Ethics in psychotherapy and counseling: A practical guide* (3rd ed.). San Francisco, CA: Jossey-Bass.

Spelke, E. S. (2005). Sex differences in intrinsic aptitude for mathematics and science? A critical review. *American Psychologist, 60,* 950–958.

Worell, J., & Remer, P. (2003). *Feminist perspectives in therapy: Empowering diverse women* (2nd ed.). Hoboken, NJ: John Wiley & Sons.

CHAPTER 4

THE IMPORTANCE OF GENDER ROLES

Chapters 1–3 presented the framework of feminist therapy through a discussion of its history, current practice, and ethical foundations. Before focusing on basic skills in feminist therapy, it is necessary to have a solid understanding of the origin and cultural meaning of gender roles. Regardless of culture, our biological gender situates us in a particular sociopolitical context. Our gender roles are our identity as a woman or a man that are learned from our culture. As you will see in this chapter, these roles impact people physically, intellectually, and psychologically. As feminist therapists, we base our practice on an understanding of these roles.

In every society, the roles for women and men are either explicitly or implicitly defined. It is important for counselors and clients alike to understand that differences in gender are primarily socially constructed and learned rather than biological (Bem, 1993; Bussey & Bandura, 2004; Hansen & Gama, 1996). In fact, during the past 30 years, gender roles in Western societies have been in a state of flux. The traditional definitions of gender roles continue to be challenged by the women and men who must live them. These socially defined roles are imposed whether the individual is male or female and regardless of an individual's personality, interest, ability, or the needs of the society. By the time individuals reach adulthood, they have been well schooled as to the types of behaviors that are acceptable for their gender. This training is so deeply internalized that women and men are unaware that societal rules are the source of their emotional upset when they experience conflicts between their learned gender roles and their own needs, values, and desires.

● EARLY SOCIALIZATION OF GENDER ROLES

Before counselors can successfully practice feminist therapy, they need to be conversant in gender-role socialization. All learning begins at home, and eventually learning is spread to other venues as we grow and mature. Early gender socialization at home and at school shapes not only gender identity but also expectations about gender roles. Parents of newborn baby girls have been found to think of their baby girls as more fragile and weaker than have parents of newborn baby boys (Karraker, Vogel, & Lake, 1995; Wester & Trepal, 2008). Parents are often quick to say that they did not treat their girls differently from their boys. We live in a culture that espouses equality. Research, however, has shown that the actual behavior of parents often conflicts with their beliefs about their behavior (Bornstein, Cote, & Venuti, 2001). When observed, parents were found to be active participants in their children's gender-defined training (Fagot, 1978; Leaper, 2002). They may send their gender-defined messages by praising children for "gender-appropriate" play and activities. In fact, Fagot and Hagen (1991) found that preschool children were praised for their gender-appropriate play and reprimanded for inappropriate gender play. Additionally, boys were discouraged from gender-inappropriate play more than their female peers. That is, parents, especially fathers, are less tolerant of their son's gender-role-inappropriate behavior than similar behavior in their daughters (Campenni, 1999; Sandnabba & Ahlberg, 1999). Imagine a young boy growing up in a household with an older sister. He plays with her and her dolls. His father never yells at his son for playing with dolls but just quietly takes the dolls away and puts them back in big sister's hands instead of his son's hands. Perhaps, dad tells his son that big boys do not play with dolls. Think about what the son learns from this behavior, especially since dad has never told his sister that big girls do not play with dolls. The son and daughter learn that there is something inherently wrong with boys who "play house" or possibly by extension are the caregivers for others. Parents also communicate gender roles by example. Some examples of this are households where the mother always cleans the house while the father always cuts the grass or where the mother is responsible for taking care of sick family members while the father is responsible for distributing weekly allowances.

Some families, however, try to be egalitarian in their approach to gender roles by creating a gender-fair (that is, gender roles are consciously disputed and/or not enforced) and nonsexist (that is, males and females are treated equitably) family environment, teaching girls and boys about equity and equal opportunity, and encouraging both their girls and boys to play competitive sports and to prepare meals (Bem, 1998; Worell & Remer, 2003). Research has shown that the children of such families are indeed more flexible in their gender roles (Weisner, Garnier, & Loucky, 1994). However, such families are at a handicap because many gender-type messages are communicated to children through television, peers, books, toys, and, most unfortunately, their schools (Wester & Trepal, 2008; Worell & Remer, 2003). For an excellent real-life discussion of a gender-fair childrearing experience, see Sandra Bem's *An Unconventional Family* (1998).

A great deal of gender-role socialization takes place with peers and in the school setting. Boys and girls may attend the same school or even sit in the same classroom, but while educators are reluctant to admit that their perceptions and treatment of boys and girls differ, it is likely that the boys and girls in the classroom are treated differently (Maher & Ward, 2002). Teachers still tend to give boys more attention, more talk time, and more feedback when they do well and to ask them higher-level questions than the girls (Gillies, 2001; Sadlker, 1999; Worell & Remer, 2003). In addition, it has been found that educators have different perceptions and expectations of children related to gender. Girls are perceived to be neat, quiet, and emotional while boys are not. Moreover, in a 1999 study of textbooks, DeZolt and Henning-Stout found that girls were portrayed as passive and fearful and boys were more likely to be adventurous and high achieving. White males tended to dominate the texts, giving students a visual message about the importance of White males.

These findings point to the fact that although much has changed in the schools since the 1970s and the feminist movement, too often girls and boys are treated differently, with boys having the advantage over girls. For example, girls are typically encouraged to take language and social sciences over advanced mathematics and science (DeZolt & Henning-Stout, 1999). Advanced skills in math and sciences are essential to many of the higher-paying, higher-prestige careers. Without these skills, girls are at a disadvantage. It is typically believed that women have little ability and interest in math and science. Research does not support this notion. Very few math differences are found between genders (Hyde, 1996; Hyde, Fennema, Ryan, Frost, & Hopp, 1990). The ones that do exist are usually very small and not relevant to career choice.

However, when girls and boys give self-estimates of their abilities, girls tend to underestimate their mathematical abilities (Beloff, 1992; Rammstedt & Rammsayer, 2002). On the other hand, girls have higher self-estimates of their artistic ability than boys. Washburn-Ormachea, Hillman, and Sawilowsky (2004) as well as Rammsted and Rammsayer (2002) suggest that these estimates are influenced, in part, by gender stereotypes. What research finds is that there are greater differences within each gender than between the genders (Worell & Remer, 2003). Therefore, women's lack of interest in mathematics and sciences seems to be a societal artifact resulting from schools' lack of support, peer pressure, and family expectations.

In the end, gender-role socialization teaches boys to be competitive, fearless, achievement oriented, and emotionally restricted—all attributes that are valued in U.S. society. Girls, however, learn to be nurturing, supportive, communicative, helpful, well behaved, and artistic—all attributes that support an achieving and successful mate. Therefore, gender-role socialization sends the message that men and boys are more important and smarter than women and girls. Societal attention, rewards, and encouragement are geared toward masculine ways of being.

● GENDER ROLES AND CAREER DECISIONS

A lifestyle decision that is often based on gender-role expectations is career choice. Although the demographics in many careers have changed from male-dominated to a more equitable representation of women, it is still unusual for women and men to choose nontraditional careers—those dominated by the opposite gender (Betz, Heesacker, & Shuttleworth, 1990; Hannah & Kahn, 1989; Herr, Cramer, & Niles, 2004). Men do not choose nontraditional careers in part because women's careers typically pay less and lower wages would interfere with their defined role of "provider" and in part because a female-dominated profession would imply a lack of masculinity—at least the definition of masculinity espoused by society (Betz, Heesacker, & Shuttleworth, 1990; Hannah & Kahn, 1989; Leung & Harmon, 1990; Judge & Livingston, 2008; Tokar & Jome, 1998). Women do not choose nontraditional careers in part because they have been socialized to believe they do not have the skills to do "men's work" and in part because these careers make demands that may interfere with their defined role of family nurturer (Judge & Livingston, 2008; Stickel & Bonette, 1991). Even though kindergarten girls state interests in nontraditional careers, by the time they are adolescents, their goals have changed. When asked about careers, both adolescent girls and boys cite traditional career choices. However, at this point, few understand how those roles have shaped and limited their choices. Some teens can identify their choices as gender appropriate but cannot identify why these are gender-appropriate roles. They seem to be unaware of the impact of society on their individual choices.

Thanks to many brave women during the past 40 years who chose to enter male-dominated fields, several of those fields now have a critical mass of women (>25%) and are no longer considered nontraditional for women. However, working in those fields still presents challenges for women (e.g., long hours, glass ceiling, lower pay scale, sexual harassment, travel, and day care). These challenges are often exacerbated by employers who have not made adjustments to meet the current needs of both their female and male employees and their families. Women who hold these kinds of positions struggle to fulfill the androcentric norms of the work world (Bem, 1993) while also striving to fulfill the more traditional demands of what was once called the "women's sphere."

SOCIETAL EXPECTATIONS OF THE GENDERS ●

In our society, women, in general, are expected to be selfless, to sacrifice their own needs for the needs of others, to be physically attractive and desirable to men, emotionally expressive, and caring. Men, however, are expected to be emotionally restrained and logical and to provide for their families. It is problematic enough that personal attributes are assigned a gender preference, but the greater issue is that these attributes are not valued equally. Feminist authors often refer to the U.S. society as a patriarchy that is "a sex/gender system [in which] men have advantage conferred on them because of their prescribed rank or societal status or both" (Robinson, 2005, p. 48). Not only are men privileged in the patriarchy, but gender-role socialization also ensures that men remain in more powerful and advantaged positions than women. More insidious is the fact that the expectations are so rigidly engendered that when women do take on some of the highly valued male gender roles, the women are not valued more; to the contrary, they are often ostracized for "trying to be like a man."

Both women and men are essential to the survival of a society, as are all the tasks that must be performed to keep the society going. However, when roles and behaviors are designed to privilege only one group of people and when they are rigidly prescribed by one factor alone, a factor over which individuals have no control, neither the privileged group nor the subordinate group is allowed the complete freedom of life experiences. As always, when one group (men) has advantages that others (women) do not, the privileged group suffers in many ways as well. The obvious problems for men include, among many, meeting the demands of unearned privilege, recognizing when women are overlooked in their favor, and being pressed to maintain the status quo. When incidents such as these are encountered by men, men can experience gender-role conflict. Gender-role conflict becomes more common as changes are made in society and as individual men risk their status and privilege in order to redefine masculinity.

The societal expectation of a woman is for her to be the family caretaker even if she is also committed to full-time work outside the home (Evans, 2006). Most women who are engaged in a career often do "women's work" (careers dominated by women), which are typically lower paying than "men's work" (those dominated by men). Moreover, most "women's work" as opposed to "men's work" was not designed to have a career ladder with steady promotions. Women who chose careers that involve "men's work" are often reminded of their breach of social norms by discrimination and sexism. Interestingly, even when women enter the higher-paying, male-dominated fields, they are still paid less than male counterparts who do the same work (Robinson, 2005).

The societal expectation for men is that they obtain a career that will support their families, and in so doing, they are usually expected to choose work over family when such choices must be made (Mahlik et al., 2003). Men cannot be perceived as emotional or in need of help, which puts them in a very precarious position when they have multiple-role stress or fatigue. Most important, men must not possess feminine qualities, as those qualities lessen their status as men. Riley (2003) reported that even with the changes in the workforce with societal movement away from some of the traditional gender roles, men are unlikely to give up on the notion that they should be the primary provider for their families. In fact, that role still seemed to contribute to their sense of masculinity. Such findings make it easy to understand that when a dual-career family is faced with promotion and relocation, it is more likely that the female member of the couple will be the one to make the move with her male partner than it is for him to move for her career (Evans, 2006; Kaltreider, 1997).

● GENDER ROLES IN U.S. DIVERSE GROUPS

Gender roles among culturally diverse groups in the United States frequently vary from the dominant European-American, middle-class culture. We will highlight some ways in which gender roles of major ethnic and cultural groups may differ from those of the dominant U.S. culture.

Historically, African American women have always worked and have never been full-time homemakers. This is primarily a result of slavery and the subsequent treatment of African Americans in the United States. In fact, the survival of African Americans in this country depended on the African American woman's economic contribution (Evans & George, 2008). Therefore, the completion of household tasks was always more important than gender-typing those tasks. It is not unusual in many African American households to see a sharing of the duties without regard to gender (Evans & George, 2008). Even so, according to Winbush (2000, p. 13), "African American women traditionally are expected to be caretakers . . . and not the primary breadwinners." Moreover, as more African Americans enter the upper classes and the upper middle classes, they take on more of the dominant culture's values, and the division of labor becomes more gender specific.

A similar migration toward the dominant culture is apparent with Latinas/os and Asian Americans. According to Vasquez (1994), machismo (the belief that a man has the dominant role in the family and that he must take charge and provide for them) is not as pronounced in the Hispanic cultures as many have espoused it to be. Today, Latinas are more likely to be single parents than they were in the past, although many still value "familismo" (a devotion to family, an idea that family members join together and help one another and that the family takes precedence—including extended family) (Raffaelli & Ontai, 2004).

According to Neal (2000), cultural expectations that women are caregivers is present among Native Americans, yet in many tribal nations, women often have influential power over the decision making of the tribe (e.g., the council of women elders). Typically, these expectations were in keeping with the occupation of communally owned land where the extended family was essential. Unfortunately, although still highly valued, the extended family structure that helped them survive is crumbling as a result of government relocation interventions, high poverty, and unemployment rates.

Asian Americans are a very diverse group with roots in various Asian cultures. The term includes, among others, individuals from Indian and other South Asian cultures, the Hmong culture of Laos, as well as third- and fourth-generation Japanese Americans. Therefore, gender-role expectations for Asian Americans may differ among the various subcultures. In fact, the term "Asian American" might be too inclusive to be valid (Chan, 2004). As feminist therapists, we must remember this as we work with Asian and Asian American clients.

Some Asian American women and men pursue professional degrees because of cultural achievement standards but live within their expected gender roles. However, lower socioeconomic status Asian American women from Korea, the Philippines, and China are more apt to be exploited as workers, particularly in the garment industry, and through their work provide the primary income for their families (Vo & Scichitano, 2004). Overall, however, as with many other cultural groups, much of women's power lies within the family. For example, Laotian women are expected to handle the family's finances as well as preserve family unity (Zaharlick, 2000). Thus, many Asian American women walk a narrow line when they give up traditional gender power and move into the public sphere. In traditional Vietnamese family structure, women are solely responsible for raising children, although in the economic and social sphere, they are considered to have little power. Women ensure their future comfort and survival by maintaining their children's loyalty to them (Kibria, 1993). Female refugees to the United States from Southeast Asian countries have had to adapt to raising their children without the assistance of extended family and to the need for securing employment outside the home for the good of the family (Zahrlick, 2000).

Looking at similarities in gender roles and expectation across cultures, one might wonder whether gender roles are biologically rather than socially constructed. However, numerous studies point toward the sociocultural learning model of gender roles. There seems to be little or no difference in aptitude and cognitive ability between women and men (Hyde, 1981, 2005; Hyde & Linn, 1988). As Hansen and Gama (1996, p. 83) so aptly put it, "Although the levels of female subordination and abuse vary from culture to culture, gender inequality is still a universal social fact (and a social shame)."

SUMMARY

Bem (2008, p. 6) argues that looking at biological factors for female and male gender differences is based on the false assumption "that biology is a kind of bedrock beyond which social change is not feasible." Her argument is that biological differences do exist, but at this point in the history of humankind, they are not truly relevant. It does not matter whether men have more muscle mass than women, when one is designing a major marketing campaign, or working in a factory that makes components for electronics, or caring for children. With this in mind, feminist therapy becomes a treatment choice for all genders.

REFERENCES

Beloff, H. (1992). Mother, father and me: Our IQ. *The Psychologist, 5,* 309–311.

Bem, S. L. (1993). *The lenses of gender: Transforming the debate on sexual inequality.* New Haven, CT: Yale University Press.

Bem, S. L. (1998). *An unconventional family.* New Haven, CT: Yale University Press.

Bem, S. L. (2008). Transforming the debate on sexual inequality: From biological difference to institutionalized androcentrism. In J. C. Chrisler, C. Golden, and P. D. Rozee (Eds.), *Lectures on the psychology of women* (4th ed., pp. 2–15). New York: McGraw Hill.

Betz, N. E., Heesacker, R. S., & Shuttleworth, C. (1990). Moderators of the congruence and realism of major and occupational plans in college students: A replication and extension. *Journal of Counseling Psychology, 3,* 269–276.

Bornstein, M. H., Cote, L. R., & Venuti, P. (2001). Parenting beliefs and behaviors in northern and southern groups of Italian mothers of young infants. *Journal of Family Psychology, 15*(4), 663–675.

Bussey, K., & Bandura, A. (2004). Social cognitive theory of gender development and functioning. In A. H. Eagley, A. E. Beall, and R. J. Sternberg (Eds.), *The psychology of gender* (2nd ed.) (pp. 92–120). New York: Guilford.

Campenni, C. E. (1999). Gender stereotyping of children's toys: A comparison of parents and nonparents. *Sex Roles, 40,* 121–138.

Chan, C. S. Asian American women and adolescent girls: Sexuality and sexual expression. In J. C. Chrisler, C. Golden, and P. D. Rozee (Eds.), *Lectures on the psychology of women* (4th ed., pp. 220–231). New York: McGraw Hill.

DeZolt, D. M., & Henning-Stout, M. (1999). Adolescent girls' experiences in school and community settings. In N. G. Johnson et al. (Eds.), *Beyond appearance: A new look at adolescent girls* (pp. 253–275). Washington, DC: American Psychological Association.

Evans, K. M. (2006). Career and life style planning with couples and families. In D. Capuzzi and M. Stauffer (Eds.), *Career and life style planning: Theory and application* (pp. 335–362). Boston: Allyn & Bacon.

Evans, K. M., & George, R. (2008). African Americans. In G. McAuliffe & Associates (Eds.), *Culturally alert counseling: A comprehensive introduction* (pp. 146–187). Thousand Oaks, CA: Sage.

Fagot, B. I. (1978). The influence of sex of child on parental reactions to toddler children. *Child Development, 49,* 459–465.

Fagot, B. I., & Hagan, R. (1991). Observations of parent reactions to sex-stereotyped behaviors: Age and sex effects. *Child Development, 62*(3), 617–628.

Gillies, W. (2001). Leadership for gender-equal education. *Principal Leadership, 3,* 35–37.

Hannah, J. S., & Kahn, S. E. (1989). The relationship of socioeconomic status and gender to the occupational choices of grade 12 students. *Journal of Vocational Behavior, 34,* 161–178.

Hansen, L. S., & Gama, E. M. P. (1996). Gender issues in multicultural counseling. In P. B. Pedersen, J. G. Draguns, W. J. Lonner, & J. E. Trimble (Eds.), *Counseling across cultures* (4th ed.) (pp. 73–107). Thousand Oaks, CA: Sage.

Herr, E. L., Cramer, S. H., & Niles, S. G. (2004). *Career guidance and counseling through the lifespan: Systematic approaches.* Boston: Pearson Education.

Hyde, J. S. (1981). How large are cognitive gender differences? A meta-analysis using w2 and d. *American Psychologist, 36,* 892–901.

Hyde, J. S. (1996). Where are the gender differences? Where are the gender similarities? In D. M. Buss & N. M. Malamuth (Eds.), *Sex, power, conflict: Evolutionary and feminist perspectives* (pp. 107–118). New York: Oxford University Press.

Hyde, J. S. (2005). The gender similarities hypothesis. *American Psychologist, 60,* 581–659.

Hyde, J. S., Fennema, E., Ryan, M., Frost, L. A., & Hopp, C. (1990). Gender comparisons of mathematics attitudes and affect: A meta-analysis. *Psychology of Women Quarterly, 14,* 299–324.

Hyde, J. S., & Linn, M. C. (1988). Gender differences in verbal analysis: A meta-analysis. *Psychological Bulletin, 104,* 53–69.

Judge, T. A., & Livingston, B. A. (2008). Is the gap more than gender? A longitudinal analysis of gender, gender role orientation, and earnings. *Journal of Applied Psychology, 93,* 994–1012.

Kaltreider, N. (Ed.). 1997. *Dilemmas of a double life: Women balancing career and relationships.* Northvale, NJ: Jason Aronson.

Karraker, K. H., Vogel, D. A., & Lake, M. A. (1995). Parents' gender-stereotyped perceptions of newborns: The eye of the beholder revisited. *Sex Roles, 3,* 687–701.

Kibria, N. (1993). *Family tightrope: The changing lives of Vietnamese Americans.* Princeton, NJ: Princeton University Press.

Leaper, C. (2002). The social construction and socialization of gender during development. In P. H. Miller & E. K. Scholnick (Eds.), *Toward a feminist developmental psychology* (pp. 129–152). New York: Routledge.

Leung, S. A., & Harmon, L. W. (1990). Individual and sex differences in the zone of acceptable alternatives. *Journal of Counseling Psychology, 37,* 153–159.

Maher, F. A., & Ward, J. V. (2002). *Gender and teaching.* Mahwah, NJ: Erlbaum.

Mahalik, J. R., Good, G. E., & Englar-Carlson, M. (2003). Masculinity scripts, presenting concerns, and help seeking: Implications for practice and training. *Professional Psychology: Research and Practice, 34*, 123–131.

Neal, B. (2000). Native American women. In M. Julia (Ed.), *Constructing gender: Multicultural perspectives in working with women*. Belmont, CA: Brooks/Cole/Thomson Learning.

Raffaelli, M., &. Ontai, L. (2004). Gender socialization in Latino/a families: Results from two retrospective studies. *Sex Roles: A Journal of Research, 50*, 287–300.

Rammstedt, B., & Rammsayer, T. H. (2002). Gender differences in self-estimated intelligence and their relation to gender-role orientation. *European Journal of Personality, 16*, 369–382.

Riley, S. (2003). The management of the traditional male role: A discourse analysis of the constructions and functions of provision. *Journal of Gender Studies, 12*, 99–113.

Robinson, T. L. (2005). *The convergence of race, ethnicity, and gender: Multiple identities in counseling* (2nd ed.). Upper Saddle River, NJ: Merrill Prentice Hall.

Sadlker, D. (1999). Gender equity: Still knocking at the classroom door. *Educational Leadership. 56*, 22–26.

Sandnabba, N. K., & Ahlberg, C. (1999). Parents' attitudes and expectations about children's cross-gender behavior. *Sex Roles, 40*, 249–263.

Tokar, D. M., & Jome, L. M. (1998). Masculinity, vocational interests, and career choice traditionality: Evidence for a fully mediated model. *Journal of Counseling Psychology, 45*, 424–435.

Vasquez, M. J. T. (1994). Latinas. In L. Comas Diaz and B. Greene (Eds.), *Women of color: Integrating ethnic and gender identities in psychotherapy* (pp. 114–138). New York: Guilford.

Vo, L. T., & Scichitano, M. (2004). Introduction: Reimagining Asian American women's experiences. In L. T. Vo & M. Scichitano (Eds.), *Asian American women: The Frontiers reader* (pp. ix–xxxvi). Lincoln: University of Nebraska Press.

Washburn-Ormachea, J. M., Hillman, S. B., & Sawilowsky, S. S. (2004). Gender and gender-role orientation differences on adolescents' coping with peer stressors. *Journal of Youth and Adolescence, 33*, 31–40.

Weisner, T., Garnier, H., & Loucky, J. (1994). Domestic tasks, gender egalitarian values and children's gender typing in conventional and nonconventional families. *Sex Roles, 30*, 23–54.

Wester, K. L., & Trepal, H. C. (2008). Gender. In G. McAuliffe & Associates (Eds.), *Culturally alert counseling: A comprehensive introduction* (pp. 430–465). Thousand Oaks, CA: Sage.

Winbush, G. B. (2000). African American women. In M. Julia (Ed.), *Constructing gender: Multicultural perspectives in working with women*. Belmont, CA: Brooks/Cole/Thomson Learning.

Worell, J., & Remer, P. (2003). *Feminist perspectives in therapy: Empowering diverse women* (2nd ed.). Hoboken, NJ: John Wiley & Sons.

Zaharlick, A. (2000). SouthEast Asian American women. In M. Julia (Ed.), *Constructing gender* (pp. 177-204). Belmont, CA: Wadsworth.

CHAPTER 5

MENTAL HEALTH AND DIAGNOSIS IN THE CONTEXT OF FEMINIST THERAPY

This chapter deals with diagnosis, which is a process that labels a client's distress. Feminist therapists recognize that diagnosing is an act of power on the part of the mental health practitioner who labels client distress. Because diagnoses and the act of diagnosis reflect the dominant paradigms of psychology, feminist practitioners must have an understanding of the social construction of mental health and pathology.

MENTAL HEALTH AND PATHOLOGY ●

Definitions of mental health and pathology reflect the dominant culture's beliefs regarding normality and mental illness. Therefore, the definition of psychological wellness or mental health embraces the beliefs and values of the group of people who control the social, political, and economic arenas—White, middle- and upper-class, heterosexual, able-bodied, Protestant males (Ballou & Gabalac, 1985; Brown, 1994; Enns, 2000). These Western cultural, White, and androcentric norms deem individual characteristics and traits such as autonomy, objectivity, control, independence, and action as descriptors of optimal mental health. Behaviors and people who do not conform to dominant cultural norms are viewed as psychologically deficient or ill. Feminist therapy refers to this process as *pathologizing* (Brown, 1994; Collins, 1998; Evans, Kincade, & Seem, 2005; Martin, 1994). In fact, women and men who behave in ways that value relationships and connections over autonomy, emotionality and nurturance over objectivity, deference and selflessness over individual control, and culture, group, or family over independence are often labeled as mentally ill or deviant (Brown, 1994; Worell & Remer, 2003). Individuals who do not belong to dominant groups often possess the previously mentioned characteristics and are often from oppressed groups (Collins, 1998; Miller, 1986). Consider a young woman in counseling because her fiancée broke up with her. This is her first time seeking help for emotional problems. She is distraught, says she cannot stop crying, and states that she cannot live without her fiancée. Is she psychologically ill? Are her responses appropriate given her position in her culture and her value system?

The power of the dominant culture in terms of defining mental health is supported by more than 35 years of research. The study by Broverman, Broverman, Clarkson, Rosenkrantz, and Vogel (1970), which is discussed in Chapter 2, exemplifies how clinicians' beliefs regarding mental health influence clinical judgments. Remember, Broverman et al. (1970) found that judgments of mental health were based on the dominant culture's definition of mental health. Adult men, on the one hand, were viewed by mental health practitioners as healthy and well adjusted because their behavior coincided with the dominant definition of mental health. Women, on the other hand, were judged as unhealthy if they behaved in adult (that is, healthy) ways. Seem and Clark (2006) conducted a study to replicate the work of the Brovermans and their colleagues to discover whether clinical judgments regarding mental health were still similar to those in 1970. Participants were counselors in training. As in the Broverman et al. (1970) study, healthy adult women were found to be significantly different from healthy adult men as well as from healthy adults. As in 1970, Seem and Clark discovered that a healthy adult man was not found to be significantly different from a healthy adult. However, participants' judgments regarding female mental health had expanded to include both traditionally feminine and traditionally masculine traits and characteristics. Interestingly, perceptions of a healthy adult man revealed little change since 1970; healthy men were described in largely traditionally masculine terms. In other words, mentally healthy women can have both male and female qualities, but mentally healthy men may only have male qualities, and the "generic" healthy adult continues to resemble the mentally healthy male with characteristics such as being strong and independent. Thus, mental health definitions may change according to the zeitgeist of the dominant culture but still tend to pathologize those who behave differently from the dominant notions of mental health.

THE ORIGIN OF PSYCHOLOGICAL DISTRESS ●

Every counseling theory posits the cause of human distress. For some, like psychoanalysis and cognitive, the cause of the problem lies within the individual, either because of intrapsychic conflicts or irrational thoughts. In contrast to the traditional view of pathology as a problem within the individual, feminist therapy assumes that the major causes of individuals' problems are external and stem from sexist and oppressive environments (Brown, 1994; Rawlings & Carter, 1977; Rosewater, 1990). When therapists examine the environment in which an individual is born and develops, they acknowledge that sociopolitical and cultural factors have a profound impact on psychological development. When we disregard the environment or context as a cause of individual distress, we dismiss the harmful impact of sexism, racism, heterosexism and homophobia, ageism, and abelism on our clients (Brown, 1994; Worell & Remer, 1992; Evans et al., 2005). When distress is viewed as intrapsychic or residing within the individual, client conceptualization and treatment planning are focused solely on the client and changing the client. This focus does not require any adjustment of the social, political, and economic structures that cause clients' pain and suffering.

In contrast, feminist therapists assert that individuals' experiences must be centered in the context of their life, that is, in individuals' experiences in the world. Counselors cannot understand clients' behaviors if they view clients only in the isolation of their individual distress. Although clients' subjective understanding of experiences is important to understanding psychological distress, feminist therapists deem it equally important to consider clients' experiences within the context of the clients' lived experiences (Brown, 1994; Evans et al., 2005; Worell & Remer, 2003). Consider the case of domestic abuse. A counselor must take into consideration more than the abuse to understand clients' experiences. If clients are from low-income or lower socioeconomic class backgrounds and are dependent on family for housing and food, then it might not be possible for them to leave abusive situations. Additionally, cultural and family values concerning domestic arrangements need to be considered. Even though it may be tempting to label the behavior of a woman who stays in an abusive relationship as dependent or masochistic, in this context, it is not a case of psychological dependency but rather one of economic necessity and the need for food and shelter. That is, endurable physical abuse may be preferable to certain homelessness. If cultural or family values are part of the decision to stay in an abusive relationship, then family obligations may override individual decisions.

In summary, feminist therapists' beliefs regarding human nature and etiology of distress impact how they view their clients' concerns. Furthermore, feminist therapists' definition of mental health includes not only symptoms presented by clients but also a wide range of client behaviors that are influenced by culture and context. These beliefs about culture and context shape how feminist therapists think about the diagnostic enterprise.

● MENTAL HEALTH DIAGNOSIS

Feminist therapists have had an uneasy relationship with diagnosis and assessment as practiced traditionally. Historically, feminist therapists rejected the idea of diagnosis because (a) it did not acknowledge oppression as a basis of client distress (Rawlings & Carter, 1977), (b) issues of power and social control were believed to be embedded in the traditional practice of diagnosis (Rawlings & Carter, 1977), and (c) it involved therapist power (via the act of labeling) over the client (Caplan, 1992). This use of power to label is the antithesis of what feminist therapy espouses; it undermines the possibility of an egalitarian relationship. Despite these concerns, contemporary feminist therapists are often required by agencies and other societal institutions to engage in the formal diagnostic process. In these cases, diagnosis is approached thoughtfully with a feminist consciousness so that the act of diagnosing does not abuse therapists' power, replicate the dominant definition of mental health, or act as a form of social control regarding client behavior (Brown, 1990; Erickson & Kress, 2005; Hernandez & Seem, 2001).

● THE MEDICAL MODEL AND DIAGNOSIS

The Diagnostic and Statistical Manual (DSM) is the most popular and widely used nosology system in the United States (Erickson & Kress, 2005; Kutchins & Kirk, 1997). The DSM "represents the dominant cultural narrative about emotionality, behavioral, and psychological problems and shapes the thinking and practice of most clinicians" (Duffy, Gillig, Tureen, & Ybarra, 2002, p. 363). Therefore, it is important to understand the historical development of the DSM and feminist criticisms of the DSM. In addition, the appropriateness of the category model that is the foundation of the DSM and its scientific rigor are explored. Finally, the impact of counselor subjectivity and bias in the diagnostic process is examined.

The concept of diagnosis is embedded in the medical model of medicine. The intent of diagnosis in this model is to help the physician determine the nature and cause of a disease or injury so that appropriate treatment may be decided. This type of analysis functions well in the physical medicine field, where a diagnosis informs the physician and patient of the problem, the prognosis, and the type and length of treatment (Albee, 2000). In the medical model, causes of physical disease are typically gender and culture free. However, to use the model of physical sciences, which uses data based on reliable and precisely measurable variables, with the diagnosis of mental illnesses, which uses data based on abstractions, such as anxiety and antisocial personality disorder, is troublesome (Duffy et al., 2002). To do so, psychiatric categories must be reliable, valid, objective, and identifiable across all populations and clinically relevant regardless of a prospective client's gender, ethnicity, religion, class, and nationality (Horsfall, 2001). Mental disorder categories, as delineated by the DSM, do not meet those criteria. Using the DSM to diagnose mental disorders does not truly parallel the strategies used to diagnose physical illness or injury. Many factors, such as culture and gender, which do not often come into play when a physical illness is diagnosed, impact the diagnosis of a mental disorder.

Brief History of the Diagnostic and Statistical Manual

It is important to remember that the DSM is written by psychiatrists, who are medical doctors. Their assumptions about human nature and beliefs about mental health and illness profoundly influence this document. In addition, changes in the manual have reflected the changes in our society. The first edition of the DSM (APA, 1952) conceptualized abnormality as the result of neurotic conflicts, reflecting its writers' assumptions about mental illness. The DSM III (APA, 1980) was revised to be atheoretical and descriptive with specific criteria developed for each disorder. The DSM III-R (APA, 1987) added axes (Kutchins & Kirk, 1997). In the DSM-IV (APA, 1994), disorders were viewed as biological illnesses with emotional overtones (Hernandez & Seem, 2001), which reflected a trend that began in the socially and politically conservative 1980s and the emergence of managed care in the 1990s (Brown, 1994). This text was also the first edition to recognize and address culture in its framework. The DSM-IV-TR (APA, 2000) focused on behavioral symptomatology and suggested the importance of drug management of mental illness over psychotherapy (Hernandez & Seem, 2001) (See Table 5.1 for DSM categories).

"Today, DSM symbolizes the institutional basis of psychiatric practice in social contexts influenced by the United States" (Fabrega, 1992, p. 6), and its history reveals that it is not necessarily a scientific document but rather a document informed by social forces and psychological theories (Kutchins & Kirk, 1997).

Table 5.1	*DSM* Categories

> Axis I: Clinical Disorders;
>
> Axis II: Personality Disorders and Mental Retardation
>
> Axis III: General Medical Conditions
>
> Axis IV: Psychosocial and Environmental Problems
>
> Axis V: Global Assessment of Functioning Scale

Source: Adapted from *Diagnostic and Statistical Manual of Mental Disorders* (4th ed.), *Text Revision,* pp. 27–28, by American Psychiatric Association, 2000, Washington, DC: American Psychiatric Press.

In fact, Kutchins and Kirk (1997) argue that the DSM is a story of the American Psychiatric Association's fight to gain respectability with the medical field and to maintain control over the mental health field. Whatever the criticism, it is important that counselors maintain objectivity and caution, and remain cognizant of the history of the DSM, when using this system to inform diagnostic practice.

Feminist Criticisms of the DSM System

Feminist therapists criticize the DSM system for three major reasons, as follows:

1. DSM's writers' focus on an intrapsychic etiology

2. The prevalence of androcentric and monocultural perspectives in the DSM despite its writers' attempt to acknowledge gender and culture

3. The influence of political agendas on the content of the DSM

1. Intrapsychic Focus

Based on a medical model perspective, the DSM continues to adhere to an intrapsychic focus. Feminist therapists contend that the DSM's intrapsychic focus does not acknowledge social inequities and contextual factors as potential causes of human pain and distress (Brown, 1994; Fabrega, 1992; Khatidja, 2005; Kupers, 1997; Marecek & Hare-Mustin, 1991; Rawlings & Carter, 1977; Russell, 1986; Worell & Remer, 1992, 2003). Thus, mental health diagnosis (as traditionally practiced) medicalizes social problems (Brown, 1992). Few diagnostic categories locate the cause of client distress within the environment (Brown, 1994; Worell & Remer, 1992, 2003). Consequently, everyday stressors or insidious trauma (Root, 1992) related to "isms" such as sexism, racism, classism, heterosexism, and so on are at best rarely acknowledged and at worst completely ignored. This intrapsychic focus overlooks critical systems, relationships, and cultural perspectives (Erickson & Kress, 2005), and it disregards the interrelationship of the social and personal spheres of people's lives (Brown, 1994; Rawlings & Carter, 1977). Misdiagnosis and/or blaming the victim may result when contextual and sociopolitical factors are minimized or ignored (Brown, 1994; Evans et al., 2005; Santos de Barona & Dutton, 1997; Worell & Remer, 2003).

2. Androcentric, Monocultural, and Class Bias

Androcentric (e.g., male-centered), monocultural (e.g., White and Western), and class (e.g. middle socioeconomic class) assumptions regarding health and pathology are built into the DSM diagnostic criteria. Many argue that these criteria tend to be biased against women (Becker, 2001; Becker & Lamb, 1994; Brown, 1994; Caplan, 1992; Dumont, 1987; Enns, 2000; Erickson & Kress, 2005; Faludi, 1991; Horsfall, 2001; Kupers, 1997; Kutchins & Kirk, 1997; Unger & Crawford, 1996; Worell & Remer, 2003) and other marginalized groups (Adebimpe, 1981; Block, 1984; Caplan, 1995; Collins, 1998; Enns, 2000; Erickson & Kress, 2005; Flaskerud & Hu, 1992; Griffith, 1996; Kutchins & Kirk, 1997; Lin, 1996; Loring & Powell, 1988; Rogier, 1996; Snowden, 2003; Thompson, 1996; Worell & Remer, 2003). This bias may lead to the diagnosis of certain types of disorders more often for women than for men, such as some forms of depressive disorder, eating disorders, panic disorders, agoraphobia, and borderline personality disorder (Becker, 2001; Kupers, 1997).

Classism and heterosexism are also entrenched in the DSM system. Landrine (1989), for example, suggests that social role or one's location in the power (social) hierarchy also accounts for the diagnosis of certain personality disorders in both women and men. In her study, participants assigned the diagnosis of histrionic personality disorder to the single, young, middle-class woman; the dependent personality disorder to the married, middle-class, middle-aged female; antisocial personality disorder to the young, lower-class man; and either compulsive, paranoid, or narcissistic personality disorders to the middle-class male. Overdiagnosis with certain disorders and misdiagnosis also are well documented for gay men and lesbians, nontraditional men, ethnic minorities, and women (Sinacore-Guinn, 1995).

Culturally biased assumptions underlie the DSM system of classification. These monocultural assumptions are the ego centrality of self, the division of the mind and body, and the view that people are treated as parts that make up a whole rather than as a whole (Kutchins & Kirk, 1997). Even though more recent versions of the DSM address cultural variations in a separate section of each diagnosis, when available, and provide a glossary of culture bound syndromes, for example, racial/ethnic biases are still entrenched in the DSM system (Caplan, 1995; Kutchins & Kirk, 1997; Snowden, 2003) (see Table 5.2).

Table 5.2	Diagnosis as a Form of Social Control

Drapetomania

In the 19th century, slaves who frequently ran away despite recapture and punishment were diagnosed with drapetomania (Fassinger, 2000; Hernandez & Seem, 2001). Diagnosing the act of seeking freedom by a specific group of people, Black slaves certainly maintained the status quo of and social control by White slave owners.

Hysteria

The term "hysteria" was applied to the floating wombs of Victorian women whose discontent was expressed in physical and emotional distress (Fassinger, 2000). Women were controlled by the interpretation of their discontent with being a wife and mother as unfeminine and unnatural. Although we are now amused by this, using women's unique biology to control their behaviors and roles still occurs.

Premenstrual Dysphoric Disorder (PMDD)

This is only applicable to females and pathologizes women for having menses. Even though research regarding this disorder is methodologically flawed, it is still present in the DSM (Enns, 2000). Men also have mood changes caused by hormones, but this behavior is not studied (Caplan, 1995; Gallant & Hamilton, 1988). Critics declare that it is not coincidental that premenstrual syndrome was resurrected again at a time when women in large numbers were entering the workforce (Kupers, 1997; Tavris, 1992). According to Chrisler and Caplan (2002), "Each time women make substantial gains in political, economic, or social power, medical or scientific experts step forth to warm that women cannot go any further without risking damage to their delicate physical and mental health" (p. 284). To raise consciousness about the political agenda of PMDD, the following diagnoses were suggested: Testosterone-Based Aggressive Personality (Nikelly, 1996) and Aggressive, Power-Driven, Exploiting Personality (Dumont, 1987) but were not taken seriously by the writers of the DSM.

Homosexuality

Homosexuality was once considered a sociopathic personality disturbance in the DSM (APA, 1952), and it was still considered a mental disorder in the DSM II (APA, 1973). In 1980, homosexuality was changed to egodystonic homosexuality in the DSM-III (APA) and eventually dropped from the DSM-IV (APA, 1994) altogether. The life of this diagnosis followed the sociopolitical climate regarding homosexuality in the United States (Bayer, 1981). Despite this change, however, pathologizing of homosexuality may still continue and is codified in less obvious forms in the DSM-IV. A clinician may deem homosexuality a mental illness by using one of the following diagnoses: Gender Identity Disorder in Adolescents or Adults, ("sexually attracted to males" and "sexually attracted to females") (DSM IV; APA, 1994, p 538) (Kupers, 1997) and Sexual Disorder Not Otherwise Specified ("persistent and marked distress about sexual orientation" (DSM-IV; APA, 1994, p. 538) (Fassinger, 2000).

Antisocial Personality Disorder

Griffith (1996) asserts that the assignment of Antisocial Personality Disorder is an attempt to label an African American male in such a way that he does not receive help from the mental health system. This labeling in turn facilitates contact with the criminal justice system for African Americans.

Smart and Smart (1997) claim that the DSM-IV (APA, 1994) is more culturally sensitive than prior revisions. This statement also holds true for the DSM-IV-TR (APA, 2000). As evidence of increased cultural sensitivity, Smart and Smart (1997) point to the addition of five new areas of information that address specific cultural features, culture-bound syndromes, a formulation for addressing cultural background, a broader definition of Axis IV (Psychosocial and Environmental Problems), and the inclusion of new culturally sensitive V codes. However, this inclusion of cultural information seems largely marginal (Hernandez & Seem, 2001), and the manual is replete with Western White cultural assumptions. For example, the Specific Cultures Features section does not refer to specific cultures. Instead, broad generalities are stated that involve few references to other cultures than the dominant White culture in the United States. The instructions for the Cultural Foundation section tell the clinician "to provide a narrative summary for the client's cultural identity, cultural explanation of illness, cultural factors related to the client's psychosocial environment and level of functioning, cultural elements of clinician–client relationship and overall cultural assessment for diagnosis and care" (DSM-IV, 1994, p. 844–845). Those instructions, however, do not indicate how this information is to be used to formulate a diagnosis of a client. Finally, monocultural assumptions remain ingrained in the Glossary of Culture-Bound Syndromes. Kutchins and Kirk (1997) contend that the cultural entries were taken out of context and stripped of meaning. They argue that no effort was made to be comprehensive or selective in the choice of entries or cultures. Certain diagnoses, such as anorexia nervosa and agoraphobia, which are primarily found in Western cultures, are not listed as examples of culture-bound syndromes.

Although cultural Axis IV Codes allow a counselor to name oppression caused by racism, for example, as an etiology, only diagnoses on Axes I and II are required for medical insurance companies. Thus, environmental and cultural causes are not viewed as "true" mental illness in the sense that they are not reimbursable. Essentially, real mental illness does not acknowledge cultural context (Brown, 1994).

Racism is also embedded in the DSM system (Brown, 1994; Kutchins & Kirk, 1997). A healthy paranoia and blunted affect necessary to survive in an oppressive environment may be misdiagnosed as schizophrenia. For example, African Americans have a higher than expected rate of diagnosed schizophrenia and lower than expected rates of diagnosed affective disorders (Adebimpe, 1981; Snowden, 2003). Furthermore, Blacks are more likely to be described as dangerous, violent, and angry given an identical presentation to their White peers (Caplan, 1995). In a study of the relationship of ethnic identity to psychiatric diagnosis in a mental health system (Flaskerud & Hu, 1992), ethnicity had a consistent and significant relationship to diagnosis. Black and Asian patients were assigned a greater percentage of psychotic disorders than Caucasian clients. Latino clients received this diagnosis even less than White patients. In contrast, Caucasian and Asian patients were diagnosed more often with affective disorders, such as depression and anxiety, than were Black and Latino patients.

3. Political Agendas/Social Control

Defining mental illness and determining the etiology of mental illness are major political issues impacted by the zeitgeist of the time (Erickson & Kress, 2005; Fassinger, 2000; Hernandez & Seem, 2001). External pressures from certain groups, professional organizations, and corporations influence the research that is conducted and the diagnoses that are included or excluded in the DSM system (Kutchins & Kirk, 1997). Because definitions of mental illness are not static and change across time, Kutchins and Kirk (1997) and Enns (2000), among others, argue that diagnostic labels are a result of social construction and consequently may be used as a form of social control

(Caplan, 1995; Chesler, 1972; Greenspan, 1993; Kutchins & Kirk, 1997; Marecek & Hare-Mustin, 1991).

Social control has a political agenda, and the political and social climate of an era influences diagnostic categories. What is deemed pathological and normal reflects the dominant groups' values and beliefs at a particular time. In the DSM nosology, women's changes in mood because of hormonal fluctuations, for example, are pathologized (e.g., Premenstrual Dysphoric Disorder), whereas men's documented changes in mood because of hormones are not (Chrisler & Caplan, 2002; Kutchins & Kirk, 1997). Thoughts and behaviors that harm individuals and society as a whole, such as homophobia, sexism, violence against women, and so on, are not codified in the DSM system as psychological problems (Kutchins & Kirk, 1997). They are not deemed pathological because they support the dominant group's policies and power.

The social acceptance of the DSM is evidenced by the fact that the DSM's approach to diagnosis is required for (a) practitioners seeking reimbursement through private and public health insurance entities, (b) researchers seeking National Institute of Mental Health research funding, and (c) academics who write textbooks about psychopathology (Kutchins & Kirk, 1997). In addition, coursework on psychopathology is often taught using the DSM as a model so that new mental health practitioners can quickly and "accurately" diagnose clients' concerns. This overreliance on the DSM shapes and limits what we know and how we interact with clients, research participants, and students.

With regard to gendered behaviors and current social roles, Kupers (1997) asserts that diagnostic criteria reflect an upper limit of tolerance for the characteristics that are socially encouraged in both sexes. For example, traditional Caucasian female gender role behavior expects females to be dependent, passive, compliant, emotional, and nurturing. Those who overconform to such traditional female behaviors are likely to be diagnosed with dependent or histrionic personality disorders (Brown, 1994; Caplan, 1992; Kaplan, 1983; Reinzi & Scrams, 1991). A examination of the list of criteria for those two disorders elucidates the connection between the criteria and feminine-gendered behavior. In the same way, overcompliance to traditional male-gendered behavior may result in a diagnosis of antisocial, paranoid, and compulsive personality disorder for males (Reinzi & Scrams, 1991). Kupers (1997) argues that mental disorders typically assigned to men and to women serve as a way to *control* the behaviors that male and female socialization encourages. Boys, for example, are encouraged to be rough, aggressive and active, sexually aggressive, adventurous, and rational, but when they become too aggressive they may receive a diagnosis of Conduct Disorder or

Intermittent Explosive Disorder. Men may receive a diagnosis of Obsessive-Compulsive Personality Disorder if they become too rational, and if they break the rules too badly in the sexual realm they receive a diagnosis of Paraphilia (see Table 5.2).

In sum, not only have the DSM categories and mental health diagnoses been historically prone to reflect social and political beliefs and power systems, but they also continue to be used in our current modes and methods of diagnosis for mental health concerns.

● POTENTIAL FOR COUNSELOR BIAS

Counselors' assumptions about gender and culture affect clinical judgment (Broverman et al., 1970; Hernandez & Seem, 2001; Seem & Clark, 2006; Worell & Remer, 2003). Such notions may result from individual beliefs and values, some of which may be unconscious (Bem & Bem, 1970), and from human processing errors (Arkes, 1981; Darley & Gross, 1983; McLaughlin, 2002; Morrow & Deidan, 1992). As a result, diagnostic bias may occur (Becker, 2001; Becker & Lamb, 1994; Broverman et al., 1970; Brown, 1994; Landrine, 1989; Reinzi & Scrams, 1991; Robertson & Fitzgerald, 1990; Seem & Clark, 2006; Seem & Johnson, 1998).

Individual Beliefs

Like everyone else, mental health practitioners are socialized by the dominant culture's values and beliefs about mental health and pathology and may acquire a nonconscious ideology (Bem & Bem, 1970) that influences the practice of diagnosis (Hernandez & Seem, 2001). Sexism, classism, racism, ageism, heterosexism, and abelism may be a part of this nonconscious ideology. A great deal of evidence points to the existence of practitioner bias and misdiagnosis because of stereotyping and ignoring the perspectives of women and people of color (Kutchins & Kirk, 1997). A feminist consciousness and an ongoing awareness of one's beliefs and values are necessary to not replicate the dominant culture's biases in the diagnostic process.

Additionally, misdiagnosis may occur because of counselors' subjectivity. The DSM is fraught with definitions and wording that are open to counselor interpretation. Various authors (Brown, 1994; Caplan, 1992; Kutchins & Kirk, 1997; Russell, 1986) identify many forms of clinician bias, which are presented as follows:

1. The DSM-IV uses terminology that allows for a counselor's own judgment (APA, 1994, p. 2). Diagnostic decisions rely on a counselor's judgment about what constitutes "mild," "moderate," or "severe" severity; "clinically significant," "persistent," "severe," and so on.

2. The DSM-IV's (APA, 1994) definition of a mental disorder makes it vulnerable to counselor bias (Brown, 1994; Caplan, 1992; Russell, 1986). A mental disorder is defined in the DSM-IV-TR (APA, 2000) as follows:

   > clinically significant behavioral or psychological syndrome or pattern that occurs in an individual and that is associated with present distress (e.g., painful symptom) or disability (i.e., impairment in one or more important areas of functioning) or with a significantly increased risk of suffering death, pain, disability, or important loss of freedom. (APA, 2000, p. xxxi)

   This definition allows for interpretation and, therefore, subjectivity in that a counselor must decide, for example, what is "significant" or what is "distress."

3. The DSM-IV-TR (APA, 2000) allows a counselor to use clinical judgment in deciding whether or not to give a diagnosis when the client's presentation of symptoms does not meet the number of criteria for a diagnosis.

   > For example, the exercise of clinical judgment may justify giving a certain diagnosis to an individual even though the clinical presentation falls short of meeting the full criteria for that the diagnosis as long as the symptoms present are persistent and severe. (APA, 2000, p. xxxii)

   Clinicians, therefore, have much leeway in determining whether a diagnosis is given and practitioner bias and subjectivity may influence diagnostic judgments.

Human Processing Errors

Humans develop cognitive mechanisms to create order and make sense of a vast amount and variety of information. Thus, psychologists, mental health practitioners, and counselors, like all humans, use gender, race/ethnicity, social class, and so on as organizational categories to understand others and draw conclusions about others based on those organizational categories (Hernandez & Seem, 2001; Unger & Crawford, 1996). People employ several cognitive mechanisms that allow them to organize and understand information; many of these cognitive mechanisms can lead to processing errors or misdiagnosis.

Inferential bias is a reasoning process that may result in selective recall (Arkes, 1981; Hernandez & Seem, 2001; Morrow & Deidan, 1992) or the use of stereotypes or vividness of data (Enns, 2000; Garb, 1996; McLaughlin, 2002). For example, a clinician may pay selective attention to detail that confirms a preexisting bias or categorizes something on the "basis of its familiarity, ease or recall or salience" (McLaughlin, 2002, p. 260). Here, a diagnostic judgment is made on the vividness or availability of information and its salience (such as social roles, family, and/or stereotype) rather than on less available information. Because the vividness of data is limiting and stereotypes are rigid, memory may be influenced by the salience of this information and result in misdiagnosis (Darley & Gross, 1983).

Fundamental attribution error is the tendency to overestimate the effect of an individual's personality and to underestimate the environmental or situational influences on behavior (Enns, 2000; Jackson & Sullivan, 2003; Morrow & Deidan, 1992); in essence, it is to locate the source of the problem within the individual and to minimize or ignore the environment as a source of client distress. This type of bias may be especially powerful for women and people of color who often have valid claims of discrimination and may often have significant environmental pressures (Morrow & Deidan, 1992).

Another human processing error is *the primacy effect*, which may lead to assessment bias (McLaughlin, 2002). With this type of bias, the counselor is influenced by the first piece of information he or she learns about the client. For example, a clinician misdiagnoses someone as a result a prior counselor's assessment. Primacy effect is similar to another processing error called *reconstructive memory* (Morrow & Deidan, 1992). Gaps in memory are filled in or altered so that whatever the clinician remembers fits with his or her current hypothesis about the client.

Counselors also are vulnerable to s*elf-confirming bias,* which is sometimes called confirmatory bias or confirmation bias (Darley & Gross, 1983; Jackson & Sullivan, 2003; McLaughlin, 2002; Morrow & Deidan, 1992). With this type of bias, a counselor focuses on information that confirms his or her hypothesis, and a client is labeled based exclusively on the focused information. Counselors may also act on a *self-fulfilling prophecy* when they proceed on the expectation they have of a client that confirms their expectation (McLaughlin, 2002).

Although such cognitive mechanisms help with data processing, they may lead to human processing errors that result in the misdiagnosis of clients. Thus, clinician awareness of these processing errors will help lessen their influence on diagnosis and diagnostic thinking.

SUMMARY

Given the reality of our world and work, feminist therapists cannot ignore diagnosis/assessment. In all probability, we will have to diagnose because of job responsibilities and to obtain third-party reimbursement. Additionally, our clients may come to us with their own formal or informal diagnoses. Clients come to us from other agencies and, sometimes, with a mental health history. Additionally, clients come to us with diagnoses obtained from media (e.g., drug company websites and television commercials) as well as from the rich and varied self-help literature (e.g., co-dependent, adult child of an alcoholic, incest survivor, and so on). Perhaps most important is that our clients, like their therapists, live in a culture that does not like ambiguity and wants solid answers to their questions. Thus, feminist therapy, which in many ways celebrates the healthy side of ambiguity and diversity, still needs to find a way to help clients understand themselves better and live more satisfying lives. Feminist therapists as competent and ethical mental health practitioners must be able to evaluate and diagnose in a manner that honors clients' experiences and acknowledges environmental impacts on mental health.

REFERENCES

Adebimpe, V. R. (1981). Overview: White norms and psychiatric diagnoses of Black patients. *The American Journal of Psychiatry, 138*(3), 279-285.

Albee, G. W. (2000). Critique of psychotherapy in American society. In C. R. Synder & R. E. Ingram (Eds.), *Handbook of psychological change: Psychotherapy processes and practices for the 21st century* (pp. 689–706). New York: John Wiley & Sons.

American Psychiatric Association. (1952). *Diagnostic and statistical manual of mental disorders.* Washington, DC: American Psychiatric Press.

American Psychiatric Association. (1980). *Diagnostic and statistical manual of mental disorders* (3rd ed.). Washington, DC: American Psychiatric Press.

American Psychiatric Association. (1987). *Diagnostic and statistical manual of mental disorders-III-R* (3rd ed.), *revised.* Washington, DC: American Psychiatric Press.

American Psychiatric Association. (1994). *Diagnostic and statistical manual of mental disorders* (4th ed.). Washington, DC: American Psychiatric Press.

American Psychiatric Association. (2000). *Diagnostic and statistical manual of mental disorders* (4th ed.), *text revision.* Washington, DC: American Psychiatric Press.

Arkes, H. R. (1981). Impediments to accurate clinical judgment and possible ways to minimize their impact. *Journal of Consulting and Clinical Psychology, 49*(3), 323–330.

Ballou, M., & Gabalac, N. W. (1985). *A feminist position on mental health.* Springfield, IL: Charles C Thomas.

Bayer, R. (1981). *Homosexuality and American psychiatry.* New York: Basic.

Becker, D. (2001). Diagnosis of psychological disorders: DSM and gender. In J. Worell (Ed.), *Encyclopedia of women and gender: Sex similarities and differences and the impact of society on gender* (pp. 333–343). New York: Academic Press.

Becker, D., & Lamb, S. (1994). Sex bias in the diagnosis of borderline personality disorder. *Professional Psychology: Research and Practice, 25*(1), 55–61.

Bem, S. L., & Bem, D. J. (1970). Training the woman to "know her place." The power of nonconscious ideology. In S. Cox (Ed.), *Female psychology: The emerging self* (pp. 180–191). Chicago, IL: Science Research Association.

Block, C. B. (1984). Diagnostic and treatment issues for black patients. *The Clinical Psychologist, 37,* 51–54.

Broverman, I. K., Broverman, D. M., Clarkson, F. E., Rosenkrantz, P. S., & Vogel, P. S. (1970). Sex-role stereotyping and clinical judgments of mental health. *Journal of Consulting and Clinical Psychology, 34,* 1–7.

Brown, L. S. (1990). Taking account of gender in the clinical assessment interview. *Professional Psychology; Research and Practice, 21*(1), 12–17.

Brown, L. S. (1992). Feminist critique of personality disorders. In L. S. Brown & M. Ballou (Eds.), *Personality and psychopathology: Feminist reappraisals* (pp. 206–228). New York: Guilford.

Brown, L. S. (1994). *Subversive dialogues.* New York: Basic Books.

Caplan, P. J. (1992). Gender issues in diagnosis of mental disorders. *Women and Therapy, 12,* 71–79.

Caplan, P. J. (1995). *They say you're crazy: How the world's most powerful psychiatrists decide who's crazy.* Reading, MA: Addison-Wesley.

Chesler, P. (1972). *Women and madness.* New York: Doubleday.

Chrisler, J. C., & Caplan, P. (2002). The strange case of Dr. Jekyll and Ms. Hyde: How PMS became a cultural phenomenon and a psychiatric disorder. *Annual Review of Sex Research, 13,* 274–307.

Collins, L. H. (1998). Illustrating feminist theory: Power and psychopathology. *Psychology of Women Quarterly, 22,* 97–112.

Darley, J. M., & Gross, P. H. (1983). A hypothesis-confirming bias in labeling effects. *Journal of Personality and Social Psychology, 44*(4), 20–33.

Duffy, M., Gillig, S. E., Tureen, R. M., & Ybarra, M. A. (2002). A critical look at the DSM-IV. *The Journal of Individual Psychology, 58*(4), 363–374.

Dumont, M. P. (1987). A diagnostic parable (1st ed.—unrevised). *READINGS: A Journal of Reviews and Commentary on Mental Health, 2,* 9–12.

Enns, C. Z. (2000). Gender issues in counseling. In S. D. Brown & R. W. Lent (Eds.), *Handbook of counseling psychology* (pp. 601–638). New York: John Wiley & Sons.

Erickson, K., & Kress, V. E. (2005). *Beyond the DSM story: Ethical quandaries, challenges and best practices.* Thousand Oaks, CA: Sage.

Evans, M., Kincade, E. A. & Seem, S. R., (2005). Case approach to feminist therapy. In G. Corey (Ed.), *Case approach to counseling and psychotherapy* (pp. 208–241) (6th ed.). Belmont, CA: Thomson Brooks/Cole.

Fabrega, H. (1992). Diagnosis interminable: Toward a culturally sensitive DSM-IV. *The Journal of Nervous and Mental Disease, 180*(1), 5–7.

Faludi, S. (1991). *Backlash: The undeclared war against women.* New York: Crona.

Fassinger, R. E. (2000). Gender and sexuality in human development: Implications for prevention and advocacy in counseling psychology. In S. D. Brown & R. W. Lent (Eds.), *Handbook of counseling psychology* (pp. 346–378). New York: John Wiley & Sons.

Flaskerud, J. H., & Hu, L. (1992). Relationship of ethnicity to psychiatric diagnosis. *The Journal of Nervous and Mental Disease, 180*(5), 296–303.

Gallant, S. J., & Hamilton, J. A. (1988). On a premenstrual psychiatric diagnosis: What's in a name? *Professional Psychology: Research and Practice, 19*(3), 271–276.

Garb, H. N. (1996). The representativenss and past-behavior heuristics in clinical judgment. *The Professional Psychology: Research and Practice, 27*(3), 272–277.

Greenspan, M. (1993). *A new approach to women and therapy* (2nd ed.). Bradenton, FL: Human Services Institutes.

Griffith, E. E. H. (1996). African American perspectives. In J. E. Mezzich, A. Kleinman, H. Fabrega, & D. L. Parron (Eds.), *Culture and psychiatric diagnosis: A DSM-IV perspective* (pp. 27–29). Washington, DC: American Psychiatric Association.

Hernandez, T. J., & Seem, S. R. (2001, Summer). Ethical diagnosis: Teaching strategies for gender and culture sensitivity. *Professional Issues in Counseling*. Retrieved April 30, 2010, from http://www.shsu.edu/~piic/summer2001/HernandezSeem.htm

Horsfall, J. (2001). Gender and mental illness: An Australian overview. *Issues of Mental Health Nursing, 22,* 421–428.

Jackson, M. A., & Sullivan, T. R. (2003). Hidden biases in counseling women. In M. Kopala & M. A. Keiter (Eds.), *Handbook of counseling women* (pp. 152–172). Thousand Oaks, CA: Sage.

Kaplan, M. (1983). The issue of sex bias in DSM III. *American Psychologist, 38,* 802–803.

Khatidja, C. (2005). From disconnection to connection: Race, gender and politics of therapy. *British Journal of Guidance and Counseling, 33*(2), 239–256.

Kupers, T. A. (1997). The politics of psychiatry: Gender and sexual preference in DSM-IV. In M. R. Walsh (Ed.), *Women, men and gender: Ongoing debates* (pp. 340–347). New Haven, CT: Yale University Press.

Kutchins, H., & Kirk, S. A. (1997). *Making us crazy: DSM: The psychiatric bible and the creating of mental disorders.* New York: The Free Press.

Landrine, H. (1989). The politics of personality disorders. *Psychology of Women Quarterly, 13,* 324–339.

Lin, K.-M. (1996). Asian American perspectives. In J. E. Mezzich, A. Kleinman, H. Fabrega, & D. L. Parron (Eds.), *Culture and psychiatric diagnosis: A DSM-IV perspective* (pp. 35–38). Washington, DC: American Psychiatric Press.

Loring, M., & Powell, B. (1988). Gender, race and DSM-III: A study of objectivity of psychiatric diagnostic behaviors. *Journal of Health and Social Behavior, 29,* 1–22.

Marecek, J., & Hare-Mustin, R. T. (1991). Feminism and clinical psychology. *Psychology of Women Quarterly, 15,* 521–536.

McLaughlin, J. E. (2002). Reducing diagnostic bias. *Journal of Mental Health Counseling, 24*(3), 363–374.

Miller, J. B. (1986). *Toward a new psychology of women* (2nd ed.). Boston, MA: Beacon Press.

Morrow, K. A., & Deidan, C. T. (1992). Bias in the counseling process: How to recognize it and avoid it. *Journal of Counseling and Development, 70,* 571–577.

Nikelly, A. G. (1992). Alternatives in the andocentric bias of personality disorders. *Clinical Psychology and Psychotherapy, 3*(1), 15–22.

Rawlings, E. I., & Carter, D. K. (1977). *Psychotherapy for women: Treatment toward equality.* Springfield, IL: Charles C Thomas.

Reinzi, B. M., & Scrams, D. J. (1991). Gender stereotypes for paranoid, antisocial, compulsive dependent and histrionic personality disorders. *Psychological Reports, 69,* 976–978.

Ritchie, M. H. (1994). Cultural and gender biases in definitions of mental illness and emotional health and illness. *Counselor Education and Supervision, 33*(4), 344–349.

Robertson, J., & Fitzgerald, L. R. (1990). The (mis)treatment of men: Effects of client gender role and lifestyle on diagnosis and attribution of pathology. *Journal of Counseling Psychology, 37,* 3–9.

Rogier, L. H. (1996). Hispanic perspectives. In J. E. Mezzich, A. Kleinman, H. Fabrega, & D. L. Parron (Eds.), *Culture and psychiatric diagnosis: A DSM-IV perspective* (pp. 39–41). Washington, DC: American Psychiatric Association.

Root, M. P. P. (1992). Reconstructing the impact of trauma on personality. In L. S. Brown & M. Ballou (Eds.), *Personality and psychopathology: Feminist reappraisals* (pp. 229–265). New York: Guilford.

Rosewater, L. B. (1990). Diversifying feminist theory and practice: Broadening the concept of victimization. In L. S. Brown & M. P. P. Root (Eds.), *Diversity and complexity in feminist therapy* (pp. 299–311). New York: Harrington Park Press.

Russell, D. (1986). Psychiatric diagnosis and the oppression of women. *Women & Therapy, 5,* 83–89.

Santos de Barona, M., & Dutton, M. A. (1997). Feminist perspectives on assessment. In J. Worell & N. G. Johnson (Eds.), *Shaping the future of feminist psychology: Education, research, and practice* (pp. 37–56). Washington, DC: American Psychological Association.

Seem, S. R., & Clark, M. D. (2006). Healthy women, healthy men, and healthy adults: An evaluation of gender role stereotypes in the 21st century. *Sex Roles: A Journal of Research, 55,* 247–258.

Seem, S. R., & Johnson, E. (1998). Gender bias among counselor trainees: A study of case conceptualization. *Counselor Education and Supervision, 37,* 257–268.

Sinacore-Guinn, A. L. (1995). The diagnostic window: Culture-and-gender-sensitive diagnosis. *Counselor Education and Supervision, 35,* 18–31.

Smart, D. W., & Smart, J. F. (1997). DSM-IV and culturally sensitive diagnosis: Some observations for counselors. *Journal of Counseling and Development, 75,* 392–398.

Snowden, L. R. (2003). Bias in mental health assessment and intervention: Theory and evidence. *American Journal of Public Health, 93*(2), 239–243.

Tavris, C. (1996). *The mismeasure of women.* New York: Simon & Schuster.

Thompson, J. W. (1996). Native American perspectives. In J. E. Mezzich, A. Kleinman, H. Fabrega, & D. L. Parron (Eds.), *Culture and psychiatric diagnosis: A DSM-IV perspective* (pp. 32–33). Washington, DC: American Psychiatric Press.

Unger, R., & Crawford, M. (1996). *Women and gender: A feminist psychology* (2nd ed.). New York: McGraw-Hill.

Worell, J., & Remer, P. (1992). *Feminist perspectives in therapy: An empowerment model for women.* Chester, England: John Wiley & Sons.

Worell, J., & Remer, P. (2003). *Feminist perspectives in therapy: Empowering diverse women* (2nd ed.). Hoboken, NJ: John Wiley & Sons.

CHAPTER 6

FEMINIST CONCEPTUALIZATION

The feminist perspective on conceptualization requires an attitude and a valuing of varieties of experience, some of which are neither traditional nor valued by the dominant society. Feminist conceptualization requires a feminist consciousness and a willingness to examine oneself consistently in terms of beliefs and values that impact work with clients. Although we can learn specific questions and techniques for conducting a feminist conceptualization, the most important element is our attitude toward clients and their concerns. If we approach case conceptualization with an attitude that values clients' lived experiences and the context of their problems, then feminist conceptualization follows naturally. However, if we fail to address the inherent power issues in the conceptualization and evaluation processes, then we cannot truly be feminist therapists, and the conceptualization process is not a feminist one.

FEMINIST CONCEPTUALIZATION: ● ESSENTIAL ELEMENTS

There are two essential components to feminist conceptualization. The first is oppositional knowledge or the obligation that feminist therapists have to question unchallenged assumptions about how the world operates. The second is feminist consciousness, which is a related concept that requires feminist therapists to question their own assumptions and biases. These two concepts are related to the political (how the world operates) and the personal (our subjective experiences) arenas—and this theme is repeated throughout feminist therapy.

Oppositional Knowledge

In the previous chapter, we addressed a feminist perspective on mental health and pathology, and we presented feminism as a "form of oppositional knowledge" (Marecek & Hare-Mustin, 1991, p. 524), which carries with it the obligation to question unchallenged assumptions and beliefs about how the world operates. Oppositional knowledge is essential to feminist conceptualization but is not usually taught to practitioners. A good place to start to understand oppositional knowledge is to read a psychology of women textbook. Such a review will provide a basic introduction to gender and how gender impacts human development and social order. Brown (1994) and Worell and Remer (2003) speak to the importance of understanding the impact of gender and culture in the lives of people.

In Chapter 4 we stated that counselors must be familiar with research on gender issues in counseling, and in Chapter 5 we discussed how gender can impact clinical judgments of mental health (see, for example, Broverman, Broverman, Clarkson, Rosenkrantz, & Vogel, 1970; Seem & Clark, 2006). Remember, these researchers found that the understanding of mental health by clinicians and counselors in training mirrors traditional male gender-role expectations and that the gender of the client influences the perceptions of mental health. Familiarity with relevant literature helps provide an understanding of the interactions of gender with race/ethnicity, sexual orientation, social class, age, culture, and other demographic variables (Brown, 1986, 1990, 1994; Espin, 1993; Greene & Sanchez-Hucles, 1997; Robinson-Wood, 2009; Worell & Remer, 2003). Knowledge of gender and personality development, especially an awareness of theories that do not promote androcentric and White European norms, is also essential, such as postmodern or constructivist approaches. Finally, an awareness of higher base rates of experiences in one gender over another and the consequent impact on the whole of that population is also critical (Brown, 1994). For example, it is important to know that females have a much higher rate of violence in their lives than do males. Thus, it is important to ask about all forms of violence (e.g., verbal abuse to rape and family violence) in female clients' lives. Knowledge about violence is only one example. Other examples include (but are not limited to) the following: Males have a higher rate of alcoholism, but females are more often diagnosed with depression, women are paid less than men but live longer, men are more likely to be in positions of power in industry and government, and women are more likely to be on diets because of societal expectations that women must be thin. It is equally important to be knowledgeable about the experiences of oppression that people of color typically face and to ask about those experiences.

Oppositional knowledge requires that counselors do not assume that their experience is the prototype for any client. Oppositional knowledge provides counselors with information that helps them move beyond their own lived experience. It helps us be in a space where we can value clients' experiences, respect our clients' definitions of their experiences, and validate those perspectives. It helps counselors believe their clients and ask about potential experiences that they might otherwise ignore or overlook.

Feminist Consciousness

Feminist consciousness requires that we hold certain beliefs and values about the world and the way it works. We do not enter any endeavor, most of all therapy, value free. Thus, we constantly examine and seek to know and understand our own biases and assumptions. How counselors view the world, make assumptions about health and pathology, as well as hold beliefs about social systems and how people grow and develop are all factors that play a central role in how we think about or conceptualize our clients and the ways in which we interact with them.

As feminist therapists, we hold certain values and attitudes about our work with clients. The four tenets of feminist therapy discussed in Chapter 2 are critical to developing and maintaining a feminist consciousness. The belief that *the personal is the political* impels us to look at our clients in the context of their lives, to consider their lived experiences in the world, and to understand that often oppression and sexism are at the root of psychological suffering. As feminist therapists, we are aware of issues of power and possible oppression in therapy sessions. We consciously seek to build *an egalitarian relationship* with clients. This attitude toward our clients requires that we respect clients and believe that they are experts about and can define their own experiences. An example of this is the act of *privileging women's experiences.* In other words, when working with women, feminist therapists do not compare female clients' experiences with the male norm of what is considered appropriate behavior, and we do not compare clients of color with White norms. Instead, when we work with individuals, our work is to define with our clients what healthy behavior is for them, regardless of gender. And finally, a feminist consciousness means that we view clients from a strengths perspective. Rather than viewing symptoms as an indication of what is wrong with the individual, we observe clients' behaviors and feelings as a method of communication about their lived experience. Feminist therapists view resiliency where other theoretical approaches might view pathology. As a result, feminist therapists help clients empower themselves by understanding the meaning of their symptoms. For example, a young man who self-injures might do this to keep his feelings of anger under control. In many ways, this is a prosocial and nonpathological act. The young man understands that he should not take his feelings of anger out on others and hurt others. Hurting himself in private allows him not to have angry outbursts in school and to maintain good grades. However, he has not yet learned how to understand his anger so that he does not hurt himself. A feminist therapist would work to ensure that the young man make necessary connections between feelings and experience, and learn a more appropriate way to express his anger.

A feminist consciousness requires that we examine our own conscious and unconscious biases and expectations regarding gender, culture, and behavior. As human beings, we bring ourselves to our relationships with our clients and to the process of conceptualization. Thus, it is imperative that we be aware of our own gender-role socialization, our own experiences with privilege and oppression, and the impact of those experiences on the way we view ourselves and the way we view and work with others who are different in whatever way from us.

Following in the tradition of racial and cultural identity theories (Cross, 1971; Atkinson, Morten, & Sue, 1979) and Downing and Roush's (1985) feminist identity model, Worell and Remer (2003) developed a model of personal/social identity development (Table 6.1). Individuals may use this model to understand where they fall on a set of dimensions and to understand how these dimensions of identity are impacted by whether they reflect social privilege or oppression or a combination of both. The authors suggest that their model reflects the "process of becoming aware, understanding, and appreciating the positive qualities of both one's own and other groups" (2003, p. 37). This model may be used as a guide to help counselors identify their level of awareness regarding oppression and privilege not only for other groups but also for themselves. Exposure to and involvement with others who are different from us will also help make us aware of our assumptions and biases. Feminist and multicultural supervision and consultation with professionals from varied backgrounds may be other ways to improve our awareness. This knowledge and awareness must occur prior to the act of conceptualization (Brown, 1990).

Table 6.1	Personal/Social Identity Model

Level 1: Preawareness

Privilege/Advantage

- Conforms to majority norms and values: believes these are universal
- Accepts cultural stereotypes of the oppressed group
- Believes own group is better than others
- Is unaware of or denies own privileged status; accepts it as normal and deserved
- Has access to valued societal resources
- Believes in a just world in which meritocracy determines personal outcomes (I deserve the good things I have in life)

Oppression/Disadvantage

- Conforms to majority norms and values
- Deprecates own group and appreciates majority group
- Accepts negative stereotypes about own group
- Is self-deprecating and self-blaming
- Has low access to societal resources
- Believes in a just world (I don't deserve more than I have)

Level 2: Encounter

Privilege/Advantage

- Becomes aware of privileged status
- Acknowledges that privilege is connected to group status
- Becomes aware of discrimination and stereotyping
- Is uncomfortable with possibility of self as oppressor
- Experiences cognitive dissonance, conflict, or guilt
- Experiences conflict with prior views of self and others

Oppression/Disadvantage

- Becomes aware of oppression as member of own group
- Has conflicting views of self and others
- Is conflicted over valuing self and valuing dominant group
- Is aware of oppressed status of one's own entire group
- Experiences relief (It's not my fault)
- Becomes angry about the injustice and harm to self and group

(Continued)

Table 6.1 (Continued)

Level 3: Immersion
Privilege/Advantage

- Becomes informed about oppressed group and their concerns
- Understands impact of discriminatory practices on oppressed group
- Appreciates positive qualities and values of oppressed group
- Instigates increasing contact with members of oppressed group
- Increases awareness of self as oppressor
- Establishes collaborative rather than competitive relations with oppressed group

Oppression/Disadvantage

- Becomes self-appreciating
- Becomes group appreciating
- Increases knowledge about oppressed group
- Increases anger at the oppression and at the oppressors
- Immerses self in activities that center on own group; excludes oppressors

Level 4: Integration and Activism
Privilege and Oppression Combined

- Is willing to share personal and public resources
- Is able to move comfortably between the worlds of both groups
- Appreciates values and qualities of both groups
- Understands social, political, and economic status of both groups
- Rejects and confronts negative stereotypes and discriminatory practices
- Works actively to instigate change toward social justice

Note: From *Feminist Perspectives in Therapy: Empowering Diverse Women* (2nd ed.) (pp. 36–37), by J. Worell and P. Remer, 2003, Hoboken, NJ: John Wiley & Sons. Copyright 2003 John Wiley & Sons.

Once a feminist therapist feels comfortable with understanding that the process of conceptualization is, in many ways, a process of questioning assumptions (assumptions about how the world works and how we as individuals view it, as well as our clients' assumptions about these concerns and their lives), then we are ready to begin the process of feminist conceptualization.

THE SKILLS OF FEMINIST CONCEPTUALIZATION ●

To improve our understanding of this process, we will examine our work through a case study. Think about this case as you read the assumptions that guide feminist conceptualization.

Case Study: Jared is a 19-year-old Caucasian male. He states that his family is Hungarian American and that many grandparents in his hometown still speak some Hungarian. He is a second-semester first-year student attending a highly regarded state university. He is referred to counseling by a professor who believes he has promise but little motivation and has told Jared that he believes Jared to be depressed.

Jared is the youngest child of a rural, working-class family. He is the first person in his extended family to attend college. He had a girlfriend throughout high school but broke up with her after his first semester in college. He played basketball in high school. He is majoring in preengineering and is receiving adequate grades but reports losing interest in his reading fairly quickly except for his Introduction to Literature course.

He reports having had a difficult time making friends because he has little in common with his classmates. In his first semester, his dialect was a source of ridicule for his roommate. Jared reports having no friends at college and says that he spends most of his free time in his room listening to music or playing online games. He reports that he is lonely and would like friends. He had an adequate social life in high school.

He also states that prior to coming to college, he had a good relationship with his father. They often went hunting together and watched college basketball on the weekends. He does not feel that close to his father now and does not confide in him. He is not sure what has changed. He continues to talk to his mother about being lonely, but she does not seem to understand what college is all about. He has one older sister who married at a young age. She has two young children and lives close to their parents. Jared is not close to her.

MAJOR ASSUMPTIONS OF FEMINIST CONCEPTUALIZATION ●

The major assumptions that guide feminist conceptualization are as follows: (a) Gender is central to any complete understanding of client distress, (b) clients' sociocultural context must be acknowledged (the personal is the political), (c) distinctions among sources of pathology exist, and (d) symptoms must be reframed.

Centrality of Gender
Within the Context of Other Salient Factors

Feminist therapy grew out of an awareness of the importance of gender-role analysis in therapy. Again, we do not enter therapy or conduct therapy without our gender being present. Gender is a significant marker in every-one's life. Gender intertwines with culture, ethnicity/race, sexual orientation, age, social class, and other social markers that form the personal and social self (Worell & Remer, 2003). Feminist conceptualization analyzes the ways in which oppression interacts with gender (Ballou, Matsumoto, & Wagner, 2002). These markers and clients' lived social experiences with these markers must be taken into account when conceptualizing. By performing a gender-role analysis during the initial conceptualization stage of therapy, we are more apt to obtain the accurate portrait of clients' lived experiences that is essential to good conceptualization. In the past two decades work has emerged on male gender role and gender-role conflict and strain. It might be helpful for Jared's therapist to become acquainted with this material. Gender-role conflict occurs when culturally prescribed gender roles have negative consequences for individuals. Gender-role strain occurs when rigid, sexist, or restrictive gender roles result in personal restrictions, devaluation, or violation of others or self (O'Neil, 2008; O'Neil, Goode, & Holmes, 1995). Although women can experience gender-role conflict and strain, they have been studied more frequently in the context of men and male gender role.

Although the process for a formal gender-role analysis will be discussed in Chapter 8, for now it is important to understand what Jared's gender means to him; that is, what are his expectations and beliefs about being a man? We would assume that Jared was taught values about what a man should be and that he either is living up to those or is not. We may also assume that gender may be related to his choice of engineering as a major over literature. Engineering is often viewed as a male-dominated profession and, thus, is an acceptable profession for a man. His response to the disrespect he receives from other male students may also be related to gender socialization. It is important to understand any privileges that Jared might have as a result of his race and gender. Perhaps in Jared's family, Jared, as the only son, is expected to attend college whereas his sister is not.

The Sociocultural/Political Context: The Personal Is the Political

"The personal is the political" is also crucial to truly understanding client experiences. A social–political understanding of client distress is necessary to avoiding viewing clients as the sole source of their problems. It is important, however, to remember that in many cases, *both* individual and environmental factors contribute to individuals' distress. Thus, anxiety can be a result of not only a toxic environment but also clients' self-talk that exacerbates their worries. It is also possible to attribute the entire problem to contextual factors. Pathological environments are proven to produce pathology in a short amount of time in normally psychologically healthy people (Collins, 1998; Worell & Remer, 2003). Although feminist conceptualization assumes that the *root* of clients' presenting problems lies in the political realm, it teases out the *various sources* of clients' distress to understand client experiences accurately.

In Jared's case, several social/political factors are involved. Jared's socioeconomic status and geographical origins make him stand out from other students at the university. Although admitting students like Jared helps increase the diversity of the university, it does not seem that a support system is in place to help such students adapt to the new environment.

Distinguishing Among Multiple Sources of Distress

In contrast to traditional conceptualization, feminist conceptualization of clients and their concerns distinguishes among three major sources of client distress (Brown, 1994, p. 142):

1. subjective pain

2. interactive experiences of problematic behavior

3. Pathology . . . placed primarily outside the person in the social and political matrix

This differentiation ensures an exploration of more than client symptoms (Brown, 1990, 1994; Enns, 1997; Morris, 1997; Worell & Remer, 2003). Not only is individual pain explored but client experiences with others and the environment that result in problematic client behaviors are also examined. The feminist therapist discovers these distinctions through such questions as these:

How does this person's status and experiences as a gendered person in her or his culture shape a particular personality or psychological dysfunction? How has the experience of reality for this particular individual led to unique ways of comprehending and coping with that reality? And, how has this individual's membership in a particular social class informed or transformed that interpersonal experience of external events? (Brown, 1986, pp. 18–20).

Understanding client distress is *always consciously* based in clients' social and political contexts (Brown, 1994) (e.g., the personal is always political). The psychosocial environment is the focus of examination when understanding clients' subjective experiences. Individual experiences are understood within the social and political forces that formed those experiences. Moreover, because people are complex, feminist conceptualization focuses on understanding the many origins of people's ways of being in the world. Brown (1990, 1992, 1994, 2000) and Worell and Remer (2003) suggest the following areas for examination with a client:

1. Invisible and sometimes unconscious ways in which patriarchy is entrenched in people's lives—identity development, styles of personal power, powerlessness, and emotional expression (Brown, 1994, 2000)

2. Experiences with oppression and privilege and their impact on development (Brown, 1990, 1994, 2000, Worell & Remer, 2003)

3. Distress—defined in relationship to an individual's own baselines and his or her own cultural and social contexts (Brown, 1992, 1994, 2000)

4. Presence and meaning of compliance and noncompliance with social norms and behavior, and subsequent reinforcements and punishments for compliance and noncompliance (Brown, 1990, 1992, 1994, 2000)

5. Abuse and trauma, both direct and insidious or repetitious (Brown, 1992, 1994, 2000)

6. Connection between various stressors (abuse, sexism, racism, homophobia, etc.) and behavior patterns such as learned helplessness and passive and dependent behaviors (Brown, 2000)

7. Gender issues and gender socialization (Brown, 1990, 1994, 2000; Worell & Remer, 2003)

8. Meaning of gender membership in client's family and the culture in which she or he was raised, in client's current social and cultural environment, and changes in the meaning of gender over the life span (Brown, 1994, 1990, 2000)

9. Meaning of client's social and personal identities (Brown, 1992, 1994, 2000; Worell & Remer, 2003)

10. Sources of strength within individuals and their cultures/environments (Brown, 1994; Worrell & Remer, 2003)

Although understanding our clients' distress may seem more complex when considered within the feminist model, it is actually good counseling practice and an extension of therapeutic skills already known and used. By examining multiple sources of distress in clients' lives, we value them and their lived experiences. We strive not to make errors of judgment as described in the previous chapter. In essence, we strive to view the "whole picture," not just a narrow snapshot of our clients while they are in distress.

The process for understanding Jared's distress is threefold, as follows:

1. We take careful stock of own biases in working with Jared.

2. We examine the three sources of client distress (Brown, 1994, p. 142):
   • subjective pain
   • interactive experiences of problematic behavior
   • pathology . . . placed primarily outside the person in the social and political matrix

3. We consider the nine areas listed previously that examine a client's way of being in the world.

REFRAMING CLIENTS' DISTRESS ●

Traditional diagnosis views symptoms as evidence of deficit, illness, or pathology (Worell & Remer, 2003). Although a focus on strengths is not unique to feminist therapy, feminist therapy's focus on resiliency is at its core (Brown, 1994). Feminist conceptualization reframes traditional views of symptoms. Symptoms are viewed "as behaviors that arise out of efforts to influence an environment that is constricting or oppressive (Enns, 1997, p. 10). Marecek (2002) views symptoms as idioms that are "culture specific, taking forms and conveying meanings that are intelligible to other members of the culture" (p. 18). She suggests that "idioms of distress can also be thought of as relational practices that accomplish certain interpersonal goals" (p. 19). In this analysis, psychological pain or symptoms are viewed as a response to a situation and/or oppression. Thus, symptoms are viewed as adaptive, creative coping mechanisms for dealing with an oppressive or harmful environment

(Enns, 1997; Worell & Remer, 2003), and these coping strategies are not viewed as pathological (Brown, 1994). Whereas these coping strategies might not be working well for clients, they are powerful communication modes about individuals' psychological pain and experiences in an oppressive environment. Thus, "symptoms" are conceptualized as a sign indicating that something is wrong with the environment or a relationship, and not the individual living within that context.

Worell and Remer (2003) suggest several ways to reframe or reinterpret symptoms as evidence of strengths. Although Worell and Remer speak of reframing symptoms in terms of female clients, we believe that reinterpretation of symptoms is beneficial for male clients too.

Women's [men's] "symptoms" are reinterpreted as follows (Worell & Remer, 2003, p. 133):

1. Behaving in accord with traditional female [male] roles

2. Representing role conflict

3. Representing a coping strategy for surviving all types of oppression and discrimination

4. Reflecting the result/consequence of female [gender] socialization

5. Representing societal pathological labeling of deviancy from traditional female [male] gender-typed behaviors

This reinterpretation of client distress helps both counselors and clients view "symptoms" as a form of adaptive communication about clients' experiences (Brown, 1994). Symptoms communicate a story about the client, a story that helps both client and counselor understand the meaning of the symptom or symptoms. For example, rather than viewing Jared's feelings of sadness, loneliness, and awkwardness as indicating individual pathology, his "symptoms" can be reframed as a communication about his experience in an environment that differs from his lived experience physically (e.g., sharing a small room with a stranger), socially (being expected to conform to the role of preengineering student as well as making new friends), and emotionally (experiencing emotional distance from friends and family). These "symptoms" are a way Jared has of knowing that something significant has happened to him (going to college) that has impacted his entire life, not just his academics. It is a way for Jared to start identifying healthy methods of coping with these changes. Helping clients reframe their view of their distress allows clients to identify their strengths and to view possibilities of empowerment and change.

The core purpose of feminist conceptualization, then, is to expand to clients' self-awareness and self-knowledge. Feminist conceptualization strengthens clients' belief that they can truly know themselves and have the right and authority to name their feelings and experiences without being labeled as different, wrong, or deviant.

PROCESS ●

The five steps to feminist conceptualization are as follows:

1. Therapist self-examination: awareness and knowledge

2. Feminist-informed history of clients' primary concerns including areas of strength as well as remedial issues

3. Generation of hypotheses regarding psychological and psychosocial distress

4. Collaborative conceptualization

5. Collaborative summary of conceptualization and diagnosis if clients' input warrants it

Step #1: Therapist Self-Examination: Awareness and Knowledge

To begin the process, we assess where we stand in terms of oppositional knowledge and feminist consciousness. As Jared's counselor, we need to be aware of our own assumptions and biases regarding men from rural, working-class backgrounds. If not, we might operate on unconscious beliefs, for instance, that working-class people tend to be poorly educated and socially inept, because these stereotypes are abundant in popular culture. Oppositional knowledge requires that we avoid a fundamental attribution error and solely look for intrapsychic or personal causes for Jared's presenting symptoms. Such an error may cause counselors to decide that Jared lacks academic ability because he lacks the necessary skills to thrive socially at college.

Feminist therapists typically do not operate under the medical model that would assume that Jared suffers from depression because of a chemical imbalance or lack of pleasant and rewarding social interactions. Counselors who operate within the medical model might suggest treatment aimed at helping Jared develop social skills (meaning middle-class skills because they are the norm) and counseling combined with medication to ameliorate the depression.

However, if we question some of our own social norms and the influences and belief systems of popular culture—that is, if we use our feminist consciousness to consider Jared—then we are aware of our social class bias and the U.S. cultural tendency to tell clients to "take responsibility" for their own behavior. Although this is often said in a well-meaning manner and can be empowering to some, it often is translated into blaming clients for their concerns and problems. Thus, if we examine our own beliefs and assumptions about therapy with this particular client, then we are in a better position to hear Jared's story without dominant assumptions influencing our conceptualization. Our feminist consciousness allows us to view Jared from many perspectives, with a focus on the sociopolitical context of his life.

Step #2: Feminist-Informed History

History taking is an important aspect of initial assessment and conceptualization. In traditional diagnosis, a patient's history informs major decisions about the diagnosis (e.g., How long have the symptoms lasted? What is their severity? Do they recur?). Feminist history taking focuses on variables that are critical to feminist conceptualization: gender, race/ethnicity, age, sexual orientation, class, spirituality, culture, and ability. These areas are explored with the understanding that "gender crosses all bounds of race, class and place" (Marecek & Hare-Mustin, 1991, p. 12). In Jared's case, a complete history would note his unprompted disclosure about being Hungarian American. We would want to explore this more and understand what it means to be a male in this subculture. We would also note his pride in disclosing his heritage and the fact that when asked to describe himself, his ethnicity was an important part of that discussion. Thus, we address both ethnicity and gender.

Understanding client "symptoms" and distress in context are at the core of history taking. Viewing symptoms and distress as signs of resiliency allows the counselor and client to answer the question, "What is the client . . . *trying* to do" with this particular behavior or coping strategy (Sarbin, 1997)? Feminist history taking focuses on the value or usefulness of clients' behaviors within the context of their lived experiences. Even behavior that counselors or therapists view as distressing or impaired (for instance, self-injurious behaviors) can be viewed as coping mechanisms that help clients meet their own valued, but unstated, interpersonal and/or intrapsychic goals (Brown, 1994). Consider again, Jared, a bright young man who has found that if he only interacts with others in online gaming, then (a) he does not have to deal with the pain interpersonal relationships can bring (for example, no one will make fun of the way he speaks), and (b) he can still participate in a game and game strategies as he did when he played basketball in high school. We ask ourselves whether Jared is depressed and his behavior pathological or whether has he found a way to ameliorate his pain and fulfill a need at the same time. In taking clients' psycho-social-cultural history, we identify their strengths as well as weaknesses. We remember that the ultimate goal of history taking is to help clients name their pain (Brown, 1994), not for us to formulate a history that fits a pattern leading to a *Diagnostic and Statistical Manual* (DSM) diagnosis.

Gender-role assessment is another important part of history taking. Brown (1986, 1990) delineates the following areas for investigation: the meaning of gender for the client, the presence and meaning of gender-role compliance and noncompliance for the client, and the clinician's response to the client's gender and the client's response to the counselor's gender. Once again, consider Jared. Jared is majoring in preengineering, which is a traditionally male-oriented field, yet the only course he is excited about is a literature course. How might this be related to gender-role conflict given his family and class background? See Table 6.2 for Brown's outline for integrating gender issues into history taking. Please note that Brown also integrates issues of privilege and oppression into her gender-role analysis. Social markers such as race/ethnicity, sexual orientation or social class may be more salient to clients' experience than gender alone. It is important to inquire about issues of marginality, oppression, and insidious "isms," such as racism, classism, heterosexism, ageism, and so on.

Table 6.2   Proposed Outline for Integrating Gender Issues into Assessment

Preassessment

Clinician familiarizes herself/himself with scholarship and research on gender and its relation to clinical judgments of mental health

- Examines literature on interaction of gender with race, class, age, age cohort, culture, and other demographic variables

(Continued)

Table 6.2 (Continued)

- Examines literature on gender and personality development, with special attention to those theories not promoting androcentric norms
- Becomes knowledgeable about experiences that occur at higher base rates in one gender than in the other and the impact of those experiences on the entire gender

Clinician examines her/his own conscious and nonconscious biases and expectations regarding gender

- Seeks supervision and consultation from colleagues who are attentive to subtle aspects of gender in countertransference
- Explores costs and benefits of compliance with, as well as changes from, preexisting beliefs, stereotypes, and perceptions of others regarding own gendered behaviors

Assessment process

Actively inquires into the meaning of gender membership for the client

- In the client's family and culture of raising
- In the client's current social and cultural environment
- Regarding changes in the meaning of gender over life span

Attends to the presence and meaning of gender-role compliance or noncompliance in the client

- Assesses what rewards and penalties have been for compliance or noncompliance, both historically and currently

Attends to the client's responses to the assessor's gender and own responses to client's gender

- Notices how issues of perceived attractiveness of one party to the other have an impact on the interchange and the assessor's opinions of the client
- Develops hypotheses about the gendered aspects of the interaction between the client and the assessor
- Inquires into the presence of gendered high and low base rate phenomenon
- Checks the diagnosis arrived at to guard against inappropriate imposition of gender-stereotyped values regarding healthy functioning

Source: From "Taking Account of Gender in the Clinical Assessment Interview," by L. S. Brown, 1990, *Professional Psychology: Research and Practice, 21*(1), 12–17.

Gender is a salient issue in Jared's life. He reports being left out of the traditional male pursuits while at home. His family of origin is slightly contemp-
tuous of his college education, while at the same time being proud of him.

THERAPIST: I know that at college you are lonely and often feel left out; is
              it different when you go home?

JARED: Yeah, I feel more relaxed, the food is more of what I know and
              like, and I sometimes see one of my friends from high school.
              He does repairs up on the interstate. But lately I'm beginning
              to feel that I don't fit in there anymore, either. My friends hang
              out with their buddies from work. Some are even getting mar-
              ried and having kids. When I come home, they sometimes for-
              get to include me. This past fall my dad, my uncle, and all my
              cousins went up to my uncle's hunting camp and forgot to tell
              me they were going. Everybody leaves me out of a lot of stuff.
              I don't even know how I feel about that. Sometimes I am so
              pissed, and other times I just don't seem to care.

When we talk to Jared, we find that his father now calls him "college boy."
This implies that college has somehow made less of a man out of 19-year-old
Jared. He is not a man in the same way cousins his age or friends from high
school are men.
      We also ask Jared about his social and romantic relationships to better
understand gender and gender roles in his life.

THERAPIST: From what you said previously, it also sounds like you don't
              have any romantic relationships right now.

JARED: I broke up with my girlfriend from home over the winter break.
              We just seemed to want different things, but mostly I think it was
              because I was away at college. And well, maybe it was because I
              was acting a little uppity. Sometimes the way she talks makes me
              cringe. She hated that and the fact that I never asked her to come
              down here to visit. I guess I thought she would embarrass me. I
              knew she wouldn't fit. I don't know; I just had a hard time putting
              the college life and the home life together. It was too hard.

From this interaction, we learn that for Jared, the class and culture conflict between college and home is so great that it interferes with his
male/female relationships. We also learn more about his coping mechanism
of letting go of interpersonal relationships that cause him distress.

Socioeconomic class and privilege have particular significance for Jared. He is both privileged and not privileged. He is an intelligent, White man. In U.S. culture, these factors grant privilege, but Jared is also strongly identified with his cultural heritage and comes from a small working-poor family in a rural area with traditional values. Class and family background are important sources of difference in his life that conflict with sources of privilege. In essence, Jared is marginalized in both college and his family and community.

His particular family and culture place college and education as something that real men do not do. This is an intersection of gender, culture, and class. Culture and class influence how one "does" gender. Many parents want their children to do better socioeconomically than they have, but to do so, they leave behind the norms and mores of their family and family's culture. To do what his family wishes and to move into the middle class, Jared has to become a lesser man in their eyes. At this point, we move into generating hypotheses because we begin to understand why Jared might be confused, in distress and more comfortable with the pain of isolating himself than with interacting with others at college.

Step #3: Generating Hypotheses

Feminist conceptualization is not a singular act but rather a process in which client content is considered only within the larger picture of the totality of clients' experiences. The therapist *and* client work collaboratively to develop hypotheses about the nature, etiology, and meanings of clients' distress (Brown, 1994). These hypotheses serve as a guide for therapy and counseling and provide a framework for answering the following question: "What does it mean for the course of therapy if the client has had X experience in Y context and is from Z culture, is reporting Q symptoms and relates to me in A and B manner?" (Brown, 1994, p. 129). Considering Jared, what does it mean for conceptualization and treatment planning that Jared and his family believe that the purpose of college is to get a professional job after graduation in a well-paying field (X), that he is the first in his family to attend college (Y), and that he is from a rural, poor socioeconomic status with little job stability (Z), that he is reporting lack of motivation and inability to concentrate on his science courses (Q symptoms), and that he comes to therapy wanting to be told how to make it better while at the same time seemingly not invested in therapy (A and B manner)? Does it mean that Jared is depressed and cannot motivate himself because of depression, or could it mean that Jared is under pressure to please his lower-socioeconomic-class family with traditional values about male and female rather than himself and is rebelling in the only manner that he believes is open to him—lack of motivation and concentration? A discussion of the various sources of distress is an important part of the hypothesis building.

THREE SOURCES OF CLIENT DISTRESS ●

In understanding any client, we always keep in mind that there are three sources of distress. We explore these sources with Jared while assessing the areas suggested by Brown (1992, 1994, 2000) and Worell and Remer (2003). Remember, hypotheses are our best guesses based on the available evidence. As feminist therapists, our evidence is our knowledge and awareness of the sociopolitical context of the individual client's life as well as individual distress.

1. Individual, subjective pain.

Jared speaks about feeling sad, down, and alone. He feels awkward at college and states that he does not fit in. He wonders if something is wrong with him. He often feels angry at his roommate but does not express this verbally. This past year, he has not sought to make friends. He listens to music, sleeps, and plays online games in his residence hall room. In high school, Jared was on the basketball team, was a good but not outstanding student, had a strong social group, and had a girlfriend. He went hunting and watched basketball with his dad.

JARED: I really miss having a place to belong. It feels like I don't belong here, but I don't belong at home any more either. I used to like doing things with my dad, but even he treats me differently— calling me "college boy." I only live 2 hours away, but I don't have any real friends left there. What's the use of going home, anyway? All I do there is sleep all day or study. I can do that here. Do you think I'm depressed? I must be. I feel awful.

Hypothesis: Jared is experiencing identity disruption as a result of being in what is essentially a new culture for him (middle-class, White, educated U.S. culture in contrast to rural, working-poor, ethnically bound, traditional U.S. culture).

Hypothesis: Because concepts of manhood fluctuate based on ethnicity and class, Jared's concept of his gender identity and what it means to be a male is being questioned, and this causes distress. He is experiencing gender-role conflict.

2. Relational experiences of troublesome behavior.

Relational experiences refer to both our relationships with others and our relationship with ourselves. Jared feels awkward and inept in social situations at college. He reports that his way of talking is often mocked by his peers. He does not know what to talk about with the other people in his residence hall, and he is afraid that he might say something about which he will be teased. Jared tells us more about what is going on:

THERAPIST: From what you are telling me, college has been a lot different from high school and not for the better. You sound pretty lonely.

JARED: That sounds right. When I told Sue, my RA, that I was having a hard time, she told me that I don't have social skills. I thought it was a rude thing to say to me. I'm at college. I had friends back home. Why would she say that? She's rude. (pause)

Hypothesis: Jared does not know the norms for social interaction at this particular place, with these particular people, at this particular time in his life. He did at one time. He has the skills and ability but cannot apply them in this situation. This causes distress and cognitive dissonance.

Realizing that class and education issues are central to Jared's distress, we focus on the experience of being the first person in his family to attend college.

THERAPIST: Tell me more about what is good and bad about being the first person in your family to go to college.

JARED: Well, it's good because my dad is always bragging to his friends that I'm going to be an engineer. It's also good because I like living in this town, where you can do things and get a job if you want. It's bad because everybody at home treats me differently—like I shouldn't like doing the things I used to do like fishing and hunting. Last fall, I went home, and my dad was going hunting, and when I said I wanted to go, Dad said that I had more important things to do and that I needed to stay home and hit the books. It's bad when my friends look at me funny when I use different words or say stuff they way people here at school do. I mostly have stopped talking about college when I go home even though I want to tell them about it. My dad doesn't seem to understand, and I don't feel close to him anymore. I miss that. Over the break, I told Sue, my sister, that I wasn't happy at college, and she yelled at me. She said I should be happy I'm at school no matter how bad it feels. She said she wants to take classes at the branch campus near us, but her husband doesn't want her to leave the kids alone. I think she's jealous; it all just feels wrong.

Hypothesis: Jared recognizes the impact attending college is having on his relationship with his father. He is confused and is receiving double messages from his father about growing up and being a man. Because of this, he experiences sadness, loss, and confusion.

3. Idiosyncratic pathology.

From what Jared has told us, several symptoms could indicate moderate depression. He feels sad, down, and alone. The following is an excerpt of a session when he was questioned about these feelings:

JARED: I want to go out and meet people. There's this guy who used to live on my floor. Now he has a house off campus. He invited everyone on the floor to a party last week. I planned to go. I took a shower and got dressed, but then I . . . I don't know, I got scared. Some of the guys who were going . . . well, I don't get along with them, and I just didn't want to put up with their sh_t—is that okay to say?—so I got online with some of my friends I play games with and never went out.

THERAPIST: What do you think your behavior means in this situation? What are some of the thoughts and feelings that might have stopped you from being with people that night?

JARED: Well, I have thought about this. Everyone goes out just to hook up, you know what I mean? That's not how I was taught. (He thinks for a minute.) Sure, I'd like a girlfriend at college, but it's different from high school. Girls here don't even seem to notice me, and I don't know why. I was thinking about this last

Friday, and I couldn't stop thinking, "What is wrong with me?" and then I just couldn't be with people and after a while I didn't even want to be online anymore. I went to sleep.

Hypothesis: Jared has traditional values about dating in the context of male/female relationships and has assumptions about college dating and interacting that may or may not be true. These values and assumptions hinder his ability and desire to meet and interact with young women.

Recently, Jared has received mediocre grades in his major courses. When asked about this, he reports that he just is not interested anymore and has no motivation. A lack of interest and low motivation could be indication of depressive illness. We explore this by focusing on his strengths; that is, what he is interested in, rather than focusing on reasons for his lack of interest in engineering.

THERAPIST: Like Professor Smith, I am impressed with your academic abilities—you have great promise as a student, but you said that you aren't really interested in the engineering class you're taking. Tell me more about what you are interested in.

JARED: Well, I like some of the engineering stuff but . . . (pause). Okay, I really like my literature class. I write stories that are based on some of the online games I play—you know, fantasy stuff.

Hypothesis: Jared is stepping outside his family's concept of his gender role (men can be engineers, but they do not write stories) and is experiencing some gender-role conflict about this as evidenced by his apparent embarrassment about his academic interests.

Hypothesis: Jared has taken all the evidence he has (i.e., few friends, rejected by young women, not interested in his major courses, left out of family male-bonding activities) and has decided that there is something about him that is intrinsically wrong. He feels disempowered. Jared has an instrumental view of the world. He believes that if he wants something, then he should be able to achieve it. If he cannot, then there is something wrong with him, not with the world. He no longer believes in his ability to impact the world.

Hypothesis: When viewed within Jared's experience and in the context of his life, his reported thoughts, actions, and emotions do not seem to be reflective of idiosyncratic depressive illness, although he experiences situations that are depressing.

Hypothesis: His lack of motivation and success in preengineering courses seems to be lack of interest. When viewed within Jared's experience and in the context of his life, these behaviors do not seem to be reflective of idiosyncratic depression, although he experiences situations that are depressing.

Step #4: Collaborative
Conceptualization (and Diagnosis)

Because feminist therapists do not want to replicate the status quo of traditional therapeutic relationships in which the therapist is the expert, they pay close attention to how labeling and diagnosis occur in therapy. A central piece to the process of feminist conceptualization is the collaborative approach to defining the problem. With Jared, we work collaboratively with him to arrive at an understanding of his distress that uses his story and past experiences as a baseline for his functioning. Together, we examine both his subjective experiences of distress and his relational experiences of troublesome behavior within his college environment and at home. His depressive symptoms are explored, but we do this within the sociopolitical context of class and gender. By engaging Jared in the process of conceptualization and paying attention to the various environmental factors that influence thoughts, feelings, and behaviors, we operate outside of the system that encourages mental health practitioners to view these behaviors as symptoms of pathology rather than methods of communication and coping with distress.

In our initial evaluation and assessment with Jared, we explore his individual subjective pain, relationship difficulties, and idiosyncratic responses to his life situations in a framework that centers on an examination of his sociopolitical milieu. The areas that we explore with him are the ways in which patriarchy is embedded in his life—ways he learned to be a man, what it means to be a man in his particular subculture as well as in the overall culture, and any privileges he has been granted as a White man; his experience with oppression—classism at college and his family's internalized classism; compliance and noncompliance, penalties, and rewards regarding working-class norms and middle-class norms; connections between the stressor of classism and his current behaviors and feelings; gender and career issues, socialization and membership, and the meaning of his social and personal identities.

As feminist therapists, when we listen to Jared, we are aware that to be a man, Jared is supposed to do what is expected of him without acknowledging feelings. As a son of rural, working-poor parents, Jared is supposed to feel honored that he is going to college. Jared's parents expect that a degree in engineering—a traditionally male field—will allow Jared to have a steady, well-paying, professional job. And it is obvious that on the intrapersonal level, Jared respects his parents and wishes to please them. Privilege, or lack thereof, is a central issue in Jared's distress. In Jared's case, it is the lack of socioeconomic privilege. Only financially secure students can afford to be worried by social and other developmental aspects of college. An awareness of privilege and oppression in all forms is central to understanding feminist conceptualization. Thus, we can reframe Jared's distress from a deficit to a coping mechanism that can help him survive classism, internalized classism, and gender and career issues. We then begin to share this conceptualization with him and to add his insights and perspective to it.

THERAPIST: Now that we have had time to get to know each other, I would like to share my impressions with you. Remember these are only impressions based on this one time we have met. I want you to think about what I say and revise it, change it, or ask questions, because this is about you, and you certainly know yourself better than I know you.

Your unhappiness and loneliness appear to be related to the conflict between the college environment and your family and background. What you have learned about yourself, about being a man and an adult, does not always fit well with what happens at college. What you learn at college does not always fit well with what you learned about yourself and your way of being in the world at home. Your family seems to have solid traditional values and beliefs about men and women, right and wrong, and so on. Some of this is good, and some can cause confusion and distress because it doesn't fit with the values and beliefs you are finding out about and experiencing at college.

JARED: Yeah, I do feel out of place. It's what keeps me from going out more or talking to people in class. It's also why I don't like to hang out with my friends back home anymore.

THERAPIST: Now, tell me if I have this right. You are from a rural background with traditional family values and a family with very little money. You grew up in a small town with a strong sense of your heritage. This also places you outside the norm at this university. There are few people from your home area or from rural areas who attend this college. On the other hand, you also have some privileges that other people at this university don't have—you are intelligent, White, and male.

JARED: It doesn't feel like I have any privileges.

THERAPIST: I know. I understand that. But, one of the privileges for you is that if you are quiet and keep to yourself, you can disappear into the background in the way that others who are not male or White may not. And you have done this. I also understand that this is painful for you and not what you really want to do. I agree that being White and male is not always easy. For instance, your roommate last year, and people like him, see you and expect you to act and sound like them. When you don't fit into the norm because of your interests and values, they oppress or tease. You don't conform or change your behavior because you value your family and their way of being. This is not a bad thing, but it means that you had to find other ways to cope.

JARED: Coping is just so hard so much of the time. Some people just make me feel so bad about myself. My mom used to talk about not liking to go to the city because she felt like she wasn't good enough. People treated her differently than at home. Now, I know what she meant. I guess that is why I don't put myself out there to meet people. But it doesn't help me to feel any better. I've tried everything I know.

The counselor and Jared talk more about the hypotheses and his beliefs about himself and fitting in. Jared seems somewhat frustrated and confused. At this point, Jared directly asks the counselor a question about his symptoms and what to do.

JARED: Do you think that I'm depressed? I've seen a lot of ads for medication for depression on television, and I think I have some of those symptoms.

Jared would like an answer to this question, and as feminist therapists we honor it and answer him. This is an essential part of sharing our conceptualization with Jared. It is also important to note that asking for medication is a culture and gender consideration for Jared. If depression is biological, which is analogous to having any other illness, then he is not responsible for his feelings. He is not weak. Weakness is an attribute traditionally tied to gender. Men should not be weak; weakness is a feminine characteristic. We know that Jared comes from an American subculture with traditional views of gender. We understand that it would be easier for him to accept the medical paradigm that defines depression as primarily an idiosyncratic illness.

THERAPIST: Jared, you do have some of those symptoms but only some, and listening to you, it seems that many of those symptoms stem directly from your current life situation. Emotional concerns are not always like physical concerns. Oftentimes what we feel and experience is due to how the world is treating us based on who we are, who our family is, where we come from, our cultural values, and so on. A good example is your roommate's not understanding your family background and where you come from and treating you poorly because of this. This can cause a great deal of distress. Also, prior to coming to college, you had no history of depression, but as we've talked together, we've developed some clear ideas about why you are currently feeling so down and lonely. Together, we can discuss and explore ways that you can gain more control over the events happening in your life and your response to them. Some of those might include medication if you don't respond to other methods. For now, let's work together to think of things that you can do, that you have control over, that might work to help you feel less alone and alienated.

JARED: I've been thinking that I should go back home and go to the technical college nearby. I know I will feel fit in because I already have friends that go there. It will be more like the old days when I was in high school. I don't really want to study engineering anyway.

THERAPIST: That would definitely solve some of your problems, but you have also discussed things that you like about college: Your dad is proud of you, you enjoy the opportunities available in town, you like your literature course, and you do computer and online gaming with some friends. Leaving college would also be a loss. How would you feel about that?

JARED: I really can't quit. I don't want to disappoint my dad; I don't really have much in common with friends back home now when I think about it. I was so excited to come to college here. I really want to stay. But, I don't know what else to do. I don't know how much more of this I can take.

THERAPIST: Well, from talking to you today, I think you have many strengths that will allow you to understand yourself better and achieve your goals. You are a bright young man. You express yourself well. You have some strong values. You have some ideas about what you want to do in life even if they are not what everybody else wants you to do. You have some very strong interests in interesting areas—gaming and literature. And, you also care about your family and where you come from. Maybe we can discuss how you might use these strengths to feel better.

As we review our conceptualization with Jared and allow him to revise and expand on it, we also review his strengths with him. We do not tell him what is *wrong* with him but rather review his areas of strength. This is an illustration of the feminist principle of focusing on increasing strengths rather than discovering pathology. We also offer Jared hope and let him know that we respect him and his experiences. We do not just assess and evaluate. Feminist therapists understand that our clients are real people who expect and deserve relationships with us. We spend time talking with Jared about marginality and ask him what it would be like if his roommate had visited Jared's home town during Jared's senior year when Jared felt socially competent and confident. This helps Jared to understand the middle-class bias he has assumed and to put his current feelings and behaviors into perspective. His roommate would not know what to talk about or how to act. In this manner, Jared leaves the initial session with a belief (or hope) that therapy will help him to solve his concerns.

Step #5 Collaborative Conceptualization and Discussion of Diagnosis (if needed)

Before Jared leaves our initial session, we review what we will be writing in our intake or initial evaluation report. We go over each point with Jared so that he can discuss or refute our hypotheses and assumptions about his symptoms. For instance, we share the hypotheses that isolating himself is a way to protect against the middle-class bias he is experiencing and that based on past experience, we know that he can socialize with others. We talk again about marginality as the source of loneliness but also as a source of his sadness. We reframe his feelings of sadness as grief or loss. He has lost the comfort he had at home before coming to college. Life will never be the same, and this is sad. We begin to discuss his academic interests and how they are threatening to him, and plans he has for the future. We place his issues in a framework of growth and development. Together, we list ways that he could expand his social repertoire to include some middle-class social skills and knowledge of middle-class norms and expectations. We include these in his treatment plan. We also talk with him about strengths, because these are an essential piece of the feminist conceptualization and our initial report. In this instance, Jared was able to articulate that his ability to live in difficult circumstances is a strength that could carry him through tough times— including his current experience with classism, was able to discuss a secret interest in literature, had strong values, and cared about his family even as he felt isolated from it. As feminist therapists, we share with him that another strength we see is his flexibility in being able to come up with his strengths and to reframe his experiences.

Our initial report and final conceptualization or diagnostic report (see Tables 6.3 and 6.4) include information on Jared's presenting problem, his strengths, his areas of growth, the impact of oppression/privilege on his life, any gender-role conflict issues, and our mutually agreed-on goals or areas to explore during counseling. As feminist therapists, we do not give Jared a label. We do not place him within a diagnostic category. We attempt to present a brief portrait of Jared that is developed collaboratively. Jared is as much an author of this report as we are.

Table 6.3 Example of Feminist Intake Written for an Agency

State University

THE COUNSELING CENTER

INTAKE REPORT

Date ___1/21/—___   Client : ___Jared___

Intake Counselor/Therapist: ___E. K. Kess___

Client Description: Jared is a 20-year-old college sophomore, 6'2" tall, with brown hair and blue eyes. He was dressed neatly and casually for the interview.

Behavioral Observations: Client was slow to smile and had some hesitancy in his speech at the start of the interview. His speech became more fluent as the interview went on. He fidgeted in the chair a great deal early in the session as well. Again, as time went on he gave more eye contact, and asked and answered questions more freely.

Presenting Problem and Relevant History (as reported): Jared was referred by his professor, who said Jared seemed depressed. Jared stated that he had lost interest in his schoolwork (except his literature course) and that he had few friends and no real desire to socialize with people at the university. He also had no desire to go home and interact with his childhood friends. He didn't know if he was depressed and asked if these behaviors meant he was.

Interpersonal/Social History: The client has few friends at the university and is ridiculed and teased by some of the students he does know. He is losing friendships at home (2 hours away) because he has grown away from them by attending college for 2 years or they forget to invite him for the same reason. He has cyber friends that he interacts with regularly. He prefers the cyber friends to the people he knows at the university.

Cultural Background: Jared grew up in a rural part of the state, where the career opportunities are scarce and family values are traditional, as are gender-role expectations. His family has been part of the working-class poor for a few generations. Although they denounce middle-class values, they still desire to achieve middle-class income and status—thus, Jared's college attendance.

Psychiatric History: Jared reports no personal psychiatric history, and he is not aware of any mental illness in his family.

Family History: Jared is the younger of two children and the first in his extended family to go to college. Jared reports strong bonds with his immediate family, though his ties with his father are weakening since he has been attending college. He maintains a good relationship with his mother. He is minimally involved with his sister and her family.

Gender Socialization: Jared's family taught him traditional gender roles and attitudes. He learned to hunt, fish, and enjoy sports either as a participant or spectator. Although his father seems proud of his college attendance, he also puts Jared down for it by calling him the "college boy." Other evidence of traditional socialization is that Jared has chosen a "masculine" profession with the potential of high earnings.

Medical History: No medical issues reported; however, Jared said he seems to sleep a lot more now than he has in the past. He wasn't sure if that was a college thing or because he was depressed.

Drug and Alcohol Use: Jared reports drinking socially on occasion and has experimented with marijuana. He does not enjoy either all that much and indulges only at parties.

Had the client been treated with psychotropic medications (for mood, ADHD, etc.) before the age of 18?

Yes _____ No __*X*__

(Continued)

Table 6.3 (Continued)

Did the client report the presence of "suicidal/homicidal" thoughts or ever having made a suicide attempt?

____ Yes   _X_ No Notes/Comments:

Client Strengths:
Jared is a bright, articulate young man who cares for his family, and his family cares about him. He is strong enough to endure all the challenges, even though they are wearing on him right now. He has come to the counseling center for assistance, which demonstrates his strength of character and resolve to make things better.

Clinical Impressions/Recommendations: (address estimated length of treatment, type of treatment, and other clinical considerations):

Jared should do well in one of the men's groups that explores, the influence of gender socialization on career/life decision making. It is especially important that he become a member of a group that is culturally diverse so that he can explore issues of classism and privilege. It is recommended that he attend 10 group sessions and reevaluate his goals at that time.

GAF (Global Assessment of Functioning) at Intake ___65___   Estimated Highest GAF Past Year: __95__

Therapist Note: Lowered GAF is due to adjustment to new environment and sociocultural realities of college.

____E. K. Kess_____   _____
Therapist Signature   Supervisor Signature

CASE ACTION   PRIORITY LEVEL :   1   X2   3
(circle or highlight one)

Terminated at Intake? ___ no ___ yes

Wait List? ____ no ___ yes date _____

Referred to Group? ___ no _X_ yes   If yes, which group? _Men's Group_____

Referred out? ____ no ___ yes

If yes, where? _____

Table 6.4 Example of How to Use Feminist Process When Using the DSM Model

Many factors come into play when conducting a formal diagnosis. Remember, the DSM system and the health-care system are focused on intrapsychic factors and place the etiology of the disease within the individual. Even though the DSM-IV-TR (APA, 2000) allows for context and environmental causes of problems via Axis IV, insurance companies reimburse only if there is a mental disorder present that is coded on Axis I.

In the case of Jared, this means that we must take into account his source of payment for services. If Jared had insurance, then we could consider giving him a diagnosis that reflects a mental disorder on Axis I. If this were the case, then an Axis I diagnosis could be 309.0 Adjustment Disorder with depressed mood, and it is considered acute. Jared is in his first year of college and is struggling with social and academic problems. He is feeling sad, lonely, and overall unmotivated regarding his engineering courses. These symptoms have been in existence for less than 6 months, which makes them acute. The stressor is identified as his difficulty with adjusting to a college environment and his subsequent social and academic challenges. His distress is significant for him because he is a first-generation college student and, thus, does not know how to navigate this new cultural environment.

If Jared were not to use insurance, then we are free to view Jared in his social context and to identify the environment as a cause of his current distress. Axis IV addresses psychosocial and environmental problems. When the psychosocial or environmental problem is the primary focus of treatment, the DSM-IV-TR (APA, 2000) instructs the clinician to code this on Axis I. In the case of Jared, we conceptualize his distress as rooted in his environment. He is a working-class individual who is now in a different culture, a middle-class one, and he is experiencing discrimination. Roommate comments about his dialect have resulted in Jared's keeping to himself and not making friends. His history of friends in high school indicates that he has the ability to make friends, so this also confirms that the etiology is environmental. So, without the issue of insurance reimbursement, Jared could be given the following diagnosis on Axis I: V 62.4 Acculturation Problem given his challenges with adjusting to a middle-class culture. Furthermore, we might also give Jared a diagnosis of V62.81 Relational Problem not otherwise specified because of his recent, since arriving at college, difficulties in relating with his father.

Jared would receive no diagnosis on Axis II Personality Disorders (V71.09) or on Axis III General Medical Conditions (V71.09). He demonstrates no evidence of significant maladaptive personality characteristics or defense mechanisms, and he also does not have any current medical conditions that are potentially relevant to understanding and treating his presenting concerns.

(Continued)

Table 6.4 (Continued)

The DSM system provides an Axis V: Global Assessment of Functioning, which allows the clinician to make a judgment regarding the impairment of the individual's functioning. Jared is given a GAF of 65 because he has mild symptoms that result in difficulty in his social and occupational, in this case school, functioning.

With Jared, his distress is defined in relationship to his social and cultural context. In assessing his distress, we come to the conclusion that his behaviors and feelings are typical for someone who is struggling to negotiate two different worlds and coming to grips with the classism and gender-role conflict in life. We discuss various ways of viewing this with Jared. At the end of the session, rather than labeling himself as depressed, Jared renames his concerns as being a "man in the middle." He explains to us that this refers to the pressure in the college environment to move into the middle class as well as his marginality in being stuck between two worlds. This naming of his pain and connecting it with his social and cultural context results in Jared feeling empowered. He leaves the initial session feeling ownership in therapy and more motivated. He chooses to return because his voice has been heard and his lived experiences are valued. In our initial report on Jared, we use his words "man in the middle" to describe his concerns.

Formal Diagnosis

Our feminist conceptualization work with Jared is built on the assumption that we work in an enlightened agency not tied to the medical model of mental health and illness. However, if our work situation requires that Jared be given a formal diagnostic label or code, then we would consider Jared's "symptoms" and possible diagnosis while keeping the limitations of the DSM system firmly in mind. For example, we understand that we could use the DSM "V" codes to diagnose Jared's concerns but believe that these codes dismiss the intensity and seriousness of Jared's distress. Additionally, V codes discuss "normal" responses rather than "healthy" or "rational" responses. From the feminist therapy perspective, Jared's distress is a healthy, or at least rational, response to a sociopolitical problem. Healthy responses are not diagnoses. In our work with Jared, our focus is on a precise and complex understanding of his distress and experience within a given social/cultural context rather than finding a category of classification or diagnosis (Brown, 1994). Out of this focus a formal diagnosis can be given. We work with Jared to develop hypotheses about the character, cause, and meaning of his distress (Brown, 1994) in accordance with the feminist conceptualization model. We view Jared as the expert on himself and work from the stance that he knows best his own experiences, his distress, and the meaning they hold for him. Jared's understanding of his distress and its meaning and our understanding hold equal weight in the diagnostic process.

Again, the feminist therapist and the client are equal experts in their own spheres of knowledge and experience, and both are considered equally. We work collaboratively to understand the meaning of his behavior rather than have the counselor give a label to his thoughts, feelings, and behavior. If differences exist between Jared's and our assessment of certain behaviors, we develop hypotheses about what this difference means to both of us and to the therapeutic relationship. For example, if as feminist therapists we saw Jared's distress as indicative of external events (racism, classism, or gender-role conflict) and Jared viewed his distress as a biological condition that indicates clinical depression, then we would arrive at a series of best guesses or hypotheses as to why our differences exist, and these hypotheses would be a part of our diagnosis. Throughout the initial evaluation, we would discuss the meaning of diagnosis and how diagnosis is done in the mental health system. We would share information from the *DSM* and other sources with him as appropriate. We would share our diagnosis with him in detail and would discuss the criteria used to arrive at the diagnosis, as well as how this diagnosis did not account for any external stressors such as classism and the impact of such a diagnosis on him. Finally, we view it as imperative to inform Jared that the use of a formal diagnosis via the *DSM-IV-TR* (APA, 2000) may well impact him later in life as it becomes part of his medical record.

If Jared's symptoms were more vegetative, if he acted on his anger more, if he were using drugs/alcohol/self-injurious behaviors to deal with his emotional issues, if he had consciously alienated more of his friends, and if he expressed *clear* suicide ideation— then we could look at a formal diagnosis. We could consider Jared's illness to be analogous to an environmentally caused physical illness. Those people who become physically ill because they live in environments that are toxic to them are truly ill. We could conceptualize Jared as being ill in this manner (our toxic society has engendered or created his symptoms) and justify a diagnosis. If Jared expressed some of the more serious symptoms listed previously, then we could feel comfortable with discussing a diagnosis of Adjustment Disorder/Depressed Mood (309.0) with him.

However, even with the possibility of some of the symptoms listed previously, we know that it is Jared's rural poverty worldview coming up against the new-to-him middle-class environment that is causing his symptoms and that should indeed be in our conceptualization report. As feminist therapists, we should never just give a DSM code even if it is all that is required. We need to find (and sometimes fight for) a way to expand on that code and explain why we give it. If we have a form to fill in by hand, then we find a way to write in the margins. If we have to add something to a computer form, then we find a way to put our comments in other fields or attach an addendum. We argue cogently with our supervisors and administrators that even if the insurance companies do not *need* more than the DSM Axis I code, we need to go beyond what is needed to

Table 6.4 (Continued)

what is accurate and ethical. As feminist mental health providers, we *need* to argue for this within our own agency to be ethical providers of service. At the very least, we can argue that we should not send anything to any payment agencies without a *full* DSM diagnostic evaluation; that is, we need to use all of the axes, especially Axis IV (Psycho-Social Stressors) and Axis V (Highest Level of Functioning) when we give a diagnosis.

Why do we choose not to give Jared a diagnosis as the case is written? Jared is not ill. His symptoms are the results of an unhealthy sociocultural environment. Jared's case is primarily about class, but it is also about oppression, race, and gender. How can that be, because we know Jared to be a White male? Jared is a White male from a background of rural poverty. In coming to college, Jared discovers that an economically impoverished rural background puts him in a one-down position with his university's middle- to upper-middle-class values. He is also discovering his power as a White man. He has male professors who wish to mentor him, and he realizes that he is fairly bright. He knows his family wishes him to "rise above" their economic level and views his scholarship to the university as the method to do that. Jared does not yet value this characteristic, and he does not understand its value to society. He considers leaving college and attending a technology school with his friends. He seems (contrary to the stereotypical male gender role) to value relationships (with his father, his family, and his friends) over "getting ahead" (this might be because of a close-knit family value system and cultural differences). Loneliness is not something that he can ignore. He is starting to recognize what he will lose by becoming the typical White, middle-class male his parents wish him to become. His engineering professor, his roommate, and other college acquaintances pressure him to conform to the typical White male gender role. As feminist therapists, we need to listen closely to him and to understand what *he* wants. If we label him with depression or even adjustment disorder/depressed mood without any other considerations, then we, too, have bought into the medical model that reifies his responses to classism, gender stereotypes, and oppression as a disease.

SUMMARY

As feminist therapists, we discuss with our clients what diagnosis and conceptualization mean to them, to us, and to all the others who will have access to that information. This is good feminist practice and is supported by the Feminist Therapy Code of Ethics (See Chapter 3). If we truly believe that Jared's (or any client's) symptoms are a result of classism, sexism, racism, or other forms of oppression, then we need to recognize our clients as equal partners in determining our assessments, conceptualizations, and diagnoses. We cannot retraumatize, victimize, or oppress them through the conceptualization process. We are not the experts in their lives and cannot—as ethical feminist therapists—act as the experts. We can act only as informed, skilled, caring professionals who recognize that all therapy is a shared enterprise and that expertise emerges from the relationship between client and therapists. So, we talk with clients openly about what it means to have a disease, because that is how others will view it once there is a diagnosis. We talk with them about their views of mental health and illness and ask them what they would like us to write on any reports we may or must generate about our interactions with them. Together, we come up with either a conceptualization sans diagnostic label or a conceptualization and a diagnostic label, but never *just* a current DSM code.

REFERENCES

American Psychiatric Association. (2000). *Diagnostic and statistical manual of mental disorders* (4th ed.), *text revision.* Washington, DC: American Psychiatric Press.

Atkinson, D. R., Morten, G., & Sue, D. W. (1979). *Counseling American minorities: A cross-cultural perspective.* Dubuque, IA: Brown.

Ballou, M., Matsumoto, A., & Wagner, M. (2002). Toward a feminist ecological theory of human nature. In M. Ballou & L. S. Brown (Eds.), *Rethinking mental health and disorder: Feminist perspectives* (pp. 91–141). New York: Guilford.

Broverman, I. K., Broverman, D. M., Clarkson, F. E., Rosenkrantz, P. S., & Vogel, P. S. (1970). Sex-role stereotyping and clinical judgments of mental health. *Journal of Consulting and Clinical Psychology, 34,* 1–7.

Brown, L. S. (1986). From alienation to connection: Feminist therapy with post-traumatic stress disorder. *Women & Therapy, 5,* 13–26.

Brown, L. S. (1990). Taking account of gender in the clinical assessment interview. *Professional Psychology; Research and Practice, 21,* 12–17.

Brown, L. S. (1992). Feminist critique of personality disorders. In L. S. Brown & M. Ballou (Eds.), *Personality and psychopathology: Feminist reappraisals* (pp. 206–228). New York: Guilford.

Brown, L. S. (1994). *Subversive dialogues.* New York: Basic Books.

Brown, L. S. (2000). Feminist therapy. In C. R. Synder & R. E. Ingram (Eds.), *Handbook of psychological change: Psychotherapy processes and practices for the 21st century* (pp. 358 – 380). New York: John Wiley & Sons.

Collins, L. H. (1998). Illustrating feminist theory: Power and psychopathology. *Psychology of Women Quarterly, 22,* 97–112.

Cross, W. E. (1971). The Negro-to-Black conversion experience: Toward a psychology of Black liberation. *Black World, 20,* 13–27.

Downing, N. E. & Roush, K. L. (1985). From passive acceptance to active commitment: A model of feminist identity development for women. *Counseling Psychologist, 13,* 695–709.

Enns, C. Z. (1997). *Feminist theories and feminist psychotherapies: Origins, themes, and variations.* New York: Haworth Press.

Espin, O. M. (1993). Feminist therapy: Not for White women only. *The Counseling Psychologist, 21,* 103–108.

Greene, B., & Sanchez-Hucles, J. (1997). Diversity: Advancing an inclusive feminist psychology. In J. Worell & N. G. Johnson (Eds.), *Shaping the future of feminist psychology: Education, research, and practice* (pp. 173–202). Washington, DC: American Psychological Association.

Marecek, J. (2002). Unfinished business: Postmodern feminism to personality psychology. In M. Ballou & L. S. Brown (Eds.), *Rethinking mental health and disorder: Feminist perspectives* (pp. 3–28). New York: Guilford.

Marecek, J., & Hare-Mustin, R. T. (1991). Feminism and clinical psychology. *Psychology of Women Quarterly, 15,* 521–536.

Morris, C. (1997). Mental health matters: Toward a non-medicalized approach to psychotherapy with women. *Women & Therapy, 20*(3), 63–78.

O'Neil, J. M. (2008). Summarizing 25 years of research on men's gender role conflict using the Gender Role Conflict Scale: New research paradigms and clinical implications. *The Counseling Psychologist, 36*(3), 358–445.

O'Neil, J. M., Good, G. E., & Holmes, S. (1995). Fifteen years of theory and research on men's gender role conflict: New paradigms for empirical research. In R. Levant & W. Pollack (Eds.), *The new psychology of men* (pp. 164–206). New York: Basic Books.

Robinson-Wood, T. (2009). *The convergence of race, ethnicity, and gender: Multiple identities in counseling* (2nd ed.). Upper Saddle River, NJ: Merrill.

Sarbin, T. R. (1997). On the futility of psychiatric diagnostic manuals (DSMs) and the return of personal agency. *Applied & Preventive Psychology, 6,* 233–243.

Seem, S. R., & Clark, M. D. (2006). Healthy women, healthy men, and healthy adults: An evaluation of gender role stereotypes in the 21st century. *Sex Roles: A Journal of Research, 55,* 247–258.

Worell, J., & Remer, P. (2003). *Feminist perspectives in therapy: Empowering diverse women* (2nd ed.). Hoboken, NJ: John Wiley & Sons.

CHAPTER 7

ESTABLISHING AND MAINTAINING THE EGALITARIAN RELATIONSHIP

Feminist therapy is deeply, fully, and consistently reflective and involves a co-creation with the client around choices and meaning-making. In addition, its commitment to an egalitarian relationship insists that the feminist therapist and the client collaboratively consider choices and consequences and arrive at mutual decisions.

—Ballou & West, 2000, p. 286

Clients and therapists mutually create a relational space where we perceive ourselves to be respected and open to growth. We do this by consciously sharing the power imbued in the therapeutic relationship. The egalitarian relationship sets a particular frame of cooperation and mutual respect around our sessions and interactions. Within this space, we are connected as complex and diverse human beings seeking knowledge and growth. We acknowledge our differences as well as our similarities. Because we are equally respected within the relationship, we are open to discussion about power and meaning. We do not make assumptions

about the other but recognize that the mutuality of the relation-
ship offers us the opportunity to ask questions freely and offer
ideas and opinions without judgment from the other. We are honest
with each other as we strive toward healthy growth for clients.

—Elizabeth Kincade, Feminist Therapist

Earlier we asked, what makes feminist therapy "feminist"? If there is one aspect of the process that is essential for therapy to be feminist, it is the ability to establish and maintain an egalitarian relationship, a relationship that focuses on the shared distribution of power within the therapeutic relationship (Ballou & West, 2000; Rader & Gilbert, 2005; Simi & Mahalik, 1997). Earlier we identified the egalitarian relationship as one of the four essential tenets of feminist therapy. When conceptualized from a feminist perspective, the therapeutic relationship strives to be as egalitarian as possible. In other words, as therapists we continually strive to balance the power in our relationships with our clients. In this chapter, we further define the egalitarian relationship and sources of power in the therapeutic relationship and present ways to establish and maintain a therapeutic relationship in which power is fairly distributed between clients and counselors.

● THE IMPORTANCE OF POWER IN THE THERAPEUTIC RELATIONSHIP

Without emphasis on an egalitarian relationship, the therapy relationship favors the power of the counselor. Therapists operate as experts regarding client problems. This places clients in a less powerful position and as recipients of counselors' knowledge. Clients' knowledge exists but is subordinate to that of the therapist. As a result of this power imbalance, counselors may function as agents of social control and (knowingly or unknowingly) enforce traditional gender-role behaviors that are constricting and unhealthy and that encourage adaptation to harmful environments (Worell & Remer, 2003). Within the feminist therapeutic framework, both therapist and client are viewed as having and using healthy power.

When we seek to balance power within therapy relationships, we reduce our chance of imposing our values on our clients (Worell & Remer, 2003, p. 71). Additionally, by balancing power we avoid replicating the power imbalances that women and other marginalized and oppressed groups encounter in society (Worell & Remer, 2003). We also avoid replicating the hierarchical structures of society (Ballou & West, 2000) that may hinder healthy growth and development. Overall, feminist therapists view the therapeutic relationship as one of mutuality and equality within the constraints of a counseling relationship. This means that feminist therapists are aware that they hold more power in the counseling relationship because of their role as mental health practitioners, a role that is based in trust, and recognize that this imbalance must exist to some extent in order for counseling to occur (Brown, 1986). If we reflect back on feminist therapy ethical considerations (Chapter 3), we know balancing power in the relationship, what can also be called the establishing and maintenance of an egalitarian relationship, is not only a tenet and technique for feminist therapists but also an ethical principle.

MENTAL HEALTH PROFESSIONALS AND ● CLIENTS IN RELATIONSHIP

Frequently, the concept of an egalitarian relationship is misunderstood and is stated as follows: The therapist and the client are equal in the relationship. The difference between being equal and sharing power may seem insignificant, but it is actually quite large. Consider these examples:

1. Tyra is coming to counseling for relationship concerns. Upon entering the office, she sits abruptly and begins listing all the negative things her partner has done this week. The therapist listens to Tyra but does not say anything. After several minutes, Tyra stops speaking. The therapist sits attentively. Tyra says, "Well aren't you going to say anything?" The therapist replies, "This is your therapy time, what would you like me to say?"

2. Tyra is coming to counseling for relationship concerns. Upon entering the office, she sits abruptly and begins listing all the negative things her partner has done this week. The therapist does not interrupt Tyra. When Tyra pauses, the therapist says, "I really get how bad it is for you; this week my partner whined about doing dishes." The therapist then shares with Tyra a list of personal complaints.

3. Tyra is coming to counseling for relationship concerns. Upon entering the office, she sits abruptly and begins listing all the negative things her partner has done this week. After Tyra's first few sentences, the therapist stops her and says, "I understand that these events were upsetting to you, but last week I asked you to make a list of pros and cons regarding your relationship. I would like to review these and your homework for this week."

4. Tyra is coming to counseling for relationship concerns. Upon entering the office, she sits abruptly and begins listing all the negative things her partner has done this week. The therapist says, "I know this is

important, but I would like you to pause for a moment and think about your feelings rather than about the instances of disrespect you've experienced this week." Tyra says, "I think its rude for you to interrupt me; I just need to get this out." The therapist is silent and then replies, "Yes, it was disrespectful, and I apologize. Before we continue, do you mind if I tell you why I felt the need to interrupt you?"

Where does the power lie in each of these interactions and which might be the most therapeutic interaction? In the first instance, the client has the greater power, in the second the counselor and client are in a friendlike equal relationship, and in the third the therapist is the expert and predominant force in the relationship. In the fourth, the counselor actively seeks ways to balance the power and responds to the client, replacing the term "rude" with "disrespectful." Whereas rude carries a value judgment, respect and disrespect are terms related to how one views oneself in a power relationship. To show disrespect to another is to show that the other does not have power over us. In this instance, the therapist attempts to equalize the power imbalance perceived by the client by being respectful of her needs and her knowledge and understanding of those needs.

In an egalitarian relationship, clients are viewed as the expert in knowing themselves, being the ultimate authority about themselves, their lives, and their needs (Brown, 2004; Worell & Remer, 2003). The therapist's stance is based on trust: trust in clients' knowledge and experience as well as trust that clients know best what they need. Although clients are experts about themselves, counselors contribute expertise to the therapeutic process. Counselors have knowledge about the counseling process; about privilege, oppression, and differences; and about how clients' locations in the social structure impact their development and presenting concerns. Furthermore, counselors model how one acts and responds in an egalitarian relationship. Counselors treat clients with respect and work collaboratively to develop treatment goals and outcomes. Counselors model for clients what relationships in which power is shared and equity is valued are like.

● PURPOSE AND INTENT OF THE EGALITARIAN RELATIONSHIP

In the egalitarian relationship, the purpose and the intent of the relationship differ. When therapists fail to see this difference, the egalitarian relationship becomes ineffective.

The *purpose* of all therapeutic relationships is to move clients toward greater mental health or personal growth. The purpose of the egalitarian relationship is similar—to move clients toward mental health or personal growth goals that are mutually agreed to by both therapists *and* clients. The *intent* of the egalitarian relationship, however, is to equally distribute power within the therapeutic relationship. Effective use of the egalitarian relationship does not confuse our intent—sharing power—with our purpose—the growth and health of our clients. Interventions within the frame of the egalitarian relationship are always in the service of our client. Consider the example of Tyra. When the therapist joins in complaining about life with the client, power is certainly shared in the relationship. The *intent* of the egalitarian relationship is fulfilled. The client's complaints and the therapist's complaints are considered equal, but the *purpose* of the relationship is negated. The focus is now on the therapist. The therapist's self-disclosure does not move the client forward in her goals. Think about the other examples of therapy with Tyra. It is only in the fourth example that both the purpose and the intent are fulfilled. Tyra's concerns and emotions are respected and treated as important. However, the therapist's role of moving Tyra toward greater personal growth is also highlighted. The therapist accepts Tyra's confrontation as legitimate and seeks to explain her motives to Tyra, thus equalizing the power balance in the relationship.

STRATEGIES FOR ESTABLISHING AND ● MAINTAINING THE EGALITARIAN RELATIONSHIP

Therapeutic approaches ask practitioners to hold values and beliefs about therapy and human nature that are congruent with the values and beliefs of the theory and practice of therapeutic approach. In general, values and beliefs differ little across approaches. We assume that clients are moving toward a healthier way of being, and we believe that therapeutic intervention will help this process. For instance, cognitive behavioral therapy is based on social learning theory (Bandura, 1986). In the various cognitive approaches, distress is conceptualized as learned thoughts and beliefs about the self and the world that are dysfunctional (Dobson & Block, 1988). Thus, people are assumed to be able to learn new, healthier thoughts and beliefs that will replace the unhealthy ones. In person-centered therapy, a primary value is the belief in clients' existence as good and whole persons (Rogers, 1987). The therapeutic attitude is one of unconditional positive regard. Strategies for working with clients are developed and used within the framework of these beliefs and attitudes.

As feminist therapists we believe that clients' distress has multiple causes, including sociopolitical factors and disruptions in meaningful relationships (Miller, 1988; Jordan & Hartling, 2002). Establishing and maintaining an egalitarian relationship is one of the primary skills in helping clients understand the value of a nonexploitative, mutual, caring, and respectful relationship. Through experiencing this relationship, clients gain greater respect for themselves and their abilities. They can function in their sociocultural milieu in healthy ways.

The egalitarian relationship is developed consciously by the feminist practitioner through feminist values and strategies. To establish and maintain the therapeutic relationship, feminist practitioners hold the following values and beliefs about counseling. First, the purpose of counseling is to empower the people who are our clients. Second, the therapy process is not arcane but an open shared process. Third, clients and therapists hold equal power and responsibility for the counseling process, and finally, a therapeutic focus on encouraging and increasing strengths is more valuable than a focus on remediating weaknesses (Ballou & West, 2000; Brown, 1986, 2004; Rader & Gilbert, 2005; Worell & Remer, 2003). Each of these areas is explored in the sections that follow.

1. Empowerment of Clients

Feminist therapists view therapy as a collaborative process, in which clients are perceived as experts about their concerns (Ballou & West, 2000; Brown, 1986, 2004; Rader & Gilbert, 2005; Worell & Remer, 2003). Viewing clients as experts honors clients' power to determine their concerns and their lived experience. At the beginning of the therapeutic relationship, feminist therapists speak to clients about their relevant values and beliefs about counseling and the change process (Worell & Remer, 2003), and about their lifestyle and background (Simi & Mahalik, 1997). As a result, clients are viewed as persons who have the right and ability to make informed decisions about entering into counseling with particular counselors. Articulation of these values minimizes the chance that therapists will impose their values on clients.

2. Demystification of the Counseling Process

The sharing of relevant beliefs and values about society by feminist therapists also helps to demystify the counseling process (Enns, 1988). Feminist therapists educate their clients about the theory and process of feminist therapy. The costs and benefits of counseling are discussed, rights and responsibilities of each party are outlined (Feminist Therapy Institute [FTI], 2005), expectations of counselor and client are discussed, and alternatives to counseling are all topics for discussion with clients at the beginning of counseling (Enns, 2000). Feminist therapists also teach clients therapeutic skills when relevant (Worell & Remer, 2003). For example, counselors may teach clients the strategies of gender-role as well as political and cultural analysis (see Chapters 8 and 9) to help clients critically examine their gender-role socialization and resulting behaviors that may be detrimental to their psychological health. Learning these skills provides clients with the means to become their own authority on their lived experience rather than to depend on mental health professionals for this information. In an egalitarian relationship where clients are respected, they do not need to ask therapists "what's wrong with me?"; rather they are supported in their search for answers about themselves through learning skills and being respected and honored for their life knowledge.

Feminist therapists work collaboratively with their clients to establish counseling goals and treatment outcomes (Worell & Remer, 2003). Decisions regarding frequency and length of treatment, payment amounts, and treatment modalities are decided together between client and counselor (Ballou & West, 2000). This collaboration also helps to empower clients to have a sense of authority in the decisions regarding their therapy. This is also an ethical principle as outlined in the FTI Code of Ethics in Chapter 3.

3. Balancing of Power in the Relationship

Feminist therapists strive not to replicate the hierarchical relationships in society. They seek to model a relationship built on mutuality and care. Thus, feminist therapists pay particular attention to power in the therapeutic relationships (Brown, 2004; Simi & Mahalik, 1997; Worell & Remer, 2003). This attention to power within the relationship is a common theme throughout our presentation of feminist therapy and is unique to feminist therapy. Again, if you look at the example of Tyra, you will see that in the final scenario, her therapist strives to share appropriate power with her and thus "engages in an ethic of respect" (Ballou & West, 2000, p. 285). When we attend to power in the relationship, we build a collaborative decision-making process between ourselves and our clients. This sense of collaboration infuses the relationship established between feminist therapists and their clients. Clients' opinions, needs, and wants matter and are closely honored by their counselors. Furthermore, counselor modeling of appropriate use of power may be a powerful antidote to the abuses of power clients may experience in life and may be especially important when the focus of counseling is on gender-related issues (Enns, 2000). Notice, again, that the feminist therapist when dealing appropriately with Tyra asks Tyra's permission before she continues.

Another way feminist therapists attempt to reduce the power imbalance in the counseling relationship is to use selective self-disclosure (Worell & Remer, 2003). Feminist therapists believe that the use of self-disclosure serves to decrease the power differential between counselors and clients, promote an egalitarian relationship, and provide clients with more role model options (Simi & Mahalik, 1997). When counselors carefully and respectfully choose to self-disclose information about their current and past life experiences, clients learn that they too can overcome challenges (Worell & Remer, 2003). For instance, when a therapist self-discloses that she too experienced acquaintance rape as a young woman, her female client hears that one can recover from rape (modeling) and that she is not responsible as this happens to other "good" people (universality); then she may be more apt to place her experience in the sociopolitical context. Even when the clients and therapists differ in terms of gender or race/ethnicity, counselor self-disclosure can help clients understand that gender-role messages they received are socially constructed and not based in biology because both the counselor and the client are struggling with cultural messages about how to be (Worell & Remer, 2003). This is a particularly useful skill when used in conjunction with the skills of gender-role analysis and power analysis that are discussed in Chapter 8.

Counselors' use of self-involving responses in the here and now of therapy allow counselors to provide feedback, share their humanness, and model effective communication skills (Worell & Remer, 2003). Counselors may share how they are impacted by clients and provide clients with valuable information about themselves and how they are in relationships. Furthermore, counselors may demonstrate their humanity by sharing their feelings regarding clients or clients' experiences. Finally, when sharing their feelings, counselors model direct expression of feelings. When the feminist therapist working with Tyra acknowledges that her intended intervention was disrespectful and apologizes, the therapist is self-disclosing. She is telling Tyra that she makes mistakes. If she then proceeded with her apology to say, "When you mentioned your struggles this week, I remembered incidents in my life that I am still angry about, and I became impatient to help you with your concerns," she would further establish the egalitarian relationship.

It is important to note that the use of therapist self-disclosure and self-involvement must be done with extreme care and only in the service of the client. In the second scenario with Tyra, the therapist began to complain about her partner. This is not an acceptable use of self-disclosure, and although it may self-disclose that the therapist also struggles with relational issues, when done in this manner, the focus shifts from the client's concerns to those of the therapist. The client is put in the position of taking care of the therapist's emotional needs. The therapeutic relationship is equal in that it contains equal partners each with equal roles in the relationship. These are not the same roles but roles of equal importance and respect.

The following guidelines are derived from the research on self-disclosure. These guidelines are not derived from the feminist literature but when combined with the FTI Code of Ethics guidelines on the use of power in therapy relationships provide a model for therapeutic and ethical self-disclosure.

1. Therapists should generally disclose infrequently. Several studies show that therapists disclose only infrequently. It may be that self-disclosure is helpful because it occurs so infrequently.

2. The most appropriate topic for therapist self-disclosure involves professional background, whereas the least appropriate topics include sexual practices and beliefs.

3. Therapists should generally use disclosure to validate reality, normalize, model, strengthen the alliance, or offer alternative ways to think or act.

4. Therapists should generally avoid using disclosures that are for their own needs, remove the focus from the client, interfere with the flow of the session, burden or confuse the client, are intrusive, blur the boundaries between the therapist and client, overstimulate the client, or contaminate the transference.

5. Therapist self-disclosure might be particularly effective when it is in response to similar client self-disclosure.

6. Therapists should observe carefully how clients respond to their disclosure, ask the clients about their reactions, and use that information to conceptualize their clients and decide how to intervene next.

7. It may be especially important for therapists to disclose with some clients more than others. (Hill & Knox, 2002)

4. Focus on Client Strengths

Human beings come to counseling seeking help, advice, and support for various issues. In our culture, asking for help situates one in a lower power position. The helpee is weak and has gone to the helper for answers and strength. Obviously, this undermines the establishment and maintenance of an egalitarian relationship. Feminist therapists recognize this power imbalance and acknowledge it with their clients. One technique that feminist therapists use to equalize this power imbalance is to assist clients in identifying and focusing on their strengths rather than on their weaknesses. Feminist therapists do not view their clients as a collection of damaged parts or syndromes but as whole human beings with both strengths and weaknesses.

In the third scenario, Tyra's therapist interrupts her and discounts her feelings. She focuses on Tyra's lack of progress in her homework rather than on Tyra's strengths, which include such things as being able to express feelings openly. In this way, Tyra is punished by her therapist, and her weaknesses are highlighted rather than her strengths. For instance, her therapist might reframe Tyra's emotionality as understanding of feelings and willingness to be open about feelings. Clients may unconsciously accept societal values about being emotional and criticize themselves rather than understanding the androcentric or ethnocentric labeling of such behaviors (Worell & Remer, 2003).

● THE THERAPIST'S PERSPECTIVE

As noted in Chapter 3, the ethical stance for a feminist therapist is one of personal and cultural awareness. As we work with clients to establish and maintain the egalitarian relationship, we are constantly in touch with our own experiences, thoughts, feelings, and knowledge about clients' presentation and issues but also about the power dynamics of the therapeutic relationship. In this section, we highlight a feminist therapist's process as she works with her client within the context of the egalitarian relationship.

Allison is a therapist in private practice. She works in a small group practice that includes an administrative assistant, a nurse practitioner, a clinical social worker, and herself—a licensed professional counselor.

Sara comes to Allison seeking help with what she calls horrible sadness. She is 57 years old and has been a junior-high-school math teacher in a large suburban school system for 35 years. She was divorced in her late 30s and never remarried. She has one son, age 30, who no longer has contact with her.

Allison has not met Sara before, although they have spoken on the phone. Even though Sara has called and made her initial appointment through the administrative assistant, Allison called to confirm the appointment, to introduce herself, and to see whether Sara had any further questions about the process of counseling. At this time, Allison also asked Sara how she likes to be addressed and briefly said that she prefers her clients to call her by her first name if they are comfortable with that.

Allison walks into the office and greets Sara by name and says, "I'm Allison." As they walk to Allison's office, Allison is aware of distance and space as this can be a power issue. During her clinical training, Allison observed therapists who stood silently at the waiting room door, beckoned to a client, and then had the client follow them down to the office in a very subordinate position. Allison always tries to walk beside her clients and to match their gait. Even before they are in the consulting room, Allison strives to be aware of her client's general mood. If it is appropriate, she will make small talk to relieve client anxiety.

Once in the office, Allison does not begin by asking Sara a series of questions about herself and her past. She understands that the process of therapy can be anxiety provoking—especially for someone like Sara, who has never been to therapy before. Additionally she knows that therapy, although an intensely private experience, essentially involves telling a complete stranger very intimate thoughts, feelings, experiences, and behaviors. Allison knows that she will ask these questions after Sara knows more about both the process of therapy and Allison as a therapist. She begins by reintroducing herself and setting the frame for therapy. She explains first that counseling is a confidential relationship and how confidentiality is a sign of respect for her, the client. The content discussed in counseling is information about her life (lived experiences), and it belongs to her. Allison also explains the limitations of confidentiality and what these are in Sara's state (and the state in which Allison is licensed). She tells Sara that if she has to break confidentiality, she will do it as respectfully as possible for Sara. She asks Sara if she has any questions and assures Sara that she really is open to questions because she understands that starting therapy can be complicated. This allows Sara to understand that she is not a passive and subordinate participant in the process. Allison answers Sara's questions honestly. When Sara asks a question that Allison does not know the answer to, Allison assures her that she will find the answer for her before the next session or sooner if she needs the information before then. Allison also discusses with Sara how she conceives of human nature and the psychotherapeutic process. She does not say to Sara, "I am a feminist therapist." Allison knows that most therapists do not start by stating their therapeutic orientation because most clients do not completely understand the nuances of therapeutic modalities. Instead, Allison talks about how she does therapy. If Sara specifically asked about therapeutic orientation, she would tell her. She explains to Sara that she believes that Sara is the expert in her own life and that she, Allison, is the expert in counseling. These are two equal areas of expertise that they will combine to come up with the best solutions for Sara's concerns. Allison says that she believes that people and their lives are complex, that she understands that lives are lived within specific cultures, and that she takes that into account with her clients. She lets Sara know that she can ask questions about any part of the process or about Allison's background at any time during their work together and that she will answer questions honestly and to the best of her ability. Allison says, "This is a relationship of equals, with much experience and wisdom to share. You are the expert in your life; my expertise is in helping achieve your goals for that life."

During the first few minutes of the first session, Allison is aware of Sara not only as a client but also as a human being in a stressful situation. She assesses Sara's level of comfort in the session through listening closely to Sara's words and tone and watching her body language. This is part of counselor expertise. Sara appears somewhat anxious about the session. Allison says, "I know that therapy, especially the first session, can be a bit stressful. It is an odd position to be in. You're here to talk about your life and feeling sad (she uses Sara's words and concepts) to a complete stranger." Sara acknowledges her anxiety but says that she feels more comfortable with Allison now that they have met face-to-face. Allison asks her whether she would like to start talking about herself now. Sara says that she would but she does not know where to begin. When observing Sara during the first few minutes, Allison does not make the assumption that Sara's anxious behaviors are trait related but recognizes the inherent anxiety in coming for counseling and checks this out with Sara. Allison knows that if she sees other behaviors that appear indicative of greater psychological distress, she will also check out her impressions with Sara. Allison does not assume that she is the expert in Sara's life and her coping strategies. She understands the sociopolitical context of clients' lives and continually strives to integrate this with her intimate, clinical knowledge of them.

Once Allison and Sara are both satisfied that Sara has enough information to continue in therapy, Allison shifts the focus from the frame of therapy to Sara's concerns by asking Sara what is going on her life right now that has led her to consider talking to a counselor. This question allows Allison to understand both the severity of Sara's issues and the endurance of them.

As shown, it is important to establish the egalitarian relationship in the first minutes of meeting your client. This is done through language, tone, types of questions, and body language. In Chapter 6 we presented the case of Jared with regard to conceptualization and diagnosis. These are important concepts and techniques to review as you develop and maintain the egalitarian relationship. The power to diagnose is one way the egalitarian relationship is jeopardized, and it needs to be consciously addressed. In Chapter 3 when discussing the FTI Code of Ethics, we also discussed types of power that therapists have over their clients and how feminist therapists are ethically obligated to attempt to disperse that power and not use it to further harm clients.

Once the egalitarian relationship is established, it is therapists' responsibility to maintain it. In some ways this may be easier in matched-gender therapeutic relationships. In feminist therapy, female–female dyad therapists have increased empathy for the client and can serve as effective role models, and the egalitarian relationship is easier to develop because there is no gender power (Worell & Remer, 2003). In the feminist therapy male–male dyad, there is also increased empathy, and the client is provided with a nonstereotyped male role model who can model egalitarian, relational behavior in therapy. When the feminist therapist is female and the client is male, the client learns to appreciate a nonstereotyped woman, and male clients may self-disclose feelings more readily (Worell & Remer, 2003). The greatest problems can develop in the feminist therapy male–female client dyad, as the gender dynamics are especially problematic in this situation. Feminist male therapists must work assiduously not to abuse their gender power over female clients. In Chapter 2 we discussed men's power over women and privileging women's experience. In our culture, men have access to greater cultural power and are often assumed to be experts. These factors can impede the egalitarian relationship. However, there are also benefits for women in these therapeutic relationships once the egalitarian relationship develops and is maintained. For instance, a nonstereotyped male therapist with a feminist orientation can provide a female client with a positive experience with a man (Worell & Remer, 2003).

Let us look again at the egalitarian relationship between Allison and Sara and how it is maintained.

Allison always reviews her notes from previous sessions before meeting with Sara (respect). Allison is on time for her sessions with Sara. However, Sara knows that because of crisis rotation schedules, there may be times when Allison is not on time. If Allison is not, she makes arrangements for Sara to know why (values Sara's time as much as she values her own). By the third session, Sara and Allison have a working therapeutic relationship that is striving toward an egalitarian one.

Sara frequently begins to speak with Allison as she walks down the hall to Allison's office. Allison diverts any personal information into small talk but remembers important details and pursues these once in the counseling room. Sara notices and asks her why she does this. Allison replies that she is uncomfortable because she does not consider the hallway private, and she wants to protect Sara's interests (therapy is an open and shared process). Sara had not thought of that as she considered the center itself a safe and private place. Once in session, Allison briefly recaps what was discussed the previous week (shows that she considers Sara's time with her important/equal power) and asks whether Sara had thought about what she wanted to talk about today (giving Sara equal voice in the relationship/equal power). Allison is aware of her body language with Sara. She answers Sara's questions honestly. After disclosing a specific and painful incident, Sara asks Allison, "Do you have children? What would you do in this situation?" Allison remembers being told in her training many years ago not to answer this kind of question directly. She was told that it gave the client too much information and could interfere with transference. As a feminist therapist, Allison recognizes the damage not answering this will do to the therapeutic power of the egalitarian relationship (open and shared process).

Allison carefully considers her reply. She says, "I don't have children." She does not explain why, nor does she apologize for not having the same experience as Sara. She knows that it is important to keep self-disclosure relevant to the issues at hand and as brief as possible. "But, I know your son is very important to you, and I have worked with others who have had similar problems. Let's take my expertise in counseling and your knowledge of your situation and together work on the problem with your son" (equal power/encouraging strengths).

In this sequence, Allison touches on the four elements of maintaining the egalitarian relationship: empowering the client, embracing therapy as an open and shared process, maintaining equal power in the relationship, and encouraging the client's strengths. In addition, she does not abuse her power and tell her client what to do, she keeps the focus of her self-disclosure on her client's needs, and she indicates faith in her client's ability to find the right answers.

SUMMARY

Establishing and maintaining the egalitarian relationship is essential to feminist therapy. After obtaining a background in feminist therapy principles and achieving a solid understanding of the sociocultural factors that define how we look at mental health, we begin to work with our clients with the egalitarian relationship in place. In this chapter, we examined the factors that establish and maintain the relationship as well as therapist behaviors.

FOR FURTHER DISCUSSION

1. Within the therapy session, what information is private and what is not?

2. What are three pieces of information that you might not share with your clients? Is there any situation when you would share these with clients?

3. What are three pieces of information that you would share with clients? Is there any situation when you would not share this information with clients?

EXERCISES AND EXAMPLES

What interventions would you use to establish and maintain the egalitarian relationship in the following situations? Be specific. What would you say or do with your client?

1. A client you have seen for 10 sessions for depression and feelings of failure tells you that she was acquaintance-raped 2 weeks ago. She waited to tell you this, she says, because she feels responsible and did not want to let you down.

2. You have seen Jeremy for 3 sessions. He is always polite and somewhat formal in session. He does not easily talk about feelings.

REFERENCES

Ballou, M., & West, C. (2000). Feminist therapy approaches. In M. Baggio & M. Hersen (Eds.), *Issues in the psychology of women* (pp. 273–297). New York: Kluwer Academic/Plenum.

Bandura, A. (1986). *Social foundations of thought and action: A social cognitive theory.* Englewood Cliffs, NJ: Prentice Hall.

Brown, L. S. (1986). From alienation to connection: Feminist therapy with post-traumatic stress disorder. *Women & Therapy, 5*(1), 13–26.

Brown, L. S. (2004). Feminist paradigms of trauma treatment. *Psychotherapy: Theory, Research, Practice, Training, 41*(4), 464–471.

Dobson, K., & Block, L. (1988). Historical and philosophical bases of the cognitive behavioral therapies. In K. Dobson and L. Block (Eds.), *Handbook of cognitive behavioral therapies.* New York: Guilford.

Enns, C. Z. (1988). Dilemmas of power and equality in marital and family therapy counseling: Proposals for a feminist perspective. *Journal of Counseling and Development, 67,* 242–248.

Enns, C. Z. (2000). Gender issues in counseling. In S. Brown & R. Lent (Eds.). *Handbook of counseling psychology* (3rd ed., pp. 601–638). New York: John Wiley & Sons.

Feminist Therapy Institute (2005). *Feminist therapy code of ethics.* Retrieved November 13, 2009, from http://www.feminist-therapy-institute.org

Hill, C. & Knox, S. (2002). Self-disclosure. In John C. Norcross (Ed.), *Psychotherapy relationships that work: Therapy contributions and responsiveness to patients* (pp. 255–266). New York: Oxford University Press.

Jordan, J. V., & Hartling, L. M. (2002) New developments in relational-cultural theory. In M. Ballou & L. Brown (Eds.), *Rethinking mental health and disorder* (pp. 48–70). New York: Guilford.

Miller, J. B. (1988). Connections, disconnections, and violations. *Work in Progress, No. 33.* Wellesley, MA: Stone Center Working Papers Series.

Rader, J., & Gilbert, L. A. (2005). The egalitarian relationship in feminist therapy. *Psychology of Women Quarterly, 29,* 427–435.

Rogers, C. (1987). The underlying theory: Drawn from experiences with individuals and groups. *Counseling and Values, 32,* 38–45.

Simi, N. L., & Mahalik, J. R. (1997). Comparison of feminist versus psychoanalytic/dynamic and other therapists on self-disclosure. *Psychology of Women Quarterly, 21,* 465–483.

Worell, J., & Remer, P. (2003). *Feminist perspectives in therapy: Empowering diverse women* (2nd ed.). Hoboken, NJ: John Wiley & Sons.

CHAPTER 8

GENDER-ROLE AND POWER ANALYSES

Before presenting power and gender analysis techniques, we would like you to consider the following two case examples.

Client 1: Sally

Complaint: Sally is experiencing shortness of breath and heart palpitations that are not medically related but that occur whenever she goes grocery shopping for her family. Sally works full time at a competitive advertising firm and usually puts in 10-hour days. When she gets home, she prepares meals (mostly things she cooked over the weekend and only has to warm up). After dinner, she cleans the kitchen while her husband and children watch television, and then she helps her 7- and 9-year-old children prepare for bed. Her husband usually arrives home before she does and helps the children with their homework. Sally is very grateful for his help—otherwise, she does not know how she could do it all. She is feeling a great deal of anxiety now because of these symptoms and feelings she experiences in the supermarket. She worries that she will not be able to continue what she calls "being a good mom and getting the dinner on the table every night."

(Continued)

(Continued)

Client 2: Joe

Complaint: Joe is a top car salesperson at a dealership, but lately his work has not been up to par. In fact, in the past few months, he has failed to make it to the top three in monthly sales—something that he has been able to do each month for the past 5 years. Last month, he was beat out of the number-three slot by a younger, less-experienced female coworker. This was devastating to Joe. Recently, Joe has experienced uncontrolled bursts of rage both at home and at work—rage that seems to come from nowhere. He has started to dread going to work and has called in sick some days when he was not physically ill. Joe spends weekends watching television and drinking beer. He begs off doing anything with his family or friends. About 7 months ago, Joe's 8-year-old son was diagnosed with severe asthma, and the family has had to make life changes to adjust to the child's illness. One day, Joe came home from a rough day at work to find his son and daughter playing with dolls. Joe went into a rage—yelling at his son. He showed signs of anger even when discussing this event at his intake interview, saying, "It's bad enough that he can't play sports; does he have to do sissy things like play with dolls just because he has to stay inside the house?"

With almost every client, counselors will find that societal pressures to meet gender-role responsibilities are part of the presenting problem. In Chapter 4, we discussed the importance of gender and its relevance to feminist therapy. We reviewed research showing that socialization into sex-appropriate gender roles starts at such an early age that we are not aware that we have internalized expectations about gender. These internalized gender-role attitudes, or gender-role schemas (Bem, 1993), often dictate our expectations about ourselves and others. Both Sally and Joe have internalized and idealized their appropriate gender roles. They criticize themselves or others for not living up to or for straying from the appropriate gender expectations. An in-depth examination of their gender-role attitudes and expectations, or a gender-role analysis, will help them to understand their own behavior and the behavior of others (Brown, 1986). In this chapter, we first examine gender-role analysis and then look at a closely related technique, power analysis. Both are based in concepts presented earlier in the book: that gender roles can cause strain and dysfunction in individuals and that patriarchy—the philosophy and system that place men in power over women—is harmful to both women and men. The processes for both skills are described in a step-by-step format with a short dialogue demonstrating the skill. After the power analysis dialogue, we present a case for you to create your own gender-role and power analysis scenarios.

GENDER-ROLE ANALYSIS ●

During gender-role analysis, Sally and Joe will be encouraged to explore the societal messages they were given as children about gender and how those gender-role messages influence their lives as adults. Such an exploration will allow them both to discover how ignorance of their quest to meet societal gender expectations is instrumental in causing the concerns they bring to their therapists' office. For example, Sally most likely will find that one cause of her anxiety is the societal expectation that women be wives and mothers and, thus, ultimately responsible for household management and child care. Joe will learn that societal definitions of masculinity have influenced his own limited ideas of what it means to be a man, which results in his anger when he believes he (or someone he loves) fails to measure up to those definitions. Both Sally and Joe may decide that to change their behaviors, thoughts, and feelings, they must accept that many of their gender expectations are unrealistic and arbitrary. In doing so, they will discover that what they previously perceived as their own gender deficiencies are actually societal deficiencies and that responsibility for change lies with society as well as with the individual.

POWER ANALYSIS ●

Gender-role analysis addresses only half the story. Because feminist therapists are committed to overcoming oppressions, it is equally important that our clients understand how power influences their lives. Both Sally and Joe will learn that another cause of their symptoms is their experience with power—assuming, abusing, and being controlled by it. Power analysis helps clients understand the influence of power on their relationships and in other parts of their lives. Feminist therapists use client awareness of power to help both Sally and Joe devise more effective responses to power.

HOW GENDER-ROLE ANALYSIS HELPS ●

The information in Chapter 4 was provided because counselors need solid understanding and knowledge of gender socialization and societal gender-role expectations before they can adequately engage in gender-role analysis. You might want to review this information at this time.

Gender-role analysis can assist clients in many ways. Counselors may use the analysis to conceptualize clients' presenting issues. Once clients and counselors discuss clients' perception of their gender roles and where these perceptions originated, clients then can determine whether these perceptions of their role are helpful or harmful. In addition, gender-role analysis is therapeutic in that it raises awareness of internalized messages about what is the correct behavior for one's gender (Israli & Santor, 2000) When abiding by these messages results in psychological distress and performance failure, clients discover that something needs to change in their lives. When clients become aware of the harmful effects of these beliefs, they are ready to start the process of "resocialization." Resocialization instructs clients in restructuring their beliefs about men's and women's roles. It prods them to "take on roles that may not be socially prescribed and to seek the reward for taking such roles internally as opposed to taking cues from the larger society" (Israli & Santor, 2000, p. 5).

The Gender-Role Analysis Technique—An Example

Gender-role analysis allows clients to recognize how gender-role expectations—their own and others—affect their thoughts, actions, and feelings. Clients can then keep those gendered behaviors they truly value and learn to discard those that they do not. Gender-role analysis can be used in individual counseling/therapy, psychoeducational settings, personal group workshops, and therapeutic group work (Brown, 1986). Worell and Remer (2003) believe that gender-role analysis is especially effective in a group setting. Group members can stimulate one another and challenge each other's beliefs more efficiently than a therapist/counselor can in an individual session. Whether it is done in a group or with an individual, gender-role analysis typically follows the six steps outlined by Worell and Remer (2003, pp. 77–78).

Step 1. Have client identify the gender-role messages he or she has received. The client should be prompted to list both direct messages (girls don't ____; boys don't ____) and indirect messages (behaviors of role models and examples from the media) (Worell & Remer, 2003).

Step 2. Have the client identify consequences of the gender-role messages he or she has listed in step 1. Both positive and negative consequences should be explored. For example, a possible positive consequence of the nurturing role is that women learn to care about people and form lasting relationships. A negative consequence of the nurturing role may be that women become overburdened with meeting the needs of others. A positive consequence of the achieving role for men may be that they have financial and emotional support for their higher education. The negative consequence of the achieving role may be that men are pressured to always compete with others and may come to view themselves as never achieving enough or being good enough.

Step 3. Have the client identify those external gender-role messages she or he has internalized. Messages are usually internalized when the client's self-talk mimics the admonitions of the significant adults who taught the gender role. A stereotypical gender-role self-talk for women might be "I cannot take that assignment and have my husband babysit the children for a week." Self-talk for men might be "I have to work late and miss school events to get that promotion. How else am I going to be able to afford to buy that house in the neighborhood my wife loves so much?"

Step 4. The client decides on the internalized messages she or he would like to keep and those to discard. Because clients have identified the benefits and drawbacks to these messages, theoretically, this task should be easy. However, some beliefs are held so strongly that even if they work to clients' detriment, they are not willing to let those beliefs go. Often, this kind of reaction is a result of deeply rooted cultural expectations and norms. It is not the therapists' job to push their clients toward changing these deeply held beliefs but to work on those that clients are willing to change because of the pain they feel.

Step 5. The client decides on a plan for changing one of the messages he or she has internalized.

Step 6. The client implements the planned change.

Case Study

The following client attended an intake interview. Her counselor Kathy reviewed the summary of the interview prior to meeting the client. Because Kathy is part of a feminist practice, all clients are interviewed from the philosophical stance on which feminist therapy is based—gender- and cultural-role socialization informs psychological health. Therefore, the intake interview is very thorough. It includes the following information: gender, age, race, ethnicity, nationality, culture, similarities and differences the family of origin has with the cultural group, occupation, class, religion, language(s) spoken, roles of family members (including significant extended family), educational background, history of child abuse—physical or sexual, and history of adult physical or sexual abuse (including rape and date rape). You may refer back to the intake interview for the client discussed in Chapter 6 for an example of an agency intake with a young man.

INFORMATION FROM INTAKE INTERVIEW

Identifying Information:

Joan is a 37-year-old single African American woman—a lawyer in a prestigious firm. She has been practicing law for about 8 years now and has been an associate at her firm for the past 5 years.

Presenting Problem:

Joan's presenting problem is that she suffers from insomnia and anxiety (her words). She has been to her physician, who has prescribed medication, but Joan doesn't want to take a pill for what she believes is a personality flaw. She believes she should be able to solve her problems and flaws without help from medication. Thus, counseling was more acceptable to her than medication. Joan has had two panic attacks—one before giving an opening statement in court and the other just before going out on a blind date. She expresses disgust with herself because all the women in her life are strong and can better handle the stresses of life. She mentions her mother, grandmother, and aunts as examples. Even her sisters, who have families as well as jobs, seem to function well. She berates herself because she has no children, no husband, and no obligations, and cannot handle the pressures she encounters in her life.

Relevant History:

Joan is a native of Virginia, and she knows that five or six generations in her family were born in Virginia. Many of her ancestors are buried in the graveyard of the church her parents still attend. She lives 3 hours from her parents and her two older sisters. Joan considers herself to be a little more cosmopolitan than many of her closest friends because she grew up in a military family and has lived in Germany and Guam. She also thinks that her sisters and parents are more accepting of different racial groups, especially White Americans. Most of her African American friends are skeptical at best of White people, and some believe White Americans are the enemy.

Currently, Joan lives a solidly middle-class lifestyle. As the daughter of an officer, her childhood was also solidly middle class. Her parents and sisters are all college graduates, and one sister has a Master's degree in engineering. In keeping with her middle-class background, her family has always spoken Standard American English. As a child, Joan was taught that the African American Vernacular English was bad English. She states that she no longer believes this, and that unlike her family, she is not judgmental in this regard. Joan does not attend church in her own community but always attends her home church when she visits her parents. She says she is a "nonpracticing Christian." Joan believes in God and prayer, but that is the extent of her spiritual life.

Joan is single and never married. She knows that this is a great disappointment to her mother, who wants and values grandchildren from all of her children; however, Joan's mother is clear that children should be born in wedlock. Joan reports that she never wanted children and does not feel pressured by her mother to "give her grandchildren," as Joan's three siblings have already done so. Joan does feel deep disappointment that she has not married. At 37, she feels that she will never get married, and that makes her very sad and lonely. Joan has dated men, some very seriously over several years, but the relationships always seemed to fade out. She has never been sexually abused or raped.

Her counselor, Kathy, is also an African American woman who is about 10 years older than Joan. Although her background is similar to Joan's in terms of race, ethnicity, and social class, Kathy must not assume that she knows Joan well. Kathy's knowledge of within-group differences and worldviews will be essential in addressing Joan's issues. Kathy has a high racial identity status level and is in the higher stages of feminist identity (issues of feminist identity and racial identity were discussed in Chapter 6; see Table 6.1). She is certain she can work with Joan. Kathy does not believe, and neither does her supervisor, that she will enter the relationship with any prejudice or bias toward the client. One potential difficulty is that Kathy will overidentify with Joan because some of Joan's issues may mirror Kathy's. If this happens, then therapy may stall, and exploration of issues will remain at a superficial level because of countertransference. Another consequence of overidentification may be that boundaries between friendship and therapy may blur. Although Kathy is a licensed professional, she belongs to a women's supervision group made up of six skilled women therapists from various mental health disciplines. Kathy discusses these concerns with her supervision group. With her supervision group's guidance and wisdom, Kathy believes she can be a benefit to Joan. Kathy's consultation with her group is in keeping with the Feminist Therapy Institute's Code of Ethics (Feminist Therapy Institute, 1999) statements about the need for consultation and ongoing supervision to provide effective and ethical therapy. You may want to review Chapter 3 for more information.

In this initial meeting, Kathy explains to Joan her own beliefs about gender roles and how they impact women. These include the basic feminist therapy tenets—that the personal is political, the therapeutic relationship is egalitarian, women's experiences are valued, and therapy empowers clients. Kathy begins the interview by initiating a gender-role analysis with Joan, which will achieve two goals. First, Kathy will learn more in-depth, specific information about Joan's worldview. This will be helpful in preventing Kathy from overidentifying with Joan. Second, beginning with a gender-role analysis allows Joan to start to separate her goals and expectations for herself from societal goals and expectations. Kathy begins the analysis by telling Joan that she wants to get a better idea of how she has been affected by societal demands.

Step 1: Have client identify the gender-role messages he or she has received.

Kathy: Joan, as we have discussed before, it is my belief as a feminist therapist that women and men are socialized in order to maintain the status quo in this society. What that means for us is that everyone in the United States is socialized to keep White males in the dominant position. All other groups must maintain subordinate positions, especially women. However, women struggle with maintaining this subordinate position the more they learn how arbitrary it is and how it hurts and limits them. I believe that struggle is the primary reason women have psychological and emotional symptoms, and the best way to overcome those symptoms is for the society to change as well as the individual.

Therefore, it is my belief that your anxiety and insomnia are the by-products of your struggle to cope with the societal and cultural restrictions that are imposed on you as an African American woman. It is important for us to explore your own beliefs about your gender roles so that we can explore ways to overcome your symptoms. The sociological and political remedies we consider may include learning more about the valuing of your own experience as a woman as well as the experiences of other women, being your own advocate, and/or becoming involved in advocating against oppression against women and/or others.

Why don't you start by telling me about how you learned and who taught you about what it meant to be a girl.

Joan: You mean what should good little girls do?

Kathy: Yes, we can start with that.

Joan: My mother always told me that good little girls stayed clean and didn't talk loudly. They do what their parents tell them. She also told me that it is all right to act like a tomboy sometimes but that I had to remember that I was a girl and I couldn't act like that all the time. I remember wondering, how would I know when I should stop being a tomboy? But when it came right down to it, I didn't have to worry—she always told me when I had stepped over the line.

Kathy: It sounds like she told you "when" sometimes when you didn't want to stop.

Joan: Yeah, sometimes she stopped me when I was having an argument with a boy or when I got too loud. She didn't mind a little loud—just not what she called boisterous. You know, acting way too much like the boys.

Kathy: You can play *with* the boys as long as you didn't play *like* a boy.

Joan: Yeah, that's it.

Kathy: Did you get messages about being a girl from anyone else?

Joan: Yes, my dad said that good little girls helped out their mothers, and they took care of their fathers. He always had me bring him water and sandwiches and stuff to show how well I could take care of him. (Joan laughs). I still bring him sandwiches.

Kathy: Sounds like it is a well-ingrained habit now.

Joan: Hmmm . . . I guess it is.

Kathy: What else?

Joan: I think we got the same spiel at school about how to behave, but I don't remember anything specific that teachers told us. I remember them yelling stuff about "Young ladies, this and young ladies that." I don't think I paid much attention to all that yelling.

Kathy: Were there other lessons you got about being a girl or a woman— about what you were supposed to do or not do?

Joan: I played t-ball with my cousins when I was 5 years old. I left for Germany when I was 7, and it was just about the time when we were going to play real little league. My dad said that even if I were going to stay here, in the United States he didn't think I should try out anyway—it would just make me more of a tomboy. I had the feeling that he wanted me to do something like piano lessons, which is what I did when we got to Germany.

Kathy: It was okay to play ball when you were very young, but the older you got the more gender-appropriate activities were acceptable.

Joan: Right!

Kathy: Any other lessons?

Joan: Of course, there was our church. They were always telling girls what they could and could not do to be a "nice young lady." Nice young ladies don't wear short skirts; nice young ladies don't make out with boys; nice young ladies don't call boys; etc. I remember my friends and I used to say behind their backs, "Nice young ladies are bored silly." They were always talking about what would make a good Christian woman. But we mostly thought that stuff was for old women and not really for us. Women and men did different things in church. I think the only things my parents did together was their Sunday school class.

Kathy: (smiles) Okay, so tell me this, were there any messages from your family or others specifically about being an African American girl?

Joan: You know, the usual. Do well in school because with a good education, you can get a good job and take care of yourself so you won't have to depend on a man to survive. Funny thing, though, even though everybody wanted you to be self-sufficient, they also let you know that having a man was better than not having a man.

Kathy: So you learned that having a man was good, but needing a man wasn't. Were there any other lessons that you remember about being a girl? Something that people showed by example, for instance, rather than somebody explicitly telling you this is how you ought to be?

Joan: One of my aunts was a beautiful woman. She had beautiful clothes, and all the men went crazy over her. She was smart and elegant, and so was her husband. I remember thinking that I really wanted to be like her when I grew up. She was feminine *and* smart—she was seemed perfect.

Kathy: Sounds like she was role model…that you could look at her and see someone you wanted to be like.

Joan: She was. I didn't know it until I was much older, but my aunt was an entrepreneur. She ran her own cleaning business and had five or six employees.

Kathy: So you learned that women could do "women's" things and still be a business owner and beautiful as well.

Joan: Yes. Most of the other women in the family didn't like her much, though. They thought she was condescending and phony. I wanted to be like her.

Kathy: The message that this role model had for you was that you could have it all, a business, a family, and beauty but maybe not the admiration of the other women in the family.

Joan: (laughs) That sounds about right.

Step 2: Have the client identify consequences of the gender-role messages he or she has listed in step 1.

Kathy: Let me recap for a moment. You were taught that girls need to stay clean, be quiet, take care of their fathers, help their mothers, be nurturing, beautiful, smart, strong, and successful but avoid masculine behavior. Can you tell me how these messages might currently influence your life? I suspect there are both positives and negatives.

Joan: I resisted some of what I learned. I never wanted to wait on a man and never did. My mom thinks that's why I cannot—in her words—hold on to a man. Maybe she *is* right. I like staying clean and neat, but I will never be quiet—my mom stopped trying to enforce that one when I was 7. On the other hand, I think I rejected that strong thing. I just don't know why it is so important to always be everyone else's rock. I want someone to take care of me sometimes.

I still think it is important to be good-looking and take care of myself. I know some of my female colleagues don't, but I guess I feel that this is the way to attract a man and fulfill my life. That lesson is one that has caused me grief! I am successful; I own a nice car and my own house, but I seem to run all the men I meet away. Being smart got me in trouble, too. My dad once told me that I educated myself right out of a husband! That can't be true; my sister Helen has a husband, and she had her Master's degree before they even met. I guess I'm stuck on this man thing—I suppose that is one lesson that has had negative consequences. I'm supposed to be married with children at 37, and I'm not even dating. How *can* I call myself successful?

Kathy: That's a lot, Joan. And, it seems that most of it is negative. Is there anything positive from these messages?

Joan: The stuff that is supposed to be positive seems to have taken on the negative—like being smart, being beautiful, and being successful.

Kathy: The positive things—like getting an education, becoming self-sufficient, and making a good salary—are what you were taught were important for an African American woman. I wonder, for example, if being clean, neat, and attractive has been helpful in your career.

Joan: (nods) Um-hmm. That's probably true now that you mention it. It's just hard for me to think of positives right now.

Step 3: Have the client identify those external gender-role messages she or he has internalized.

Kathy: We learn a lot from others about what our gender roles should be, but only some of those messages become part of our own thinking. You listed a number of messages you learned as a child about what girls do in order to be girls and women—stay clean; be quiet; take care of their fathers; help their mothers; be beautiful, smart, successful, and independent; avoid masculine behavior; and have men in their lives. Are there any of those messages you learned about being a girl that are part of your *own* thinking? In other words, have you internalized any of these messages? Usually, you can tell whether you've internalized a message when you start telling yourself the same things that perhaps your mother or some other significant person might have told you.

Joan: I guess I'm always telling myself that I ought to do more to be a good daughter and kick myself when I make excuses not to see my parents. I'm so independent I always think, "You can do it yourself. No need to ask someone to help you." But the message that bothers me the most is that I keep telling myself that my life is meaningless without a man in it.

Kathy: You have internalized the belief that success means having a husband and family as well as a prestigious career, and having only one of those two—career rather than family—means that you have not succeeded. Does that sound right?

Joan: I think that is right. I really don't think I'm that successful because I have failed at what everyone else seems to have found so easy to do—find a man and get married. Why do I think marriage is such a measure of success? What's wrong with me?

Kathy: I think a better question is what is wrong with a society that would devalue a person's career accomplishments to the extent that she would feel like a failure.

Joan: I've never thought of it that way, but it makes sense. Odd, I think about societal impact on my clients but don't seem to be able to do it for myself. Why should I feel like a failure? I've worked hard to get where I am in my career. I'm not a total failure at life.

Kathy: How do you think society benefits from such a practice?

Joan: You're asking how society can benefit from making women think they need a man to be successful and fulfilled. I don't see how society would benefit more by my being a wife instead of a lawyer or even in addition to being a lawyer. (pause) You know, I once heard someone say that before the feminist movement, there was only one career in the family, and both husband and wife worked to see that his career was successful. The man's career couldn't help but take off. I think that is still happening because most of the wives that I know follow their husbands when their jobs call for relocation. If I were to marry and take on a supportive role with my husband, then my male colleagues, who have wives to support them, would be certain to get partnerships in the firm before I ever could. Come to think of it, very few of the firm's partners are women, and there are no other African American women partners. This is a perfect way to maintain the status quo.

I cannot believe that I've bought in to all of this. All this time, I've been thinking of what a disappointment I have been to my mother, what a failure I've been not to do what everyone else seems to have done, how lonely I am because I don't have a man, and how guilty I feel because I've achieved success in a career that frightens men away. I *am* accomplished and bright, and that is what should matter. No one can take that away from me, even if I don't have a man in my life. I have other things…important things. I know that. I just don't think I ever believed it.

Step 4: The client decides on the internalized messages she or he would like to keep and those to discard.

Kathy: Am I right to think that this is a belief that you would like to change?

Joan: That seems like a good idea. I don't have a clue why I still believe these messages even when rationally I don't agree with them. I let other people make me feel that I have to apologize for being single and childless. Worse yet, sometimes people look at me with pity— many ask me why is it someone like me hasn't been married. Do they really think I planned it this way? (She pauses.) Uh-oh, there I go again thinking that something is wrong with me and my life as it is.

Kathy: Long-held beliefs are hard to overcome, but if you are willing, I can help you with it.

Using the strength-based techniques of solution-focused counseling, as well as cognitive-behaviorally oriented techniques, Kathy helps Joan develop a plan to resocialize her gender roles so that she can learn to put aside the beliefs that are harming her. The integration of feminist therapy techniques with other therapeutic modalities is discussed in Chapter 10. Next, we present some ways that these techniques can be used with Joan within a feminist framework.

Kathy: Joan, was there ever a time when you knew something in your head, but you didn't really believe it in your heart, but you were able to resolve it?

Joan: I know it is going to sound like I'm singing the same old tune, but the first thing that comes to mind is when my last boyfriend Tim broke up with me. He told me he found someone else, and I knew it intellectually, but I couldn't believe he really meant to choose her over me.

Kathy: How were you able to resolve it?

Joan: First, I had to hit bottom, which was getting caught stalking him and his new girlfriend. That was incredibly horrible. Then, I concentrated on getting over him. Whenever I found myself thinking about him or wondering what he was doing, I would call a friend or write a letter I wouldn't mail, or write in a journal, or watch the comedy channel, or anything that would get my mind off him. I would talk to myself (not out loud or anything) and tell myself to get a grip, that life can and will go on. That I was an attractive, wonderful person and it was his loss that we weren't together anymore. Pretty soon, I was thinking of him less and less and not having to do those things so much. The day I realized that I had gone two days without thinking of him once, I knew I was on my way. I felt good, like I accomplished something major.

Kathy: Joan, that is fantastic. You were using tools that we counselors recommend to clients all the time to resolve those kinds of issues. How do you feel about applying some of those same strategies to your thoughts about needing a husband to make you successful?

Joan: Do you think it will work? It doesn't seem like the same thing at all.

Kathy: No, it isn't the same thing, but you really seemed confident in your ability to use the skills mentioned, and those skills can be applied to a lot of different issues and concerns. Would you be willing to try to use one or two?

Joan: Sure, I think I would like to try journaling and talking myself out of it.

Kathy: That is wonderful, Joan. When you are able to abandon those ideas that underlie your anxiety, you are likely to find that your insomnia and panic attacks will subside as well.

Kathy and Joan continue their therapy relationship, focusing on deep breathing and other ways to manage anxiety as well as confronting negative self-statements. Kathy and Joan also talk about their relationship as client and therapist. Kathy shares some of her struggles as a professional African American woman with Joan, but only to the extent that it is in service to Joan's awareness of herself as a healthy and functioning woman who can confront and escape from internalized and negative gender-role expectations. Confronting gender roles and beliefs is woven into the ongoing process of their therapy together.

Gender-role analysis can also be effective in groups. A common type of group therapy in counseling is the interpersonal group, which is composed of both women and men. Remer and Remer (2000) designed an exercise to help clients identify gender-role messages within this type of group setting. In the "alien invasion exercise," male members of the group are told they are aliens who will visit earth as women, and they have to be trained in how to behave and how to think as women. The women in the group teach the "aliens" all the rules and gender-role messages on being female. Remer and Rotosky (2001) encourage the adaptation of this exercise for individual therapy, using an empty chair to represent the alien being taught.

SUMMARY: GENDER-ROLE ANALYSIS ●

In our previous discussion on gender and gender roles (Chapter 4), we spoke in favor of the position that gender refers to the constellation of psychological attributes that are not physiologically determined. Caring, achievement, nurturance, math ability, language ability, and reasoning belong to all of us, regardless of gender, and are shared equally among the human population. It is the sociocultural context that creates differences. An examination of that sociocultural context is at the core of feminist therapy. The skillful use of gender-role analysis provides therapists with an understanding of clients' negative self-statements, self-fulfilling prophecies, and ineffective coping mechanisms. It also provides clients with a way of understanding themselves as part of a greater system. Through this awareness, they may come to realize that what they have internalized as personal weaknesses, flaws, or diseases may actually be societal problems that affect many. The way to lasting change is through societal change in addition to personal change. In other words, the personal is the political.

● POWER ANALYSIS

It is unusual to read feminist literature and fail to find mention of power. An understanding of power is as essential to feminist therapy as an understanding of gender. Androcentric cultures not only endorse the valuing of men but also assume that males are the norm or the neutral condition (Bem, 1993) and define what is normal and healthy. In U. S. society, this means "White male," and anyone other than a White male is afforded less power and viewed as less powerful and more insignificant. Women are the second sex, but so too are all others who stray from the narrowly defined path of gender (de Beauvoir, 1961), such as gay, lesbian, bisexual, and transgendered (GLBT) individuals.

The discourse on power has, however, evolved. On the one hand, the traditional masculine conception is to have power over people and things (Robinson, 2005). Power is viewed as a finite resource that must be amassed in greater and greater quantities by anyone who wants to be a valued person in society. This leads to competition for power. The more power one person has, the less others have. On the other hand, feminist theory and practice posit that power is an unlimited resource of indefinite size, and the more that it is shared, the more of it everyone has. However, we live in a society formed by androcentric, patriarchal norms that ascribe power to positions over others and acquisition of items that are most often related to the masculine role. This is the traditional conception of power and all of its consequences with which we are familiar (Robinson, 2005). As long as there is a belief in a finite amount of power and as long as White men are socialized to exhibit characteristics that allow them to acquire that power, women and others who do not fit the narrow, societal definition of male will stay in a subordinate position. The same strategies that keep the status quo for women in gender roles operate to keep other oppressed groups from gaining power as well (e.g., people of color, people with disabilities, and GLBT individuals).

Power is heavily influenced by gender socialization, and men are expected to use power strategies that reflect the preferred male characteristics of individualism, competitiveness, and aggressiveness. Therefore, on the one hand, the expected power strategies for men are coercive, expert, and reward based. Women, on the other hand, are not really expected to acquire power, so the strategies they typically use reflect their socialized role as individuals who are nurturing, passive, and gentle. Although these expectations may be changing, Tepper, Brown, and Hunt (1993) found that when women use "male" power strategies and men used "female" strategies, they lost credibility and influence with others. This is one of the ways that our culture discourages changes in role expectations. Interestingly, however, Keshet, Kark, Pomerantz-Zorin, Koslowsky, and Schwarzwald (2005) did not find stereotypical expectations of power when individuals held high-status positions.

The assumption can be made that when there is strong legitimate power, the manner in which that power is exerted is irrelevant.

Other subordinate groups have used similar strategies as those used by women, in general, to gain advantage. The power strategies used are not out of character with the one-down position; in fact, sometimes that one-down position is exploited, such as in the use of powerlessness or helplessness and personal resources (Johnson, 1976).

DEFINITIONS OF POWER ●

Before a power analysis can be performed, mental health practitioners need to have an understanding of social power. A great deal of research has been conducted regarding social power in the last few decades in an effort to improve our understanding of how people use and abuse their power status. Originally, French and Raven (1959) proposed a taxonomy of five bases of power or influence. However, in 1959, the description of power was entrenched even more in patriarchy, and the notion that anyone in a subordinate position (e.g., women and minority men) could exercise power was not even considered (Raven, 1992). Paula Johnson's (1976) critical work on women's use of power from a subordinate position pointed out that women exercised power and influence over others but in such a way that those being influenced were not aware of that influence. The subtle use of power can be described as manipulation and coercion, but these indirect methods are effective in the short term and are types of power that women are socialized to view as acceptable. In subsequent articles, Raven (1992, 1993, 2008) incorporated many of Johnson's ideas; therefore, the six bases of power are currently conceptualized in a more complex manner. Table 8.1 lists the bases of power and the stereotypical uses of each based on whether one is in the dominant or subordinate position.

Coercive power is described as "one's ability to manipulate the behavior of others," and reward power is defined as "power whose basis is the ability to reward" (French & Raven, 1959, p. 156). Both reward and coercive power can be personal or impersonal. Impersonal reward power is used when one is given something valued and tangible (pay raise or prize, money) in return for a new behavior. Personal reward power is the ability to give something valued and intangible such as praise, approval, or affection.

Legitimate power is "power which stems from internalized values in P which dictate the O has a legitimate right to influence P and that P has an obligation to accept this influence" (French and Raven, 1959, p. 159). In this case, P refers to a person and O to the social agency or agent that has power over that person. For instance, one's boss (O) would have formal legitimate

| Table 8.1 | Bases of Power and Stereotyped Usage by Dominant and Subordinate Groups |

Basis of Power	Dominant	Subordinate
1. Coercive power: Impersonal (tangible rewards or threats such as money and position)	X	
Coercive power: Personal (intangible rewards or threats such as personal favors and appreciation)		X
2. Reward power: Impersonal	X	
Reward power: Personal		X
3. Legitimate power: Legitimate position (superior position in a formal structure)		X
Legitimate power: Power of reciprocity (obligation to help those who help us)	X	X
Legitimate power: Power of equity (compensatory norm)	X	X
Legitimate power: Power of responsibility (obligation to help those who cannot help themselves)	X	X
4. Expert power (expertise is respected, faith in superior insight)	X	
5. Referent power (identification with others)		X
6. Information power: Direct (explanation is given, understanding the reason)	X	
Information power (explanation is implied or assumed, understanding is implied or assumed)		X

Source: Adapted from Raven, B. H. (2008). The bases of power and the power/interaction model of interpersonal influence. *Analyses of Social Issues and Public Policy, 8,* 1–22.

power over an employee (*P*). Legitimate reciprocity is "you scratch my back, I'll scratch yours," and legitimate equity power is compensatory. Legitimate responsibility and dependence type of power is influenced by the fact that *O* really needs *P* or that helpless others need *P*. Also in this category would be the use of helplessness as a power tactic. The statement, "I can't, would you?" illustrates this.

Expert power is the extent to which "*P* evaluates *O*'s expertness in relation to his [or her] own knowledge as well as an absolute standard" (French & Raven, 1959, p. 163). If an individual is perceived to be an expert, then he or she will have the power to influence another's behavior. Raven (1992) has updated the definition to include positive expert power to describe behavior that is changed to emulate the expert and negative power as behavior that is changed or continued despite the expert.

Informational power can be direct or indirect. Informational power is defined as the power based on information "that the influencing agent (*O*) can present to the target (*P*) in order to implement change" (Raven, 1993, p. 235). The information can be divulged directly or indirectly (hints, innuendo, or overheard conversation) (Raven, 1992, 1993).

Referent power operates when the "target of influence . . . would comply because of a sense of identification with the influencing agent or a desire for such an identification" (Raven, 1993, p. 233).

In the United States, subordinate groups are those who are not White, able-bodied, heterosexual, middle-class, Protestant males. Typically, members of subordinate groups have limited power, and it is not unusual for subordinates to believe that they are powerless. According to Collins (1998), those who are in the subordinate position will get to know those in power to anticipate the resources to which they may be given access. When those who have legitimate power abuse that power, the subordinate groups are oppressed, excluded, and denied those resources. On a brighter note, however, several authors state that analyzing abuses of power and reframing one's thinking about one's powerlessness can be empowering to subordinates (Brickman, 1984; Pinderhughes, 1989).

The discussion of power in this chapter is focused primarily on responses to individual, one-on-one power interactions. Although individuals can manipulate their own use of power, the more insidious manipulations are those that are done by institutions, societies, and cultures. We have made mention throughout this chapter and the entire book about the patriarchal society we live in and how laws, policies, and practices in our society are all designed to maintain male privilege even though this is psychologically harmful to both women and men. Similarly, our society is designed to maintain White privilege even though this is psychologically harmful to all. When these privileges are threatened, the response is quick and forceful. People and organizations in the subordinate position are verbally denigrated, sometimes physically abused, and legitimate rights are taken away from them. This kind of power can seem insurmountable, but it can be breached.

If we think back to our discussion of the feminist and civil rights movements and the limitations that were forced on women and minority men through laws and discriminatory practices, we can find clear evidence of how powerful institutions can be changed. Unfortunately, that power was not obliterated; it still exists even though the evidence of it is not defined as clearly as it was during the 1960s and 1970s. Feminist therapists work with clients to help them identify how institutional power affects them and how they respond to it. Chapter 8 addresses these areas. In working with individuals, however, Worell and Remer (2003) suggested several steps that lead to effective power analyses (see Table 8.2).

Table 8.2	Steps to Performing a Power Analysis

According to Worell and Remer (2003 p. 78), the following steps should be followed to conduct a power analysis.

Step 1. Have client review current definitions of power and choose one that she or he believes best describes his or her own definition. This can be accomplished by creating a worksheet or handout such as Table 8.1.

Step 2. Give the client information on the various bases of power. Again, a previously printed handout (Table 8.1) would be helpful.

Step 3. Review with the client the access different groups have to the types of power listed in the handout of powers.

Step 4. Review with the client the strategies individuals use to exert power and possible alternative strategies. Client identifies the strategies she or he uses to exert power.

Step 5. Have client identify how socialization, societal expectations, and external and internalized forces such as sexism, racism, ageism, heterosexism, and so on affect his or her use of power. Have the client review any messages that she or he has internalized that affect his or her use of power.

Step 6. Have clients do a cost-benefit analysis of the different power strategies and then decide which strategies she or he will want to add to or delete from his or her own toolbox.

Because the first three steps are informational in nature, the dialogue below with Kathy and Joan begins in the middle of step 4 after they have discussed how the power strategies of others (including men) have influenced Joan's behavior and have moved on to Joan's use of power.

Kathy: I know all of this seems like you are back in school, but I needed to go over all of that information to get to where we need to go next in your counseling. What I would like to do now is to think about all those uses and abuses of power we've discussed and see if you can list for me all of the ways you have power and how you exert your power.

Joan: I'd knew you'd get to that sometime. I've been thinking of that as we've been talking. One thing about being a lawyer is that you learn a lot about people and how to press their buttons. I guess that is a use and abuse of power. I would say that at work, I use almost all these forms of power in some way or another with either clients, judges, or colleagues. (pause) In my personal life I use personal and impersonal rewards, legitimate equity, dependence, and reciprocity.

Kathy: That is quite impressive, Joan. How would you say that you are most likely to exert that power your personal life? Directly, indirectly?

Joan: Most of the time, I'm pretty direct. My friends typically expect it from me. I'm a pretty assertive person.

Kathy: What about with men or boyfriends?

Joan: With my dad, I'm still his little girl; I don't usually use any kind of power. However, I use flattery and begging, which is a kind of power. With men I date, I'm the same way. I would say that I am indirect with my dealings with men more often than I am direct. Maybe I learned that being assertive is too threatening to men that are important to me, that I will be punished or drive them away. But I'm not that way with White men. Not unless they are older—my father's age or older. With White men my own age, I act like I do with my friends—up front and assertive. Maybe I don't view White men as possible boyfriends? I don't think I'm that way with Black men I don't date. (She pauses.) That's interesting.

Kathy: You are way ahead of me. That is the next thing I want to explore with you—are there messages you internalized from your childhood about being a woman that influence your current use of power?

Joan: There are messages about being a good Black woman I guess. I remember most of these from my mother and aunts. It was about supporting your man.

Kathy: That is probably a culturally influenced gender role, don't you think? An important factor in African American culture is that men are devalued in our society, so it is important that they find some value at home.

Joan: Yeah, and you would think in the 21st century, this wouldn't still be an issue, but it is. It seems like such an old-fashioned notion, though. I'm not sure what I want to do with that one. I remember those college conversations and strategy sessions with girlfriends, and they were almost always about what you don't want to do to scare your man away. Maybe I act that way with men because I think if I don't, they will leave.

Kathy: From what you've said, it appears that those fears about never finding or keeping a man were pretty widespread among you and your friends. Tell me, how do you feel about yourself when you use these indirect approaches with men? Is it okay with you or do you want to kick yourself in the morning?

Joan: (laughs) To tell you the truth, I've been doing it for so long, I don't even know. I suppose when I look back on some of my relationships, there were times when I wish I had just said no or just asked for what I wanted. I could have used my legitimate power with them, and I didn't. I would nag and complain and beg. Now that I think of it, I wanted to kick myself after doing some of those things (smiles).

Kathy: So is it safe to say that these are some of the behaviors you want to put away?

Kathy and Joan add these behaviors to the list that Joan would like to change in her future. These analyses will assist Kathy and Joan in deciding on her treatment plan. Part of the plan would be for Joan to design ways that she can get involved in advocating for change in socialization for the young women in her church youth organization. This piece is critical for Joan to accept her own resocialization. In the African American population, the number of eligible African American men, in any socioeconomic group, is far fewer than the number of eligible African American women. This "shortage" has caused many stressors on both women and men and can be linked to several discriminatory practices against African American men, such as their overrepresentation in American prisons. Another way that Joan can get involved, as a member of the criminal justice system, is to advocate against profiling African American men and for equity in sentencing for African American males.

SUMMARY

In this chapter, we discussed two unique and essential techniques in feminist therapy—gender and power analyses. Gender socialization has an enormous impact on the lives of everyone; however, because it occurs from the time an individual is born, few people are aware of that impact. Feminist therapists help educate their clients on gender socialization to facilitate four of the basic tenets of feminist therapy—*the personal is political, valuing women's experiences, striving for an egalitarian relationship*, and *empowerment.* Gender and power analyses are very effective and useful tools in feminist therapy. Understanding the effect of gender socialization and the influence of power is the first step for clients receiving feminist therapy. These analyses assist counselors and clients in identifying the effects of gender and power on clients' lives. Once these analyses are complete, the information gleaned from them will help with treatment planning and resolution of the problem.

ADDITIONAL READINGS AND MATERIALS FOR CONSULTATION

Athenstaedt, U. (2003). On the content and structure of the gender role self-concept: including gender-stereotypical behaviors in addition to traits. *Psychology of Women Quarterly, 27,* 309–318.

Berliner, P.M. (1992). Soul healing: A model of feminist therapy. *Counseling and Values, 37,* 3–13.

Enns, C. Z. (1993). Twenty years of feminist counseling and therapy: From naming biases to implementing multifaceted practice. *The Counseling Psychologist, 21,* 3–87.

Gillespie, B. L., & Eisler, R. M. (1992). Development of the feminine gender role stress scale: A cognitive-behavioral measure of stress, appraisal, and coping for women. *Behavior Modification, 16,* 426–438.

Hill, M., & Anderson, G. (2005). Feminist therapy practice: Visioning the future. *Women & Therapy, 28,* 165–176.

Hill, M., & Ballou, M. (1998). Making therapy feminist: A practice survey. *Women & Therapy, 21,* 1–16.

Horne, S. G., & Mathews, S. S. (2004). Collaborative consultation: International applications of a multicultural feminist approach. *Journal of Multicultural Counseling and Development, 32,* 366–378.

Marecek, J., & Kravetz, D. (1998). Putting politics into practice: Feminist therapy as feminist praxis. *Women & Therapy, 21,* 17–36.

Moradi, B., Subich, L. M., & Phillips, J. C. (2002). Revisiting feminist identity development theory, research, and practice. *The Counseling Psychologist, 30,* 6–43.

Morrow, S. L., & Hawxhurst, D. M. (1998). Feminist therapy: Integrating political analysis in counseling and psychotherapy. *Women & Therapy, 21,* 37–50.

O'Hare-Levin, M. (2000). Finding a "lower, deeper, power," for women in recovery. *Counseling and Values, 44,* 198–213.

O'Neil, J. M., Helms, B. J., & Gable, R. K. (1986). Gender-role conflict scale: College men's fear of femininity. *Sex Roles, 14,* 335–350.

Rawlings, E. I. (1993). Reflections on "Twenty years of feminist counseling and therapy." *The Counseling Psychologist, 21,* 88–91.

Sagara, J., Ito, Y., & Ikeda, M. (2006). Gender-role attitude and psychological well-being of middle-aged men: Focusing on employment patterns of their wives. *Japanese Psychological Research, 48,* 17–26.

REFERENCES

Bem, S. L. (1993). *The lenses of gender: Transforming the debate on sexual inequality.* New Haven, CT: Yale University Press.

Brickman, J. (1984). Feminist, nonsexist, and traditional models of therapy: Implications for working with incest. *Women & Therapy, 3,* 49–67.

Brown, L. S. (1986). Gender-role analysis: A neglected component of psychological assessment. *Psychotherapy, 23,* 243–248.

Collins, L. H. (1998). Illustrating feminist theory: Power and psychopathology. *Psychology of Women Quarterly, 22,* 97–112.

de Beauvoir, S. (1961) *The second sex.* New York: Bantam Books.

Feminist Therapy Institute. (1999). Feminist Therapy Code of Ethics (revised). Retrieved November 13, 2009, from http://www.feminist-therapy-institue.org

French, J. R. P., Jr., & Raven, B. (1959). The bases of social power. In D. Cartwright (Ed.), *Studies in social power* (pp. 150–167). Ann Arbor, MI: Institute for Social Research.

Israli, A. L., & Santor, D. A. (2000). Reviewing effective components of feminist therapy. *Counselling Psychology Quarterly, 13,* 233–248.

Johnson, P. B. (1976). Women and power: Toward a theory of effectiveness. *Journal of Social Issues, 32,* 99–100,

Keshet, S., Kark, R., Pomerantz-Zorin, L., Koslowsky, M., & Schwarzwald, J. (1993). Gender, status and the use of power strategies. *European Journal of Social Psychology, 36,* 105–117.

Pinderhughes, E. (1989). *Understanding race, ethnicity and power: The key to efficacy in clinical practice.* New York: Simon & Schuster.

Raven, B. H. (1992). A power/interaction model of interpersonal influence: French and Raven thirty years later. *Journal of Social Behavior and Personality, 7,* 217–244.

Raven, B. H. (1993). The bases of power: Origins and recent developments. *Journal of Social Issues, 49,* 227–251.

Raven, B. H. (2008). The bases of power and the power/interaction model of interpersonal influence. *Analyses of Social Issues and Public Policy, 8,* 1–22.

Remer, P., & Remer, R. (2000). The alien invasion exercise: Creating an experience of diversity. *International Journal of Action Methods: Psychodrama, Skill Training, and Role Playing, 52,* 147–154.

Remer, P., & Rotosky, S. (2001). Practice talk: The fears of labeling ourselves feminist practitioners. *Feminist Psychologist, 28,* 30.

Robinson, T. L. (2005). *The convergence of race, ethnicity, and gender: Multiple identities in counseling* (2nd ed.). Upper Saddle River, NJ: Merrill Prentice Hall.

Tepper, B. J., Brown, S. J., & Hunt, M. D. (1993). Strength of subordinates' upward influence tactics and gender congruency effects. *Journal of Applied Social Psychology, 23,* 1903–1919.

Worell, J., & Remer, P. (2003). *Feminist perspectives in therapy: Empowering diverse women* (2nd ed.). Hoboken, NJ: John Wiley & Sons.

CHAPTER 9

SOCIAL CHANGE AND EMPOWERMENT

Consider the case of Sara. When Sara was a sophomore in college, she was invited to a male student's residence hall to study for a biology test. After some initial small talk, the young man attempted to force her to have sex with him by throwing himself on her while she sat on his bed reading from her biology book. Sara's experience with acquaintance rape has led her to avoid men in as many situations as possible, including ones that should be defined as social and safe. Two years after college, when Sara is working for a corporation and is frequently in mixed-gender groups, she finds that when alone with male colleagues or working on teams with men, she is tongue-tied and, as she puts it, on the verge of panic. After several sessions, her therapist suggests Sara volunteer to work in an agency that assists women in abusive situations and advocates for women who have been raped. Sara trains for work on the agency's hotline. When her therapist first suggested this, Sara asked, "Won't working with rape and abuse victims just make me more afraid of men?" However, after discussing and processing her fears with her therapist, she volunteered only after being assured that there were only women and young children at the shelter. After 6 months of being a part of the volunteer agency, Sara reports that in a recent business meeting, she was able to express herself clearly and without stammering to a male colleague. Her therapist replies: "You no longer feel powerless. You are helping other women remain safe and become strong, and you are working for an agency with the goal of changing society so no woman is raped."

If the personal is the political, then we must also consider that personal change is accomplished through political action or working toward social change.

● FEMINIST THERAPY, PRIVILEGE, AND SOCIETY

Emerging from the grassroots of feminist activism to overcome oppression of women, feminist therapy has challenged the traditional psychotherapy definition of mental health illness and the treatment of girls and women. Feminist therapy has made oppression, the act of denying privilege to others, the focus of its work. Feminist therapy has sought to effect not only social change in counseling and psychotherapy but also change in the greater society. In short, feminist therapy has sought, and still seeks, to create a healthy society in which healthy individuals can flourish. This focus reflects one of the core tenets of feminist therapy—the personal is the political. Feminist therapists believe that clients' presenting problems are "inextricably connected to the social, political, economic, and institutional factors which influence personal choices" (Enns, 2004, p. 11). This basic tenet demands that feminist therapists make a "commitment to social change that supports equality for everyone" (Worell & Johnson, 1997, p. 69). Feminist therapists work for social change at a variety of levels: individual, community, policy, and interpersonal (Ballou & West, 2000), within larger society and within counseling sessions. As indicated, social change can involve both clients and counselors. Indeed, the Feminist Therapy Institute Code of Ethics (see Chapter 3) presents this as an ethical principle.

Why are feminism and feminist therapy still concerned with oppression and the lack of privilege? Hasn't the United States come far as a country in terms of addressing, for example, racism and sexism? Doesn't the fact that we have a president who is an African American and have had more than one woman as the Secretary of State indicate that oppression is no longer an issue or at least does not impact large groups of people anymore? Despite some obvious gains (e.g., broadened opportunities for people of color and women's gains in politics and employment), oppression exists today; major groups of people still lack significant privilege while masculinity and, in particular, white masculinity still carry significant privilege. Almost 50 years after the Second Wave of United States Feminism and the Civil Rights Movement, we see oppression in many forms, many subtle and some overt. Groups who remain oppressed today are people of color; females, regardless of color; people with disabilities; people who are poor; sexual minorities; and non-Christians. Today feminist therapists are concerned with oppression of all kinds, including racism, classism, ableism, ageism, and heterosexism.

It is unfortunate that after a 40-year push for multiculturalism, when the term "women" is used, most people, including women of color, assume it to mean White women. Therefore the discussion of gender discrimination is primarily assumed to be about White women. Today, there is broad support among women and men for the position that gender discrimination is a thing of the past and that all inequalities have been eliminated or the ones that are left are unimportant. Therefore, although people may be sympathetic toward other oppressed groups, they often feel little concern for the plight of women because they believe that White women have successfully closed the gender gap in privilege especially when this is measured by salary. Specifically, it is difficult for most people to summon sympathy for someone whose annual salary is more than $100,000 but who has been denied promotion to the highest levels of management because of gender discrimination. These are the kinds of stories that the public typically hears. There is little or no publicity about the oppressive conditions that the average White woman or woman of color experiences. The beliefs about women's progress are, in actuality, myths that need to be challenged. The fact is that the number of women who fit in the high-salaried category mentioned above is minuscule. It is far more likely that the average woman client is oppressed because of her gender. Table 9.1 enumerates several points of information that indicate that women are still an oppressed class.

Table 9.1	Why Women Remain an Oppressed Class in the United States

1. *No pay equity.* Women, in general, earn $0.77 for every $1.00 men make. African American women earn $0.75, and Latinas earn $0.66 for every dollar men make. Even when a male enters a female-dominated profession, he earns more than women in that field (Atkinson & Hackett, 1998).

2. *Poverty.* The majority of families living below the poverty line are headed by women (U.S. Census Bureau, 2008).

3. *Low wages.* Female-dominated professions (K–12 teaching, nursing, etc.) continue to be the lowest paid in the country (U.S. Census Bureau, 2008). Research states that people believe "women's" work is worth less (in terms of dollars) than "men's" work (Alksnis, Desmarais, & Curtis, 2008). Salaries tend to fall in male-dominated professions when more women enter the field (Reskin & Roos, 1991).

4. *Glass ceiling.* Women are concentrated in midlevel management jobs and rarely get promoted to high-power positions (glass ceiling) (Herlihy & Watson, 2007).

5. *Perceived lack of competence.* Women continue to be perceived as incapable of handling high-level management positions (Alksnis, Desmarais, & Curtis, 2008).

(Continued)

Table 9.1 (Continued)

6. *Sexual harassment.* Approximately 35–70% of working women have been sexually harassed.

7. *Double duty.* Although 59% of all women work outside the home, they spend more time on child care and household duties than men (Evans, in press; Gilbert & Rader, 2008).

8. *Teacher neglect.* Teachers continue to reward boys at a higher rate than girls (Maher & Ward, 2002).

9. *Counselor bias.* Research shows that counselors, today, are influenced by gender-role stereotypes (Eriksen & Kress, 2008).

Source: Adapted from Evans, K. M. (2010). Advocacy and women. In M. J. Ratts, J. A. Lewis, & R. L. Toporek (Eds.), *The ACA Advocacy Competencies: An advocacy framework for counselors.* Alexandria, VA: ACA.

Oppression causes psychological distress (Enns, 2004; Worell & Remer, 2003). McAuliffe et al. (2008) point out that members of oppressed groups may experience some of the following effects of oppression:

- Emotional abuse: A poor child being teased about wearing second-hand clothes that the original owner recognizes.
- Isolation: The person in a wheelchair who has to enter a building by the truck loading dock instead of the front door like all of the people he or she is with.
- Sexual abuse (stereotyping): The gay middle-school teacher who hides his sexuality for fear that he may lose his job because of people's belief that being gay is the same as being a pedophile.
- Economic abuse: The Muslim or Jewish person or other non-Christian who has to use vacation time to observe religious holidays when all the Christian religious holidays are paid for by the employer in addition to vacation time.
- Privilege status: The assumption that women cannot handle the highest level positions in the corporate world or in the country.
- Threats/violence and intimidation: Racial profiling by law enforcement that results in men of color being routinely stopped for offenses overlooked in other groups.

FEMINIST THERAPY AND SOCIAL JUSTICE ●

In 1991, Paul Pedersen suggested multiculturalism as the force that moved the fields of counseling and psychotherapy toward inclusion of oppressed groups in theory, research, and practice. However, there was not much movement toward the feminist ideal of social justice until the dawning of the 21st century. At this time, there was a proliferation of publications promoting social justice counseling, which "includes empowerment of the individual as well as active confrontation of injustice and inequality in society as they impact clientele as well as those in their systemic contexts" (http://counselorsforsocialjustice .com). In 2003, the *Counseling Psychologist* sponsored a social justice forum at the Counseling Psychology convention that was primarily in response to the challenge of counseling, community, and liberation psychologists to bring social justice into the purview of psychological practice (Goodman et al., 2004). American Counseling Association (ACA) members were equally active in pushing for increased social action on the part of counselors. In 2003, this organization endorsed advocacy competencies created by Counselors for Social Justice, a suborganization of the ACA (see Table 9.2). Since the beginning of this century, mental health practice has evolved from recognizing and understanding oppression to working toward the reduction and elimination of oppression. In Table 9.2, you will note the letters in parentheses after the advocacy competencies. We believe that feminist therapy is the basis for social justice work and counseling. Thus, we have examined these advocacy competencies and have identified the feminist techniques that they illustrate.

Table 9.2 Advocacy Competencies

Feminist Therapy Techniques

A/C:	Feminist Assessment and Conceptualization (Chapters 2, 3, 5, and 6)
PA:	Power Analysis (Chapters 2, 3, 8, and 9)
GRA:	Gender-Role Analysis (Chapters 2, 4, 6, and 8)
CA:	Cultural Analysis (Chapters 2, 3, 6, and 9)
SA:	Social Action (Chapter 1, 3, 7, and 9)
EME:	Establishing and Maintaining the Egalitarian Relationship (Chapters 2, 3, and 5–7)

(Continued)

Table 9.2 (Continued)

Feminist Therapy Tenets

PIP (tenet):   Acknowledging the Sociopolitical Context (Personal Is Political)
E (tenet):   Recognizing, Valuing, and Supporting Strengths/Empowerment
PEO (tenet):   Privileging Experiences of Oppressed Groups/Privileging Women's Experiences
ER: (tenet):   Equalizing the Power in the Relationship (Egalitarian Relationship)

Client/Student Empowerment Counselor Competencies

In direct interventions, the counselor is able to:

1. Identify strengths and resources of clients and students (CA, PA, GRA, A/C; PEO, PIP, E).

2. Identify the social, political, economic, and cultural factors that affect the client/student (CA. PA, GRA, A/C; PEO, PIP).

3. Recognize the signs indicating that an individual's behaviors and concerns reflect responses to systemic or internalized oppression (CA, GRA, PA, A/C; PEO, PIP).

4. At an appropriate development level, help the individual identify the external barriers that affect his or her development (GRA, PA, CA; E, PIP).

5. Train students and clients in self-advocacy skills (GRA, PA, CA, SA, EME; ER, E, PIP).

6. Help students and clients develop self-advocacy action plans (GRA, PA, CA, SA; E, PIP).

7. Assist students and clients in carrying out action plans (GRA, PA, CA, SA; E, PIP).

Client/Student Advocacy Counselor Competencies

In environmental interventions on behalf of clients and students, the counselor is able to:

8. Negotiate relevant services and education systems on behalf of clients and students (EME, SA; E, PIP).

9. Help clients and students gain access to needed resources (SA, EME; ER, E, PIP).

10. Identify barriers to the well-being of individuals and vulnerable groups (A/C, CA, GRA, PA; EME; E, PIP).

11. Develop an initial plan of action for confronting these barriers (GRA, PA, CA, SA; PIP, E).

12. Identify potential allies for confronting the barriers (PA, SA; PIP).

13. Carry out the plan of action (PA, SA; PIP, E).

Community Collaboration Counselor Competencies

14. Identify environmental factors that impinge on students' and clients' development (GRA, PA, CA, A/C; PIP, PEO).

15. Alert community or school groups with common concerns related to the issue (SA; E, PIP).

16. Develop alliances with groups working for change (PA, SA; PIP, PEO, E).

17. Use effective listening skills to gain understanding of the group's goals (PA, SA; EME; ER).

18. Identify the strengths and resources that the group members bring to the process of systemic change (A/C, CA, PA; E, PEO, PIP).

19. Communicate recognition of and respect for these strengths and resources (EME, SA; E, PEO).

20. Identify and offer the skills that the counselor can bring to the collaboration (A/C, EME, SA; ER).

21. Assess the effect of counselor's interaction with the community (A/C, SA; PEO, PIP).

Systems Advocacy Counselor Competencies

Authors' note: Although not specifically discussed in the text, feminist therapy tenets and change techniques can be applied to working with systems and organizations.

In exerting systems-change leadership at the school or community level, the advocacy-oriented counselor is able to:

22. Identify environmental factors impinging on students' or clients' development (A/C; PEO, PIP).

Table 9.2 (Continued)

23. Provide and interpret data to show the urgency for change (A/C, SA; E, ER, PEO, PIP).

24. In collaboration with other stakeholders, develop a vision to guide change (SA, EME; E, PIP, PEO, ER).

25. Analyze the sources of political power and social influence within the system (A/C, SA; PIP, PEO).

26. Develop a step-by-step plan for implementing the change process (PA, SA; PIP, PEO).

27. Develop a plan for dealing with probable responses to change (PA, SA; PIP, PEO).

28. Recognize and deal with resistance (A/C, EME; ER, PEO).

29. Assess the effect of counselor's advocacy efforts on the system and constituents (A/C, EME; E, ER, PEO, PIP).

Public Information Counselor Competencies

In informing the public about the role of environmental factors in human development, the advocacy-oriented counselor is able to:

30. Recognize the impact of oppression and other barriers to healthy development (A/C, PA, CA, GRA; PIP, PEO, E).

31. Identify environmental factors that are protective of healthy development (A/C, PA, CA, GRA; PIP, PEO, E).

32. Prepare written and multimedia materials that provide clear explanations of the role of specific environmental factors in human development (A/C, GRA, PA, CA; PIP, PEO).

33. Communicate information in ways that are ethical and appropriate for the target population (A/C, GRA, PA, CA, EME; ER, PIP, PEO).

34. Disseminate information through a variety of media (SA; PIP).

35. Identify and collaborate with other professionals who are involved in disseminating public information (SA; PIP, PEO).

36. Assess the influence of public information efforts undertaken by the counselor (A/C, SA; PIP).

Social/Political Advocacy Counselor Competencies

In influencing public policy in a large, public arena, the advocacy-oriented counselor is able to:

37. Distinguish those problems that can best be resolved through social–political action (A/C, GRA, PA, CA, SA; PIP, PEO, E).

38. Identify the appropriate mechanisms and avenues for addressing these problems (PA, SA; PIP, PEO).

39. Seek out and join with potential allies (PA, SA; PIP, PEO, E).

40. Support existing alliances for change (SA; PIP, PEO, E).

41. With allies, prepare convincing data and rationales for change (SA; PIP, PEO, E).

42. With allies, lobby legislators and other policymakers (SA; PIP, PEO, E).

43. Maintain open dialogue with communities and clients to ensure that the social/political advocacy is consistent with the initial goals (SA, PA; PIP, PEO)

Source: Adapted from Lewis, J., Arnold, M. S., House, R., & Toporek, R., (2003). Advocacy competencies. Retrieved December 10, 2009, from http://counselorsforsocialjustice.com/Advocacy%20Competencies %20Domain%20Outline.pdf

Social justice is reflected in the work that feminist therapists do to subvert the systems of oppression, whether in the larger sociopolitical context or within a single counseling session. Addressing the larger social context, feminist therapists may be involved in the whole range of activities that challenge the status quo and work to address oppression. For example, one of the authors is a board member of a professional organization division to address gay, lesbian, bisexual, and transgendered issues. Involvement in social change may take several different forms, from individual therapy to community involvement to professional involvement to political activism.

As is apparent from Table 9.2, many of the skills outlined in the ACA Advocacy Competencies are skills that feminist therapists have used for years. For example, the first category is *Client/Student Empowerment Counselor Competencies*, which focuses on empowerment. Empowerment is one of the four tenets on which feminist therapy lies. It is a major part of the social change strategy in feminist therapy and will be discussed in detail in the next section. A commitment to the four basic tenets (the personal is political, empowerment, egalitarian relationships, and valuing women's experiences or the experience of oppressed groups) and the application of assessment/ conceptualization, gender-role, power, and cultural analyses and social action/ empowerment techniques allows mental health professionals to enact all of the ACA advocacy competencies.

● FEMINIST THERAPY AND EMPOWERMENT

The need for social change and social justice is addressed with clients in counseling sessions by helping clients become empowered to make changes in their own lives. Another major goal of feminist therapy is to help clients see themselves as agents of change on their own behalf (Enns, 2004), which is done through empowerment.

Feminist therapy views empowerment as the process by which individuals, groups, families, organizations, and communities become aware of their ability to address personal, interpersonal, and institutional factors that affect their physical and emotional health (Worell & Remer, 2003). Empowerment is "a process of changing the internal and external conditions of people's lives, in the interests of social equity and justice, through individual and collective analysis and action that has as its catalyst a political analysis" (Morrow & Hawxhurst, 1998, p. 41). There are two ways in which empowerment is used in feminist therapy: self-learning and social change activities (Enns, 2004; Worell & Remer, 2003). Empowerment involves political analysis. Feminist therapists help their clients analyze "personal and interpersonal realms that are the focus of current psychotherapy and social/political structures and processes that either enhance or limit one's access to an empowered life (Morrow & Hawxhurst, 1998, p. 42). According to Morrow and Hawxhurst (1998), there are three dimensions of empowerment: personal, interpersonal, and social/political. The personal domain entails the focus of traditional therapies—the intrapsychic and intrapersonal areas of individuals' experiences. With feminist therapy, however, this realm includes an analysis that focuses on helping clients claim or reclaim and maintain power and control over parts of their lives. The interpersonal domain addresses individuals' experiences of powerlessness and power that occur at the relational level. Issues of power, dominance, and privilege based on social position and status are explored. Self-blame may occur when the social/political dimension is ignored. Morrow and Hawxhurst (1998) argue that it is "necessary to understand the nature of privilege and power relations in regard to, for example, gender, race, class, ethnicity or sexual orientation in order to achieve empowerment at the personal and interpersonal levels" (p. 45).

Morrow and Hawxhurst (1998) identify three conditions that are necessary for empowerment to occur: *permission, enablement, and information.* This requires that the feminist therapist explore with clients their sense of *permission* to have the right, for example, to be involved in an egalitarian relationship. Morrow and Hawxhurst (1998) identified these questions to explore with clients: ""May I? Do I have the right? What am I entitled to? Am I worthy?" (p. 45). These questions are explored at the personal, interpersonal, and sociopolitical dimension.

Enablement addresses the questions of "Can I?" and "How can I?" (Morrow & Hawxhurst, 1998, p. 46). This involves examination of abilities, skills knowledge, and resources in the personal domain. Mentoring or support for individuals through actions such as networking or support groups takes place at the interpersonal level. Enablement at the social/political dimensions means identifying and having access to resources and opportunities that empower the individual. This may take the form of implementation and enforcement of policies such as Affirmative Action.

Information, according to Morrow and Hawxhurst (1998), addresses the questions of "What do I need to know? What are the questions that I do not know to ask? Where do I find the information that I need?" (p. 46). With all three dimensions (personal, interpersonal, and social/political), it is the power of information that can be used to expand the possibilities for individuals.

In sum, feminist therapists help clients gain the awareness, knowledge, and skills to address their life issues. This empowerment is done in counseling sessions. Empowerment encompasses the actual engagement in some activity or action that influences the structures and systems that support oppressive conditions that harm individuals. Clients who take action feel less powerless or empowered, which leads to feeling better about themselves. Remember the vignette with Sara that opened this chapter.

The feminist skill of empowerment through social action can also be seen in various cognitive behavioral modalities that seek to ameliorate depression by having clients learn firsthand that they are not powerless. For instance, Meichenbaum (1992) cites a case where a young child accidentally shot and killed his sister with a family gun. In therapy for severe depression, as well as for remorse and guilt, the mother of these children did not start to come to terms with living with the death of her child until she became involved in community activism for gun safety. Using community activism as a mechanism for regaining power or a sense of power in has long been a technique in feminist therapy. For instance, a client who has been sexually abused as a child attends a community action event (The T-Shirt Project) to promote awareness of childhood sexual abuse. Other examples of this technique include rape and torture survivors working with other survivors to increase awareness and change laws. Additionally, individuals who have been harassed because of differing sexuality benefit psychologically from being involved in efforts to raise awareness, change laws, and gain acceptance. These are ways that involvement in social action activities increases mental health. This is a central technique in feminist therapy.

● THE CURRENT ZEITGEIST OF SOCIAL CHANGE AND FEMINIST THERAPY

There is some suggestion that feminist therapy practiced in the 21st century does not include the notion of radical social change. Morrow and Hawxhurst (1998) contend that this core tenet of feminist therapy has become less important as feminist therapy has become integrated into mainstream psychological practice. Enns (1993) states a commitment to social change is no longer a part of feminist therapy. Israeli and Santor (2000) question whether it is necessary or even beneficial to combine therapy with social change.

Empirical research on this is inconclusive. In a study that examined the ways in which feminism impacted the therapeutic practice of 20 feminist therapists, Marecek and Kravetz (1996) found that these therapists adapted feminist elements in their work to conform to the psychotherapy culture. They focused on individuals' experiences and mental lives with goals of self-discovery and fulfillment rather than on social change. In contrast, in a survey of experienced feminist therapists to examine how they integrate feminist principles into their practice, Hill and Ballou (1998) found that these therapists saw social change as a part of their treatment planning.

We believe that social change, as a core tenet of feminist therapy, must remain in the actual practice of feminist therapy. The idea and practice of social change is a radical and subversive act—one that has changed how counseling is practiced and the larger social context. Without social change, feminist therapy becomes co-opted by the dominant psychology culture and loses its ability to make both individual and societal transformations. The eloquent words of Morrow and Hawxhurst (1998) express our belief about the absolute necessity of the tenet of social change as a value and as therapeutic activity. Feminist therapy is "a field of practice that we hope can combine personal healing with political transformation" (p. 40).

The following dialogue is an illustration of empowerment with an identified feminist therapist.

CLIENT PROFILE

Client Name: Dhriti A.

Age: 26

Occupation/Education: M.S. in Information Technology

Family History: Raised in India; family of origin is upper class. They live outside Mumbai. Parents are together; has three sisters and no brothers. Reports being close to her sisters. Marriage was arranged by her mother. When she married, Dhriti had just completed her graduate degree, and her husband was in his second year of medical school. The couple is waiting until after her husband completes his training to have children. They continue to live in international housing on the university campus. She works full time for the university as a technology specialist.

Presenting Problem: Reports poor relationships with co-workers. She feels that they take advantage of her work ethic at the same time that they also sexually harass her.

Kendra had seen Dhriti for 10 sessions. What follows is the conversation at the end of the tenth session.

Dhriti:	I've been wanting to talk to you about something. (pause) Sometimes my husband and I argue. We really argue a lot, and sometimes he slaps me. I sometimes hit him back with a dishcloth or something, but when I do that, he gets really mad, and it can hurt.
Kendra:	Dhriti, this is distressing. I have to say that I am not that familiar with Indian culture. Tell me. Is it acceptable in India for men to strike or discipline their wives?
Dhriti:	I don't think this is acceptable in any culture. But it is certainly known to happen. My auntie used to talk about her husband beating her too, and she would just say, "but it is my lot as a woman to be beaten." I never believed it would happen to me.
Kendra:	How badly has he hurt you?
Dhriti:	A couple of times, I couldn't go to work.
Kendra:	That is very scary, Dhriti, I am worried about your safety.
Dhriti:	I'll be all right. I know how to handle him most of the time.

(Continued)

(Continued)

Kendra: It's those times you don't that I worry about you. Tell me, Dhriti, what do you know about spousal abuse? And about spousal abuse laws?

Dhriti: I know nothing of the laws here, and I don't know much about them at home either.

Kendra: Spousal abuse is not acceptable in the United States. In fact, it is now a crime. Although, it wasn't so long ago that police would not do anything when a husband and wife were physically fighting.

Dhriti: I think it's probably still that way in India.

Kendra: It isn't that way here. I am concerned for your safety. I'd like to give you some information about women who are battered, and then I'm going to ask you to go ahead and find out more about this for yourself, okay?

Kendra gave her client some basic information about spousal abuse and about how society contributes to this kind of oppression. Kendra invited Dhriti, a well-educated woman, to do some research on domestic violence in India and suggested that they talk further about cultural expectations there. Kendra hoped that these activities would empower her client, but she also knew that she had to be careful not to impose her own cultural values onto her client, so she, too, did research on domestic violence in the Indian subcontinent. They discussed their findings in their next session.

Dhriti: Kendra, you will not believe what I found out. I actually found a research study that was done 7 years ago. Can you believe it, 45% of women in India are slapped or hit. What was really surprising is that the more education they have, the more likely it is that they will be abused.

Kendra: This information seems to have caught you by surprise.

Dhriti: I had no idea this was so prevalent. I didn't know because I only had the one aunt who even talked about it. My father is so good to my mother and to my sisters and me. He loves us like we are boys. The good thing that I found out was that women are doing something about it. There are courses in self-defense, and they even have shelters for women who are battered.

It was at this point that Kendra knew that her client had been empowered by what she had learned. Through her gender and power analyses,

Dhriti seemed to gather a great deal of strength from knowing the effects of her own socialization and saw her greatest asset as her family, a fairly influential family in Mumbai.

Kendra: If you were at home in Mumbai, what would you do if K. hit you?

Dhriti: He would not hit me if we were living at home. I would tell him that I would tell my father that he hit me for no reason. He's afraid of my father.

Kendra: Your father isn't here, though. So how will you keep yourself safe here?

Dhriti: Sometimes threatening to tell my father works here as well. He respects my father very much. I don't know what I will do, but I'm learning that there are some options.

Kendra: Is one of those options to leave K.?

Dhriti: My mother would never forgive me. She arranged our marriage, and she would be devastated and feel like a failure.

Kendra: So let's look at what some of your options are.

Kendra and Dhriti made a list of Dhriti's options and the positive and negative consequences of each. Kendra also gave Dhriti the telephone numbers of the domestic violence hotline and shelter in their area. At their next meeting, Kendra and Dhriti talked more about spousal abuse among Indian women.

Dhriti: I spoke to people at the domestic violence shelter. They were very nice. They didn't try to make me come in or anything, but they did say they would help me if I needed them. They were very nice.

Kendra: That is wonderful Dhriti. I'm glad you took that step. It sounds like you felt pretty good about it too.

Dhriti: It was very scary, but I admit it made me feel better.

Kendra: You know I was thinking about the other Indian women on campus, and I wonder if any of them are aware of this kind of help.

Dhriti: I was thinking the same thing—if 45% of the women at home are abused especially by educated men, then maybe that is happening here as well.

Kendra: How would you feel about helping them learn what you have learned?

(Continued)

(Continued)

Dhriti: I don't think any of them would tell me that was going on in their houses.

Kendra: Probably not, but what if you just put out flyers from the center where women could easily see them?

Dhriti: Yes, I could do that.

It so happened that Dhriti also volunteered to coordinate and manage the bulletin board in the entry of the international student housing area. She hung the domestic violence poster in a prominent spot. Dhriti reported to Kendra that even though she could not yet make a decision about leaving her husband, she felt that she might have helped others who were worse off than herself to do so. She also reported that she did not feel as help-less as she did previously, knowing that the shelter was available to her right now if she needed it but also knowing that there was a movement in India to curb domestic violence toward women.

Kendra worked with Dhriti on how she could remain safe. She also explored with her the lament she had heard from her aunt that a woman is "just a woman" and it is a woman's lot to be abused by men. During this time Dhriti was able to see how her problem with co-workers was not that she was too argumentative or too passive (both of which she had been accused of by co-workers) but that she found her work situation "unsafe" because several of her male co-workers were the same ethnicity as her husband.

Eventually, Dhriti volunteered to work at the domestic violence shelter during the evenings that her husband worked the night shift at the hospital. She learned that her problems were shared by others and that her experi-ences helped her to help other women. She began to feel more competent as both a professional and a person. Kendra asked Dhriti, "If you can take care of others and help them at the shelter, what is stopping you from being able to take care of yourself?" Dhriti reported that she did not want to stay in the United States if she left her husband, and if she left now, that was what she would have to do. Dhriti told Kendra that the abuse was not esca-lating and that she was able to keep herself safe. She stated that if she felt in true danger, she would call 911 and/or leave for the shelter. Furthermore, Dhriti reported that she had already expressed dissatisfaction with the mar-riage to her sisters, whom she missed a great deal. She knew that in a month her younger sister was coming to the United States to look at graduate schools and would stay with Dhriti and her husband. It was unlikely that her husband would abuse her while her sister was visiting. She would then return to Mumbai with her sister and discuss her situation with her family.

Both Kendra and Dhriti were empowered by this course of therapy, and both became social action agents. Through this encounter Kendra became aware that there was nothing official set up at the university to address domestic violence issues among international students, nor was there anything in place for the families in that community that may need counseling. Kendra made it her project over the next year to provide these kinds of services to the international students and their families. She, working with a local agency as well as the university police, was especially careful to make it easier to report domestic violence. Presentations on violence, in general, and domestic violence, in particular, were given in the international students housing area as well as information on counseling for victims of abuse as well as for the abusers.

Through involvement with social action, Dhriti was able to identify internalized negative self-statements that were part of her culture ("I'm nothing but a woman and do not have the right to be treated well"), despite having been raised in a progressive, well-off family with a father who "treated his daughters as if they were sons." She was also able to better understand her mother's position within the family and her culture and why her mother was highly possessive of the power she did have—such as arranging this "good" marriage for her daughter. She was able to work out a solution for herself that honored her family (she returned home), her culture, and her own needs as a person. She spoke about contacting agencies in Mumbai and continuing her volunteer work at home.

SUMMARY

In feminist therapy, social change, empowerment, and social action are all considered therapeutic interventions. The feminist tenet that the personal is the political informs these three interventions. By understanding the sociocultural context, feminist therapists know that individual change alone cannot bring lasting psychological health. The culture in which an individual lives must also be healthy. Thus, working toward social change is imperative for individual change. Being involved in social action that impacts one's culture empowers the individual and helps to bring about social change.

REFERENCES

Alksnis, C., Desmarais, S., & Curtis, J. (2008). Workforce segregation and the gender wage gap: Is "women's" work valued as highly as "men's"? *Journal of Applied Social Psychology, 38,* 1416–1441.

Atkinson, D. R., & Hackett, G. (1998). *Counseling diverse populations* (2nd ed.). New York: McGraw-Hill.

Ballou, M., & West, C. (2000). Feminist therapy approaches. In M. Braggio & M. Hersen (Eds.), *Issues in the psychology of women* (pp. 273–297). New York: Kluwer Academic/Plenum.

Enns, C. Z. (1993). Twenty years of feminist counseling and therapy: From naming biases to implementing multifaceted practice. *The Counseling Psychologist, 21*(1), 3–87.

Enns, C. Z. (2004). *Feminist theories and feminist psychotherapies: Origins, themes, and diversity* (2nd ed.). New York: Haworth Press.

Eriksen, K., & Kress, V. E. (2008). Gender and diagnosis: Struggles and suggestions for counselors. *Journal of Counseling & Development, 86,* 152–162.

Evans, K. M. (2010). Advocacy and women. In M. J. Ratts, J. A. Lewis, & R. L. Toporek (Eds.), *The ACA Advocacy Competencies: An advocacy framework for counselors.* Alexandria, VA: ACA.

Gilbert, L. A., & Rader, J. (2008). Work, family, and dual-earner couples: Implications for research and practice. In S. D. Brown & R. W. Lent (Eds.), *Handbook of counseling psychology* (4th ed., pp. 426–443). Hoboken, NJ: John Wiley & Sons.

Goodman, L. A., Liang, B., Helms, J. E., Latta, R. E., Sparks, E., & Weintraub, S. R. (2004). Training counseling psychologists as social justice agents: Feminist and multicultural principles in action. *The Counseling Psychologist, 32,* 793–837.

Herlihy, B., & Watson, Z. E. P. (2007). Social justice and counseling ethics. In C. Lee (Ed.), *Counseling for social justice* (2nd ed.) (pp. 181–199). Alexandria, VA: American Counseling Association, 2007.

Hill, M., & Ballou, M. (1998). Making therapy feminist: A practice survey. *Women & Therapy, 21,* 1–16.

Israeli, A. L., & Santor, D. S. (2000). Reviewing effective components of feminist therapy. *Counselling Psychology Quarterly, 13,* 233–247.

Lewis, J., Arnold, M. S., House, R., & Toporek, R., (2003). Advocacy competencies. Retrieved December 10, 2009, from http://counselorsforsocialjustice.com/Advocacy%20Competencies%20Domain%20Outline.pdf

Maher, F. A., & Ward, J. V. (2002). *Gender and teaching.* Mahwah, NJ: Lawrence Erlbaum.

Marecek, J., & Kravetz, D. (1996). *A room of one's own: Power and agency in feminist therapy.* Presented at the 104th annual convention of the American Psychological Association, Toronto, Ontario, Canada.

McAuliffe, G. (2007). *Culturally alert counseling: A comprehensive introduction.* Los Angeles, CA: Sage.

Meichenbaum, D. (1992). Evolution of cognitive behavior therapy: Origins, tenets, and clinical examples. In J. K. Zeig (Ed.), *The Evolution of psychotherapy: The second conference* (pp. 114–128). New York: Brunner/Mazel.

Morrow, S. L., & Hawxhurst, D. M. (1998). Feminist therapy: Integrating political analysis in counseling and psychotherapy. *Women & Therapy, 21,* 37–50.

Pedersen, P. B. (1991). Multiculturalism as a generic approach to counseling. *Journal of Counseling and Development, 70,* 6–12.

Reskin, B. F., & Roos, P. A. (1991). "Feminization" of fields a result of several factors. *Chronicle of Higher Education, 38*(5), B4.

U.S. Census Bureau. (2008). *Facts for features: Women's history month.* Retrieved December 12, 2009, from http://www.census.gov/PressRelease/www/releases/archives/cb08ff-03.pdf

Worell, J., & Johnson, N. G. (Eds.). (1997). *Shaping the future of feminist psychology: Education, research, and practice.* Washington, DC: American Psychological Association.

Worell, J., & Remer, P. (2003). *Feminist perspectives in therapy: Empowering diverse women* (2nd ed.). Hoboken, NJ: John Wiley & Sons.

CHAPTER 10

FEMINIST THERAPY IN CLINICAL PRACTICE

Throughout this text, the goal is to convey the viability, merits, and usefulness of feminist therapy. Although techniques have been presented that are unique to feminist therapy, other techniques have also been discussed. However, feminist therapy is driven more by its philosophy and values than by its techniques (Murdock, 2004). The practice of feminist therapy not only encourages individualized treatment for clients but also leaves room for therapists to develop their individual approaches to treatment. To bring feminist theory alive in practice, most feminist therapists combine it with other techniques and theories (Herlihy & McCollum, 2007; Worell & Remer, 2003).

Worell and Remer (2003) suggest that some therapists use feminist therapy as their only theoretical approach while others may choose specific techniques from other theories that are congruent with the client's needs. Still others integrate feminist philosophies and techniques with other orientations. In their 1998 survey of feminist therapists, Hill and Ballou found that feminist therapists use a variety of techniques from hypnosis and autobiography to cognitive restructuring and dream analysis to carry out their feminist philosophies.

Feminist theory and philosophy have roots in humanistic, cognitive behavioral, and psychodynamic theories (Fodor, 1993; Sharf, 2008; Worell and Remer, 2003). The humanistic school of counseling and psychotherapy is the source of several feminist principles in that it puts an emphasis on the phenomenological world of the individual and on his or her ability to change and acquire self-direction. Rogers's (1951) core conditions of unconditional positive regard, genuineness, congruence, and empathy can be seen in the feminist principle of the egalitarian relationship, which focuses on the therapist's regard for the client (Enns, 2004; Waterhouse, 1993).

Fodor (1993) states feminist therapists have been using cognitive behavioral techniques since the 1970s to educate clients and modify their socialized, gender-specific thinking. Cognitive behavioral influences include the ideas that what is learned can be unlearned and that belief systems can be changed through reframing and cognitive restructuring. Using assertiveness training, for example, feminist therapists helped women learn that their beliefs in self-sacrifice and self-denial for others were actually detrimental to themselves as well as to others. Letting themselves get worn thin by all their responsibilities and denying themselves any joy actually kept them from being their best selves with their families and other important people in their lives.

As far as psychodynamic approaches are concerned, feminist theory is consistent with the concept of social influence of Adlerian therapy and with attachment and self-development concepts of other approaches (Corey, 2009; Fodor, 1993). It can be argued that psychoanalytic and psychodynamic approaches influenced theories of feminist therapy more in terms of what not to do in therapy than in terms of what therapists should do, although there are theorists and therapists who have found ways to marry psychodynamic therapy with feminist therapy.

Theoretically, feminist therapy is considered a postmodern approach. It accepts the postmodern concept that there is no single reality. "There is "no one 'right' feminist theory or epistemological position about women, and . . . women's multiple realities, experiences, and roles is central to feminist theory building" (Porter, 2005, p. 143). In addition, the focus on political and power issues in postmodern approaches easily connects with feminist therapy, as does the belief in the client as expert on his or her own life.

In feminist therapy, practitioners can use a wide range of therapeutic techniques, but the expectation is that they remain committed to the basic feminist therapy tenets and that the techniques used do not undermine those tenets (Worell & Remer, 2003). A feminist therapist, therefore, is one who believes in the principles of feminist philosophy and who may add techniques from other therapies (e.g., rational emotive behavior therapy [REBT]) he or she believes will enhance his or her work with clients. Similarly, the REBT therapist may want to use a feminist therapy technique like gender-role analyses because he or she strongly believes clients can benefit from understanding the sociocultural rewards for the irrational thoughts and behaviors they want to change. The REBT therapist will still believe that the cause of a client's upset is intrapsychic and reject the feminist belief that the cause of emotional and psychological upset is the imposition of unfounded gender-role expectations. Those who use feminist therapy techniques (e.g., gender analysis) but who do not follow the philosophies of feminist therapy are not truly feminist therapists.

Although feminist therapy is essentially a postmodern theory, feminist therapists use aspects of many traditional theories; most of these techniques require adaptation when used in feminist practice. It is left to the feminist practitioner to determine how to integrate other theories into the feminist perspective. What follow are models of systematic strategies for integrating theories.

INTEGRATING THEORIES ●

In recent years, integrated theoretical approaches have become more accepted in counseling and psychotherapy. Recent inclusion of chapters on integrated approaches in most theory textbooks (Corey, 2009; Corsini & Wedding, 2007; Sharf, 2008) support this. In addition, more than 95% of the respondents to a Psychotherapy Networker survey (2007) stated that they used integrative approaches with their clients. We need to be aware, however, that integration of approaches differs from haphazard combinations of techniques and theories. This practice is referred to as "technically eclectic" or, more disparagingly, as "seat of the pants" therapy, where therapists choose specific techniques from a variety of different theoretical approaches based on what they perceive to be the individual needs of their clients. This type of strategy is unacceptable because it leads to theoretical confusion and questionable practice (Corey, 2009). There are more acceptable ways of integrating both theory and practice. These methods include theoretical integration, common factors approach, and assimilative integration.

Theoretical integration involves combining at least two existing theories. There are a few techniques for doing this. *The common factors approach* allows therapists to use elements, common to several theories, that have been proven effective with clients. This is a common approach but tends to be atheoretical. *Assimilative integration* occurs when therapists have clearly chosen a specific theory (such as feminist therapy) but are open to incorporating concepts and techniques from other schools of thought. The integrative theoretical approach focuses on common theoretical elements, rather than on practice elements. This chapter focuses on assimilative integration and integrative theory.

● ASSIMILATIVE INTEGRATION

Worell and Remer (2003) developed and used empowerment feminist therapy as the feminist basis for integrating other theories with feminist therapy. Their approach most resembles the assimilative integration model, and they suggest following a series of steps in order to integrate a second theory when practicing empowerment feminist therapy. These feminist therapists and authors illustrate how theorists may commit to one specific theory (in this case, empowerment feminist therapy) and find ways of fitting the concepts of a second theory into the belief and values of the original theory. The recommended steps are as follows:

1. Identify the sources of bias in the theory

As stated, most theories require some adjustment to fit with feminist therapy principles. In the examples that follow, we will review some of the major, and problematic, differences between feminist therapy and other popular therapeutic orientations.

Psychoanalytic therapy has been criticized by feminist theorists as a result of such concepts as Oedipal issues, penis envy, and the narrow interpretation of women as passive, dependent, and masochistic (Fodor, 1993; Sharf, 2008). Additionally, psychoanalytic therapy violates the basic feminist therapy tenet of sharing power equally in the therapeutic relationship, the egalitarian relationship. In the psychoanalytic model, therapists are knowledgeable, sometimes wise, and know what is best for clients. Clients are in subordinate positions.

Although the Freudian approach to therapy is still referred to as psychoanalytic psychotherapy, theories based on some aspect of psychoanalysis (e.g., ego) are referred to as psychodynamic theories (Archer & McCarthy, 2007). Psychodynamic approaches, such as object relations, cause concern for some feminist therapists because women and men are viewed differently. Although classical psychoanalysis focuses on the sexual underpinning of parent–child relationships, object relations theory focuses on the early relationships between the infant and his or her primary caregivers. However, the focus is generally on the mother/child relationship rather than equal emphasis on father/child (Fodor, 1993; Worell & Remer, 2003). Attachment theory, however, focuses on how early childhood bonds with caregivers create models for adult interaction with others. Again, the mother is the focus of this early bonding (Archer & McCarthy, 2007).

In addition, psychodynamic approaches primarily focus on intrapsychic forces at work within clients, which cause distress. Worell and Remer (2003) suggest that this implies that it is only clients who need to change and that little or no attention is given to the environmental factors that may influence individuals' lives and perspectives. When environmental factors are harmful to clients, they are often encouraged to cope with the environment or leave it. The concept of actively working to change a toxic environmental or sociopolitical factor, for instance, women's lack of pay equity, is rarely addressed as an appropriate topic for the counseling office.

Although popular with some feminist therapists for certain issues, for example, assertiveness and depression, there are problems from a feminist perspective with cognitive behavioral approaches. Behavioral, cognitive, and subsequently cognitive behavior therapies evolved as objective alternatives to the subjective nature of psychoanalytic approaches. Although focused on helping clients change behaviors and thoughts that are unproductive and harmful, cognitive behavior therapies also disregard social, cultural, economic, and political issues. They require intrapsychic accommodations and pathologize clients' thinking as irrational or distorted (Enns, 2004; Worell & Remer, 2003). Cognitive-behavioral approaches are also criticized for focusing only on client change without mention of societal change. Finally, the assessment as to what is rational and what is not is based on masculine definitions.

Humanistic and person-centered therapies have been criticized by feminist therapists because of their emphasis on self-reliance and personal responsibility to the exclusion of social and political influences on an individual's behavior (Enns, 2004). Although the person-centered approach is compatible in terms of the client/counselor relationship, as Enns stated, it is "not sufficient for feminist therapy that connects the personal and the political" (p. 74).

Postmodern theory is the newest theoretical point of view that is becoming very popular and can best be described as the antithesis of objective (modern) approaches, such as behaviorism. Postmodernists could personify the phrase "it depends." To postmodernists, for example, the truth depends on the teller's perspective, and what may be true for one person may not necessarily be true for someone else (Sharf, 2008). Feminists often have difficulty with some postmodern views because of the underlying belief that there is no one truth—truth and, therefore, reality is constructed on fluctuating perceptions. Each individual's reality differs somewhat. Subscribing to that concept might mean discarding a belief in the oppression of groups of people based on gender and cultural socialization. Social constructivism, a concept related to postmodernism, suggests that people create meaning in their lives based on their individual truths and that there are "shared meanings that people in a culture or society develop" (Sharf, 2008, p. 18). There is similarity between feminist therapy and many of the social constructivist views (e.g., solution-focused therapy and narrative therapy). The major difference between social constructivism and feminist therapy is that feminist therapy maintains a strongly held value and belief that oppression of groups is not acceptable and will encourage clients to do something about it. However, some postmodern, constructivist models might argue that there is no absolute right or wrong, only what an individual constructs given his or her "reading" of reality at a certain time and place. An example would be women who do not perceive themselves as being oppressed—as that is not their reality, sexism would not be addressed with them in some social constructive approaches, but it would be the focus of conversation in feminist therapy.

2. Restructure the biased components of the theory

Once you have identified the approach you wish to integrate with feminist therapy, you need to look carefully at the theory behind the therapy. What are its theoretical underpinnings, and what implicit or explicit bias is present? As shown, in traditional psychoanalytic theory, bias is often explicit. Women are perceived as damaged men, therapists are viewed as experts who are not to be questioned, and so on. The bias in other theories is less obvious. For instance, in cognitive behavior therapy (CBT) and its variants (rational emotive behavior therapy [REBT], for instance), reasoning based in emotion is perceived as flawed and often damaging. Ellis (1962) writes about rational and irrational thoughts. Yet, we know that in many societies women are the "holders" of emotion and are expected to make reasons and judgments from an ethic of care (Belenky, Clinchey, Golberger, & Tarule, 1986; Gilligan, 1982). Worell and Remer (2003) deal with the problem of labeling client thoughts as distorted or irrational by suggesting renaming the offending words or questioning clients about the origins of their beliefs—whether they were the result of socialization or were just misinformed. For instance, a male client might believe that it is weak to cry. Is that an irrational belief, or is that the way he was socialized? Rather than convince clients of the irrationality of their beliefs that are consistent with their culture, Worell and Remer suggest using a technique such as gender analysis to find the biases and stereotypes that negatively affect clients.

3. Determine the viability of the theory

Not all approaches fit easily into therapists' personal value systems as well as into how they interpret their commitment to various aspects of feminist therapy. There are times, when after examining sources of bias in the theory underlying a therapeutic approach, therapists find that to use that approach with feminist therapy, their value system as well as the values and theoretical basis of feminist therapy are severely compromised. So many changes are needed for the theory to fit into feminist theory and philosophy that it cannot be recognized as the original theory. In that case, the theory is not viable for integration with feminist therapy. In short, at this point, therapists ask themselves whether this is a theory and approach that is right for them and their values. Do they believe that the theory and approach work?

4. Identify compatibility with feminist criteria

Theories being considered for integration need to be carefully evaluated for compatibility with feminist therapy (Worell & Remer, 2003). This is similar to step #3 but differs in that therapists are examining the theoretical underpinning of the therapeutic approach under consideration for integration for compatibility with the theoretical underpinnings of feminist therapy. Step #3 deals with whether therapists perceive the theory as having use in the real world when combined with feminist therapy. To be compatible, the theory should be gender free, multicultural, interactionist (show interaction between the individual and his or her environment), and reflective of lifelong development.

5. Highlight feminist components from the chosen theory and add components from other theories

At this point, it is useful to make a list. List the techniques and principles you value about feminist therapy. Make a list of your own feminist values. Then, make a list of the techniques and principles you value from other theories and approaches. List possible sources of bias. Be aware of these sources of bias as you build your integrated feminist approach to therapy.

Once all the adjustments are made, it is good to go back and reevaluate the integrated theory and approach for compatibility with feminist theory and approach.

THEORETICAL INTEGRATION ●

Theoretical integration is an excellent approach for someone who has made no commitment to a specific theory but who is in fact attracted to two or more theories. Rather than being haphazardly eclectic, the integrative approach is a reasoned and thoughtful combination for counselors prefer to create their own personal theory of counseling. When learning about theories, it is not uncommon for counselors-in-training to choose a different theory as "the one" for them as each new theory is presented in class. Eventually, we have to decide which theory is most compatible with our own beliefs. With the integrative approach, therapists are not limited to choosing one theory. Instead they are encouraged to combine theories to best meet their idea of the best approach.

Halbur and Halbur (2006) recommend several steps to follow to find one's integrative approach to counseling and psychotherapy. The initial steps focus on self-exploration, self-reflection, and self-knowledge. It is extremely important for mental health practitioners to know their values and beliefs about what is important in counseling, in people, in the country and the world, and in life. It is also important for them to know their style, their preferences, and their personality. All of these factors influence not only what they think about how people react to psychological upset and trauma but also how their lives can be made right for them. Once counselors have a good handle on their worldview and view of psychological well-being, they can review theories of counseling and psychotherapy to determine which fits best with those views. It is helpful at this point for counselors to find a mentor from those theoretical orientations who can inspire them and work with them (Halbur & Halbur). It is also helpful to read the original works from psychological and therapeutic theorists and writers. Counselors then test their philosophy, beliefs, and values about the world in real life situations. This is not necessarily with clients but in their real lives and situations. For instance, if therapists believe that oppression causes mental distress, they might monitor how they interact with servers in restaurants and others whom society deems to be in a subordinate role. This self-monitoring supports the idea that values can only truly be called values when one acts on them. Of course, all therapists' values about counseling cannot be addressed in real life, but counselors can get a better idea of how they naturally interact with people and whether their behavior coincides with what they believe. Figure 10.1 illustrates the process of integrating feminist therapy with other schools of thought.

The illustration of the Halbur and Halbur (2006) model that follows uses solution focused therapy (SFT) and feminist therapy. SFT is classified as one of the social constructionist approaches to counseling and psychotherapy. In SFT, the therapist helps to change the client's focus from the problem to the solution (Corey, 2009). The counselor believes that the client holds the answers to his or her own problems and the skills to implement the solution (Archer & McCarthy, 2007). It is the counselor's job to help the client discover what he or she already knows and thus co-create new solutions (Corey, 2009).

Figure 10.1 Halbur and Halbur (2006) theory integration model with feminist therapy

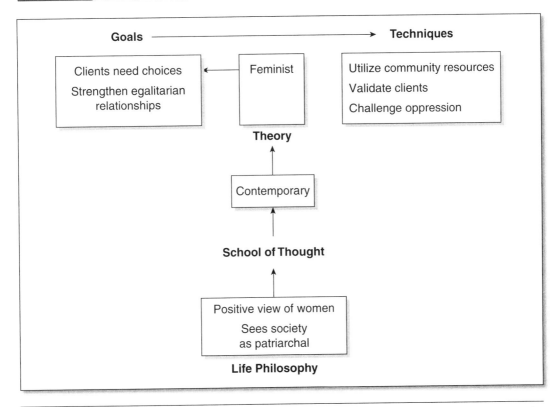

Source: Adapted from *Developing your theoretical orientation in counseling and psychotherapy,* by D. A. Halbur and K. V. Halbur, 2006, p. 75. Copyright 2006 Pearson.

THE CASE OF MORGAN ●

Morgan is a recent graduate in school counseling where her program promoted solution-focused counseling. Although Morgan believes SFT is excellent for the high-school setting where she works, she also finds it frustrating when dealing with the issues of her culturally diverse students and with the adolescents she sees every day. She is interested in integrating some feminist concepts and techniques into her solution-focused practice.

Morgan is attracted to SFT because it is a brief therapy that is positive and based on the experiences the client has already had regarding problem solving. In SFT, (a) the client is the expert on his or her life; (b) it is not necessary to know a great deal about a problem to develop a solution to it; (c) when a client discusses a problem, solutions evolve; (d) when counseling focuses on positives and possibilities, change occurs; (e) change is constant; and (f) right and wrong are relative, not absolute.

SFT is primarily focused on changing client behavior without blaming anyone for the problem. It does not address the power differential between clients and others or socially stereotyped behavior and demonstrates less awareness of issues of hierarchy, power, and abuse of professional privilege than feminist approaches (Dermer, Hemesath, & Russell, 1998).

What follows is Morgan's professional journal as she tries out this new idea.

January 15, 2009

I just got back from a great school counseling conference and got a lot of ideas about working with adolescents with solution-focused counseling. I'm using SFT with my high-school students, but I'm feeling like something is missing by using this strategy with them. I like SFT, but I wonder whether another therapy would be more suited to my needs. I see a lot of adolescent girls who have really ingrained stereotypical ideas of femininity and gender roles that lead to physical fights among them—especially when it involves relationships with boys. I'm thinking some form of feminist therapy might be more appropriate for them.

February 8, 2009

I've just finished reading two books on feminist therapy and several articles by the theorists themselves that stimulated me in some ways, and in other ways they tended to turn me off. I suppose that it is the jargon that is being used that is frustrating me, but I really like a lot of ideas that I have been reading about. There are so many hardships that my students have had to endure that are a reflection of poverty, sexism, and racism, and I would like to take that into account when I work with them. I think it would be empowering to them if I acknowledged those issues and talked about what they can do in that context. I hate ignoring those barriers when my students don't bring them up as issues.

February 25, 2009

I just read a great book on integrating theories, and they said that I should do some self-exploration before trying to choose concepts to use in my own theory. Here are my thoughts.

I believe what I've been taught in school about what counseling is and is not. For example, I work in the schools and have been told that counseling must be time limited. I really can't get to know my clients as individual people. I often don't get more than a few minutes to spend with my clients, and much of my contact with them is about how they can succeed in school. I have also been taught that being a counselor with adolescents, I must also be an authority figure—someone they respect. Although I work with adolescents and believe that they should be respectful of me as an adult, I believe in giving my students respect as well. I don't think that we can be equals, but I want to minimize that up/down relationship. I want them to feel that they have power and that they are their own best source of problem solving. I do adhere to SFT because I have seen it work and know that behavioral change is very important. But, after working with adolescents for a couple of years, many of them have questions that go deeper than just what they do; they want to know where it came from and how they keep it from coming back. So I believe that understanding is important, and if that means revisiting the past, then we should definitely do that.

My supervisors have asked me to write about what I would change about myself, my neighborhood, my city, my state, and my world. Wow. I certainly do enough complaining about all of the above; you'd think I would have that list at my fingertips. Let's see. What I'd like to change about myself is the fact that I cannot seem to stick to a healthy diet and that I cannot stop volunteering for everything. Hmm. Sounds like the same problem—too much of a good thing. I guess I just need to know my limits. What I'd like to change about my neighborhood is that I wish it were more diverse and that people were friendlier toward one another. I would change my city by making transportation more accessible to everyone in the city, hiring more teachers to create positive learning environments for children, and encouraging others to be more environmentally conscious. I'd change the country by ensuring that "liberty and justice for all" was truth and not just for the privileged, that no one goes to bed hungry from poverty, and that we dump the electoral college for the popular vote. I'd change the world by making war obsolete—we'd find less destructive ways to settle disputes, and I would use the resources spent on war to feed the hungry across the world.

I'm supposed to get some themes from these ramblings, and looking over my writing, I can identify themes about caring, justice, and, okay, food. The food part is more of that caring piece, I suppose. I guess how these themes relate to what I want to happen with my clients is the reason I am attracted to feminist therapy because things should change, and if my clients are on the receiving end of injustice, then they need to see what they can do to change that and they should feel empowered to do so.

When I took the quiz on which theories I lean toward, my highest scores were cognitive behavioral, person-centered, and integrative. I'm not surprised with the scores on person-centered counseling (PCC) because of the values I listed above. They fit better with PCC. There weren't any categories for SFT or FT, but I was surprised to see that my score for behavioral therapy was lower than CBT because I like using SFT so much. I think that my concerns about what clients think about what they do may mean that I definitely need to integrate more concepts into my work with clients than what is required for SFT alone. I like that I got such a high score on integrative because it means I'm open to the ideas of other theories and gives me more permission to think about combining SFT and FT.

From my readings on feminist therapy, I see that the items I agreed with most that seem to fall under person-centered therapies were those that fit with some of the beliefs of social feminists and cultural feminists. I believe that to be truly empathic toward my clients, I need to understand their experiences with oppression, especially multiple oppressions. I can also empathize with clients whose expertise and strengths are overlooked because they are feminine characteristics. I guess I was looking at person-centered therapy in a way that required I just had to care about my clients, but now I see that I need to care in a way that is helpful; there is more I need to learn.

The last piece I was supposed to do was to capture myself with a client or with people to see how I actually "live" my philosophy. I found that with clients, I am definitely person-centered. I focus all my attention on them, and it is all about them, I am focused on having an accepting environment for them. What I seem to do is to listen to their stories and empathize, but I always end up asking them what they want to do about it. That's the behavioral part. I don't do challenges to thoughts with clients, but I do it with my friends and family, so I guess I'm more cognitive with them. I think I am creative, too, which is where the integrative stuff comes in because I like to think of different things to do with people and with clients—something out of the box.

I didn't really learn anything new about myself with this process, but it helped to put theory into perspective with who I am. I remember my supervisor always talking about using myself in therapy. I guess that is part of what she was talking about. I can't use myself as an instrument if I don't really know how to implement myself into the theory.

March 5, 2009

I've done a couple of cool things. I went to a one-day seminar on SFT, and I have joined a supervision group for licensure. One of the people in my group is a feminist therapist. This is terrific. She is getting private supervision from a feminist therapist, so now I have a couple of people to talk to about feminist therapy. I also joined an SFT online group for school counselors. The focus in this group is on the challenges counselors have using SFT in their schools. They are more focused on creating solution-focused schools, which

I think is a great idea, but I also think they should include some feminist ideas. I keep putting the plug in for understanding people in the context of their lives and the effects of socialization. A couple of people join in the conversation. It's just like chipping away until you get to the good stuff.

April 10, 2009

Well, it is spring break from school. My goal is to write up my own theory based on all that I have learned so that it meshes with who I am and the clients I work with. This is really the hard part, but I guess I've done most of the work, so I will just focus on the outline that my theories instructor gave us to write the "My Theory" paper. It should include basic concepts, goal of counseling/psychotherapy, role of the counselor, role of the client, techniques, and evaluation. I'm going to try to write on one of these topics every day.

BASIC CONCEPTS ●

1. The personal is political—both society and clients need to change to combat oppression.

2. Oppressed groups' (women; ethnic minorities; gay, lesbian, bisexual, transgender, and questioning [GLBTQ]; and people with disabilities) experiences should be clearly understood, valued, and brought from the margins to the center.

3. Oppression of women/girls transcends culture, and counseling must be gender fair.

4. Clients must be empowered to change themselves and their environment/world.

5. The client is the expert on his/her life own life and is capable of constructing solutions to his/her own problems. At times clients need some assistance in making that happen.

6. Counseling is based on learning, focused on client strengths, creating solutions, and examining and correcting the negative effects of socialization (gender, race/ethnic, and sexual).

7. For counseling/therapy to be effective, the counselor must be genuine, warm, and empathic. The client/counselor relationship should be respectful, trusting, and collaborative.

I think these concepts go together. I may have to tweak them a bit, but this is the foundation of my theory.

April 11, Goals of Counseling

1. Facilitate clients' awareness of the role played by oppression, oppressive socialization, and the internalization of oppression in their problems.

2. To change client views of problems and encourage them to use their own power to effect solutions to those problems.

3. For client and counselor to establish concrete goals and achievable objectives toward problem solution.

My goals may seem a little vague, but I think they should be more general than specific so that I will have a wider range of techniques for achieving the goals.

April 12 Techniques

1. Empathic listening.

2. Gender, power, and cultural analyses.

3. Positive solution talk, reframing, cognitive restructuring, and scaling questions.

4. Miracle Question; use of exceptions to the problem to create the "Miracle."

5. Social action planning.

I think I have listed too many techniques, but all of them may not be necessary with all clients to achieve therapy goals. Furthermore, none of them clash with what I believe about counseling.

April 22, 2009

I tried my new theory on my first client. She is a 15-year-old African American sophomore who was referred for fighting with another girl over a boy. I have had some interaction with this student before—academic planning and changing schedules. I tried to keep in mind my newly recognized philosophy and goals. It was important that I establish a positive counseling relationship with her first. Our first session went very well. I was up front with her about what I was going to do, and I used self-disclosure to help minimize the power differential in our relationship. Since I have been using the skills of solution focused counseling with my clients, that part is pretty much second nature. I've practiced feminist therapy techniques only in conjunction with colleagues in my supervision group. This is my first time talking to a client about the effects of socialization on her behavior. It was important that it be done in a way that was not over her head but also not condescending. I said, "You know, fighting is something people frown on, but it is interesting that when girls fight, it seems to make people even more upset." Just that statement started her talking about her own gender-role socialization. From there we were able to talk about how that socialization affects her behavior. It was very cool. Before she left, we worked out our counseling goals. She seemed eager to come back. I was very pleased. I really think my integrated theory is going to work.

May 30, 2009

School is over next week, so I am winding down. I have finished my work with my first client, and I have a good grasp on what I want to do with my students next year. I liked figuring out who I am as a therapist and how to integrate the theories that seem to work for me and my clients. Feminist therapy helps me address the larger, sociocultural issues with them, whereas SFT allows me to facilitate behavior change. I am surprised how much more exciting working with my students has become. I look forward to the next academic year so I can use this integrated theory—FT and SFT—with more clients.

SUMMARY

It is important that practitioners feel free to use feminist therapy in a way that works best for them and their clients, and the integrative approaches discussed in this chapter were designed to facilitate that goal. It is generally frowned on to incorporate techniques and concepts randomly into one's practice, but feminist theorists expect that in the implementation of the theory, other theories and schools of thought can be very effective. It is hoped that even if counselors choose not to use the approaches presented in this chapter, that some thoughtful, systematic method be used to address client problems.

REFERENCES

Archer, J. J., & McCarthy, C. J. (2007). *Theories of counseling and psychotherapy: Contemporary applications.* Upper Saddle River, NJ: Merrill.

Belenky, M. F., Clinchey, B. M., Golberger, N. R., & Tarule, J. M. (1986). *Women's ways of knowing: Development of self, voice, and mind.* New York: Basic Books.

Corey, G. (2009). *Theory and practice of counseling and psychotherapy* (7th ed.). Belmont, CA: Brooks/ Cole, Cenage Learning.

Corsini, R. J., & Wedding, D. (Eds.) (2007). *Current psychotherapies* (7th ed.). Belmont, CA: Thomson Brooks/Cole.

Dermer, S. B., Hemesath, C. W., & Russell, C. S. (1998). A feminist critique of solution-focused therapy. *American Journal of Family Therapy, 26,* 239–250.

Ellis, A. (1962). *Reason and emotion in psychotherapy.* New York: Lyle Stuart.

Enns, C. Z. (2004). *Feminist theories and feminist psychotherapies: Origins, themes, and diversity* (2nd ed.). New York: Haworth Press.

Fodor, I. G. (1993). A feminist framework for integrative psychotherapy. In G. Stricker & J. R. Gold (Eds.), *Comprehensive handbook of psychotherapy integration* (pp. 217–235). New York: Plenum Press.

Gilligan, C. (1982). *In a different voice: Psychological theory and women's development.* Cambridge, MA: Harvard University Press.

Halbur, D. A., & Halbur, K. V. (2006). *Developing your theoretical orientation in counseling and psychotherapy.* Boston, MA: Pearson.

Herlihy, B., & McCollum, V. (2007.) Feminist theory. In D. Capuzzi & D. R. Gross (Eds.), *Counseling and psychotherapy: Theories and interventions* (4th ed.) (pp. 338–358). Columbus, OH: Merrill/Prentice Hall.

Hill, M., & Ballou, M. (1998). Making therapy feminist: A practice survey. *Women & Therapy, 21*(2), 1–16.

Murdock, N. L. (2004). *Theories of counseling and psychotherapy.* Upper Saddle River, NJ: Pearson.

Porter, N. (2005). Location, location, location: Contributions of contemporary feminist theorists to therapy theory and practice. *Women & Therapy, 28,* 143–160.

Psychotherapy Networker survey. (2007, March/April). The top 10: The most influential therapists of the past quarter-century. *Psychotherapy Networker Magazine,* pp. 24-37. Retrieved May 27, 2010, from http://www.psychotherapynetworker.org/component/content/article/81-2007-marchapril/219-the-top-10

Rogers, C. (1951). *Client-centered therapy.* Boston, MA: Houghton Mifflin.

Sharf, R. S. (2008). *Theories of psychotherapy and counseling: Concepts and cases* (4th ed.). Belmont, CA: Brooks/Cole, Cenage Learning.

Waterhouse, R. L. (1993). Wild women don't have the blues: A feminist critique of "person-centered" counseling and therapy. *Feminism and Psychology, 3,* 55–72.

Worell, J., & Remer, P. (2003). *Feminist perspectives in therapy: Empowering diverse women* (2nd ed.). Hoboken, NJ: John Wiley & Sons.

CHAPTER 11

CRITICAL CASE STUDIES

The purpose of this book is twofold: (a) to introduce mental health professionals and students to the theory and principles of feminist therapy and (b) to provide practitioners and students with solid grounding in and understanding of basic feminist therapy skills. Throughout the book, we have presented clinical case studies that illustrated how and why feminist therapy is indicated and how and why it is the treatment of choice for a wide variety of clients. We wove theory into practice knowing that in feminist therapy the two cannot be separated. One cannot learn effective feminist therapy skills without having a background in and understanding of feminist therapy theory. One must have a worldview that looks at social as well as individual concerns in the lives of clients. This is necessary in order to best conceptualize clients' lives and concerns and to plan client treatment. Feminist therapy is a model of social and individual change. In feminist therapy, these cannot be considered separately.

THE TENETS OF FEMINIST THERAPY ● AND FEMINIST THERAPY SKILLS

One of the most effective ways to become proficient in any form of mental health work is to learn from the experience of others. This is especially true in feminist therapy. As we discussed previously, feminist therapy asks practitioners to be self-reflective and self-aware. We learn from our own stories and the stories of our clients. Unfortunately, we cannot sit down with the readers of this book and discuss our experiences. Instead, we present four critical case studies. We have organized these case studies by the basic tenets of feminist therapy that are presented in Chapter 2.

1. Egalitarian relationship

2. Empowerment: Helping clients acknowledge and use their power in meaningful ways

3. Privileging of women's experiences/privileging the experience of oppressed groups (weighting female/oppressed group and male/dominant group experiences of the world equally)

4. The personal is political: Consideration of the social–political context and the importance of social action

As stated previously, feminist therapy grows out of a philosophical stance: feminism. The tenets of feminist therapy are the basic principles of this philosophy adapted to therapeutic work. The skills presented in this book (including applying ethical principles to the work of feminist therapy) are based on these tenets. In the following case studies, we identify the skills used as the feminist therapy tenet is applied to a case. All these cases are based on the clinical experiences of the authors.

● EGALITARIAN RELATIONSHIP

Client Profile

Client Name: Trey S.

Age: 35

Cultural Background: African American, working-class family of origin

Occupation: Skilled laborer/construction worker

Family History: Single. Close to his family of origin. Parents have been married for 40 years and are in good health. One older sister.

Presenting Problem: Grief and anger concerns.

Trey comes to therapy for grief issues related to the death of his long-term girlfriend Shawna 6 months ago in a car accident. Shawna was on vacation with friends at the time of her death, and Trey was not with her.

Trey recognizes that he misses her and that he feels somewhat guilty because he was not with her when she died. However, until 2 weeks ago, he thought that he had, in his words, moved on. He has begun dating again, he has talked with her family, and so on.

Two weeks ago, Trey became angry with a fellow worker and threatened him while on the job. He has been sleeping late and has not been punctual in arriving at this job. This past week, he yelled at his supervisor and then started to cry. His supervisor gave him the number of the company's Employee Assistance Program (EAP) counselor. Trey knows that his job is on the line. His supervisor said that he is a good man and that he does not want to lose him, but if he does not shape up, he will not be on the crew at the next job.

Lynn, the EAP counselor, meets with Trey the first time. She is a middle-class Jewish woman who was raised in New Jersey by parents who were public-school teachers. She has counseled African American men from Trey's company before and believes she can establish good rapport with him from their first meeting. Trey acknowledges his fear about being in counseling. He does not want to cry again. He fears that if he cries, then he is weak and somehow his life will be ruined.

Lynn acknowledges with Trey that his job is indeed on the line and that there is pressure on him to "succeed" in counseling, but Lynn also acknowledges that Trey is unsure that counseling is what he needs.

Intervention: Lynn asks Trey to talk about his reluctance about counseling. Trey is somewhat belligerent and angry, but Lynn understands his anger—both at the death of his girlfriend and now at having to be in counseling. She recognizes how difficult it is for him as a man to seek help and that it is often even more difficult for African American men if they have been socialized not to trust Whites—especially not with anything personal. Lynn does not dismiss Trey's anger as inappropriate. Lynn suggests to Trey that counseling will be like working on a team at work. Together, they will develop a plan for counseling that includes Trey's thoughts and feelings about his life as well as Lynn's expertise in understanding emotional concerns. Trey will have much input and control into this process, and together they will create and/or discover solutions for Trey (*skill: establishing and maintaining an egalitarian relationship*).

Outcome: At the end of the first session, Trey announced that although he still felt anxious about counseling, he was willing to come back. He stated that he felt that Lynn would work *with him* as a partner in counseling and not as a boss or supervisor telling him what to do or what he was doing wrong. That is, he recognized that the relationship between his counselor Lynn and himself was one of merged expertise and mutual respect, *an egalitarian relationship*.

● EMPOWERMENT

Client Profile

Client Name: Carissa A.

Age: 20

Cultural Background: Anglo/Latina, lower middle class. Raised as a Catholic, although her Anglo father has never joined or attended the Catholic Church.

Profession/Occupation: Full-time college student majoring in fashion merchandising; works part time as a salesperson at a clothing store.

Presenting Problem: Emotional difficulties and lack of self-esteem after an acquaintance rape.

Carissa is a 20-year-old college junior. She seeks counseling at her university counseling center because of emotional difficulties after an acquaintance rape. She reports sleeping poorly, no longer taking pleasure in being around people, and crying frequently. She tells her counselor Shanti that she had slept with this man once before and trusted him. Furthermore, she feels abandoned by her sorority sisters, who have told her that she is overreacting and do not believe that she was raped. Shanti is a third-generation Indian-Canadian American who has been counseling in the center for several years. Living in California, she has learned much about Mexican American culture and has counseled students from mixed cultural backgrounds. She is careful to let Carissa tell her story and include any cultural messages and values that are important to her. Shanti validates Carissa's feelings of anger and hurt and assures her that her feelings indicate that this was indeed rape. Carissa says that the resident assistant she spoke with in her residence hall has urged her to bring her concerns to the university's judicial system. She wants to do this but feels unsupported by her social group and states that she wants the support of a counselor while her case goes through the system.

Shanti talks with Carissa about how she can help Carissa. Mainly, Carissa requests help dealing with her feelings of powerlessness and loss of control. Shanti and Carissa discuss those aspects of Carissa's experience that are currently out of her control. Carissa talks about the rape itself, the postrape emergency room procedure, the way her sorority sisters are treating her, and her own feelings and thoughts. Shanti and Carissa work together to identify Carissa's feelings and to begin to find ways for her to feel less helpless and out of control.

Intervention: The university's women's center is sponsoring a "Take Back the Night" march. Shanti mentions this to Carissa in the context of Carissa's experiences. Carissa likes the idea of some kind of action to end male violence against women, but she is afraid to participate. She tells Shanti that this would announce to world that she was raped, and she is unsure whether she is strong enough to do this. Shanti shares more information about the march with Carissa. Together, they discuss how much participation in this activity might be comfortable for Carissa. Shanti assures Carissa that she has control over her decision to attend or not and that Shanti will not pressure her to attend. Carissa says that she will attend the activities before the march and listen to the speakers. She does so. One of the speakers is an ex-sorority member who talks about how her sorority did not want her to report a sexual assault by a fraternity member. Carissa seeks her out before the march starts and talks to her. They share experiences and march together.

Outcome: In the next session, Shanti mentions that Carissa seems less hopeless and more motivated than in previous session. Carissa tells Shanti that through attending the Take Back the Night activities, she found a new friend with similar experiences and that together they have volunteered to train for the local rape crisis line. Carissa reports that she feels more in control of feelings, thoughts, and behaviors. She reports feeling more hopeful than in previous sessions. *She has been empowered to regain control over her life.*

THE PERSONAL IS THE POLITICAL ●

Client Profile

Client Name: Mary M.

Age: 45

Cultural Background: White, middle class with middle-class family of origin from the Midwest.

Profession: Certified Public Accountant (CPA). Employed full time for the past 10 years.

Family History: Married for 15 years with two children.

Presenting Problem: Depression and low self-esteem.

Mary comes to therapy seeking help with depression and what she terms "self-loathing." She states, "I can't seem to do anything right." Mary tells her therapist that her relationships with her husband, children, family, and friends are caring and sustaining. She is a CPA at a large national firm and quite pleased to work in this particular firm. She does not understand why she has become depressed and feels poorly about herself and her ability to function.

Lindsey, her therapist, is also White, but she is in her mid-thirties and comes from a slightly higher socioeconomic background. She and Mary spent time talking about their similarities and differences, and both agreed that this relationship was workable. Lindsey spends a few sessions exploring Mary's feelings and thoughts about herself and her world. Lindsey comes to understand the context of Mary's life. Mary seems satisfied and sure of herself in her social and family life. However, Mary cannot talk about work without crying slightly or her voice catching in anger. The therapist acknowledges that a major part of Mary's identity is being a CPA and a professional. Both Mary and Lindsey acknowledge that the source of Mary's distress is what is happening to her at work. Mary states that she feels invisible and that her ideas are not listened to in meetings. Employees who have been with the organization for less time than she has seem to have more voice and input. Mary focuses on her real and imagined deficiencies in attempting to understand this situation and asks Lindsey to tell her what is wrong and how to correct the problem. Lindsey discusses with Mary why it is important that she have input into the therapeutic process. She explains that they are a team and will solve Mary's concerns together. Mary learns that she is not invisible in the counseling session and that her ideas are valued. Lindsey then talks with Mary about Mary's skills and the satisfaction she receives from being in her profession. She helps Mary take pride in accomplishments she has already made. Then, they begin to discuss Mary's current professional position and the environment in which she works. Mary states that she feels "out of the loop" in office meetings. She does not get the perks and promotions that her colleagues receive. She does not understand this because she recognizes herself as competent in her knowledge and ability. She does come to understand how working in an environment that does not appreciate her skills and ability can lead to low self-esteem.

Intervention: Mary is asked to keep a journal of her work experiences especially with regard to meetings and interactions with colleagues. In addition, Mary is asked to notice how often women speak in meetings and what they speak about. Mary returns to Lindsey's office and notes that in meetings, very few women spoke during the meeting but did speak afterward to individuals. The only woman who spoke repeatedly is an unmarried woman who spends twice as many hours at the office as any other employee. Mary also noted that most of the clerical staff in the office are women and that many of the male professionals seem to treat female professionals as if they are clerical staff.

Outcome: With Lindsey's help, Mary comes to understand the etiology of her distress as grounded in deeply ingrained cultural stereotypes about male and female roles in the workplace. She does not need to take personal responsibility for her invisibility in the workplace. It is not that she is not trying hard enough but rather that the personal (her feelings of depression and low self-esteem) is political (gender bias and ingrained stereotypes in her workplace that maintain the political status quo).

VALUING THE FEMALE EXPERIENCE/PUTTING ● FEMALE EXPERIENCE IN THE CENTER

Client Profile

Client Name: Sara R.

Age: 51

Cultural Background: White, middle class. Working-class family of origin. Client is a first-generation college graduate.

Profession/Occupation: High-school principal, 20 years of professional experience.

Presenting Concern: Lack of motivation, general dissatisfaction with her life, existential issues, unhappiness.

Sara comes to counseling citing a lack of motivation and low-level depression. She tells Eric, her therapist, that her father died at age 53 around this time of the year. Sara has been thinking about his early death and has begun to wonder about her own mortality. She is 51 and thinks about what she would do with the next 2 years of her life if she knew she would only live until 53.

Eric is a feminist therapist, and Sara is surprised to hear him say that. She also thinks that his therapeutic orientation is a perfect fit for what she is going through in her life. Sara shares with Eric that she is a well-respected professional woman who has done very well in her career; she is well respected by colleagues and those in her profession. She tells him that she enjoys her job and finds great satisfaction from it. She has a good social life and supportive friends. When asked about intimate relationships, Sara states that she has been married for 20 years to her second husband. They have one adult child. Eric remarks that Sara seems fairly content, and Sara reports she actually sought counseling because she realized that if she only had 2 years left to live, she would not want to spend it with her husband. Sara begins to cry. Eric sits with her. She states that she is mainly upset about her own behavior. She has known for some time that the relationship did not give her what she wanted but did not have "the guts" to leave. She states, "I should have known, I should have been brave enough to just do it and live on my own. I shouldn't have needed him or that relationship and now I have wasted 15 years of my life."

Intervention: Eric and Sara explore Sara's relationship with Billy, her husband. They talk about how the relationship has slowly eroded. Eric gently confronts Sara about her valuing autonomy and "bravery" over caring for Billy and her daughter. They talk about maintaining the "okay" relationship so that Sara's daughter's environment was stable. They discuss some of the positives in the relationship.

Outcome: Sara leaves therapy with an understanding of the importance of the task that she did for 20 years in keeping the relationship and the family together. She understands that it was neither about bravery nor about not being independent enough but rather about valuing the connections between people. This way of viewing the world and our work in it was, in the past, primarily a female way of being and was dismissed or viewed as deficient by psychology and counseling. By putting this experience in context and valuing it, Eric and Sara have made a female experience central in Sara's understanding of her thoughts, feelings, and behaviors.

● CRITICAL CASE STUDIES AND ETHICAL IMPLICATIONS

Three of the case studies presented in this chapter are now considered for their ethical implications, counselor/therapist responses, and resolutions of ethical concerns/dilemmas. As you read the cases with the slightly amended information, think about the ethical decision-making models discussed in Chapter 3 as well as application to the ethical code of your primary professional association and the Feminist Therapy Institute (FTI) Code of Ethics (1999).

Client Profile

Client Name: Trey S.

Age: 35

Occupation: Skilled laborer/construction worker.

Family History: Single. Close to his family of origin. Parents have been married for 40 years and are in good health. One older sister.

Presenting Problem: Grief and anger concerns.

Trey comes to therapy for grief issues related to the death of his long-term girlfriend Shawna 6 months ago in a car accident. Shawna was on vacation with friends at the time of her death, and Trey was not with her. Trey recognizes that he misses her and that he feels somewhat guilty because he was not with her when she died. However, until 2 weeks ago, he thought that he had, in his words, moved on. He has begun dating again, he has talked with her family, and so on.

Two weeks ago, Trey became angry with a fellow worker and threatened him while on the job. He has been sleeping late and has not been punctual in arriving at this job. This past week, he yelled at his supervisor and then started to cry. His supervisor gave him the number of the company's Employee Assistance Program (EAP) counselor. Trey knows that his job is on the line. His supervisor said that he is a good man and he does not want to lose him, but if he does not shape up, he will not be on the crew at the next job.

The EAP counselor Lynn meets with Trey the first time. Trey acknowledges his fear about being in counseling. He does not want to cry again. He fears that if he cries, then he is weak and somehow his life will be ruined.

Lynn acknowledges with Trey that his job is indeed on the line and that there is pressure on him to "succeed" in counseling, but Lynn also acknowledges that Trey is unsure that counseling is what he needs.

Ethical Dilemma: Lynn is hired by the company. Part of the agreement between her agency and the contract with Trey's company is that she will submit a final report of Trey's progress and suitability for his position, if asked. Lynn believes that if Trey knows this limitation of confidentiality, then he will either quit counseling (which she believes will be effective) or will not fully participate in the counseling process, thereby ensuring that she does not submit a positive progress report.

Resolution: As a feminist therapist, Lynn employs the FTI Code of Ethics as additive to the ethical code of her primary professional association. The FTI speaks to power differentials in the relationship and overlapping relationships. Both are issues in this situation. As a feminist therapist, Lynn trusts that her client is an expert in his own life and needs. She recognizes that to be an ethical feminist therapist, she will explain to Trey what it means that she is an EAP counselor and what her responsibilities are to the company. She also explains to him how and why she believes that therapy will be useful for him. Together, Trey and Lynn discuss what the limits of confidentiality are in this case. Lynn states that her final report to the human resources department will be a collaborative effort between the two of them if he continues in therapy with her; however, Lynn also presents Trey with the option to see a counselor not affiliated with the corporation and offers to facilitate this referral. When he reports that there are financial difficulties, she tells him that she can work with him to find a counselor who has a need-based sliding scale. Trey reports that he would like to work with Lynn and that he trusts her based on her honesty.

Client Profile

Client Name: Carissa A.

Age: 20

Profession/Occupation: Full-time college student majoring in fashion merchandising. Works part time as a salesperson at a clothing store.

Presenting Problem: Emotional difficulties and lack of self-esteem after an acquaintance rape.

Carissa is a 20-year-old college junior. She seeks counseling at her university counseling center because of emotional difficulties following an acquaintance rape. She reports sleeping poorly, no longer taking pleasure in being around people and crying frequently. She tells her counselor, Shanti, that she had slept with this man once before and trusted him. Furthermore, she feels abandoned by her sorority sisters, who have told her that she is over-reacting and do not believe that she was raped. Shanti validates Carissa's feelings of anger and hurt and assures her that her feelings indicate that this was indeed rape. Carissa says that her resident assistant has urged her to pursue the issues and bring her concerns to university's judicial system. She wants to do this but feels unsupported by her social group and states that she wants the support of a counselor while her case goes through the system.

Ethical Dilemma: After speaking with Shanti, Carissa feels validated and believed. Shanti refers Carissa to the local rape crisis center for follow-up medical attention and legal information. Carissa then learns that she is pregnant. She tells Shanti that, through the rape crisis center contacts, she has set up an appointment to terminate the pregnancy. Shanti's belief is that abortion is the taking of a human life.

Resolution: As a feminist therapist, Shanti must choose between her beliefs and the beliefs and desires of her client. The FTI Code of Ethics addresses issues of therapist accountability to herself and her client. The FTI also asks therapists to focus on understanding cultural diversity and oppression. First, Shanti consults with a trusted clinical colleague about the dilemma. She discusses the issues not only in terms of her own belief system but also with a focus on the cultural context of rape and pregnancy for Carissa. Next, she seeks out additional information about rape-related pregnancy through readings and/or further consultations with experts in the area. In session with Carissa, she helps Carissa clarify her beliefs. When Carissa stands firm on her decision, Shanti states that she respects Carissa but cannot help her further with this particular issue and, after consultation with her colleague and the rape crisis center, makes the referral to another therapist. Shanti checks in with Carissa to make sure she understands the difference between her belief that Carissa's actions are wrong and her caring for Carissa. She is honest with Carissa about why she cannot work with her *at this time on this issue.* She strives not to use her therapeutic power to change Carissa's decision.

Client Profile

Name: Mary M.

Age: 45

Profession: Certified Public Accountant (CPA). Employed full time for the past 10 years.

Family History: Married for 15 years with two children.

Presenting Problem: Depression and low self-esteem.

Mary comes to therapy seeking help with depression and what she terms "self-loathing." She states, "I can't seem to do anything right." Mary tells her therapist that her relationships with her husband, children, family, and friends are caring and sustaining. She is a CPA at a large national firm and quite pleased to work in this particular firm. She does not understand why she has become depressed and feels poorly about herself and her ability to function.

Lindsey, her therapist, spends a few sessions exploring Mary's feelings and thoughts about herself and her world. Lindsey comes to understand the context of Mary's life. Mary seems satisfied and sure of herself in her social and family life. However, Mary cannot talk about work without crying slightly or her voice catching in anger. The therapist acknowledges that a major part of Mary's identity is being a CPA and a professional. Between Mary and Lindsey, they acknowledge that the source of Mary's distress is what is happening to her at work. Mary states that she feels invisible and that her ideas are not listened to in meetings. Employees who have been with the organization for less time than she has seem to have more voice and input. Mary focuses on her real and imagined deficiencies in attempting to understand this situation and asks Lindsey to tell her what is wrong and how to correct the problem. Lindsey discusses with Mary why it is important that she have input into the therapeutic process. She explains that they are a team that will solve Mary's concerns together. Mary learns that she is not invisible in the counseling session and her ideas are valued. Lindsey then talks with Mary about Mary's skills and the satisfaction she receives from being in her profession. She helps Mary take pride in accomplishments she has already made. Then they begin to discuss Mary's current professional position and the environment in which she works. Mary states that she feels "out of the loop" in office meetings. She does not get the perks and promotions that her colleagues receive. She does not understand this because she views herself as competent in her knowledge and ability. She does come to understand how working in an environment that does not appreciate her skills and ability can lead to low self-esteem.

Ethical Dilemma: By the fourth session, Lindsey recognizes that Mary is one of the clients she looks forward to meeting with. Mary is a bright, well-informed professional woman of a similar age as Lindsey. Lindsey recognizes Mary's struggles as she has had similar issues in her career path. Mary makes a great deal of progress in both self-awareness and assertion in her work environment. Counseling is successfully ended after 10 sessions. After a month has gone by, they run into each other at a local coffee shop. Mary joins Lindsey at her table and they begin to talk about common interests.

Ethical Dilemma: Feminist therapists recognize that there are many overlapping relationships in the lives of their clients. Furthermore, feminist therapists recognize that therapeutic relationships are real relationships. The FTI Code of Ethics states the following:

> Feminist therapists recognize the complexities and conflicting priorities inherent in multiple or overlapping relationships. The therapist accepts responsibility for monitoring such relationships to prevent potential abuse of or harm to the client (FTI, 1999, p. IIIA).

The FTI also advocates that feminist therapists self-monitor public and private statements and comments and recognizes that the client's confidentiality is primary. While having coffee with Mary, Lindsey is aware that she is still accountable for not causing harm to or abusing clients, even if the relationship has ended. She remains aware that she is not Mary's friend, although they do not have to avoid each other at the coffee shop. Additionally, Lindsey wonders what was so attractive about her relationship with Mary and why she was willing, on a personal level, to engage in an acquaintanceship with Mary after therapy had ended. She recognizes and acknowledges a lack in her life from not having close relationships with other successful professional women. She knows that she does not want to "use" Mary for this purpose because of the inherent power imbalance within their prior therapeutic relationship. Lindsey seeks out a support and consultation group for female therapists that also includes social interaction. Mary and Lindsey continue to run into each other occasionally and even have coffee together if time and circumstances permit, but Lindsey remains aware that she is always in a position of potential power over Mary having once been her therapist. She does not seek to have her own needs met by her interactions with Mary.

CASE STUDIES FOR DISCUSSION

Now that we have finished learning (a) ways of being a feminist therapist, (b) feminist therapy theory, (c) feminist therapy ethics, and (d) the skills and techniques of feminist therapy, it is time to refine our knowledge and skill.

Presented next are case studies that cover a wide variety of areas and a format (Table 11.1) for applying feminist therapy techniques. Following this we offer a format for developing your own case studies for feminist therapy. This is also a model for how to approach clients from a feminist perspective.

1. Jim is seeking counseling on the advice of his girlfriend Sue. He states that throughout their 2-year relationship, there have been frequent arguments about "minor" issues. This happens on the average of once a week. He reports that Sue is responsible for beginning the arguments by "picking on" him. Until last week, the arguments were limited to yelling and door slamming by both of them. However, Jim states that in their last "fight" he became so angry he grabbed Sue, shook her, and left bruises on her shoulder. Jim states that Sue has told him he needs counseling to deal with his temper and tendency toward violence. She has made this a condition of staying in a relationship with him.

2. Alice has been referred for a possible eating disorder. She comes to the session in loose, oversized clothes but immaculately groomed. She seems small for her height, but it is difficult to tell. She does not make eye contact with you throughout the initial session. She states

that she is in your office because other people are concerned about her and have told her to come to counseling. When asked how she feels about this, she just shrugs and says nothing. Her scores on a standard instrument for depression (The Beck Depression Inventory) indicate a moderately high level of depression. She has endorsed the item that indicates that she thinks about suicide. However, she denies depression.

3. Ellen is a 25-year-old White, Anglo-Saxon Protestant female graduate student referred for "anxiety attacks." When she has a paper to submit or an upcoming examination, she cannot concentrate and experiences her heart as "racing." She has left classrooms feeling that she cannot breathe. Ellen is certain that her work is below average and that everyone will find out that she does not belong in a doctoral program. She finds she is particularly anxious with a demanding and critical African American male professor.

Ellen grew up in a predominantly White middle-class neighborhood in the Midwest U.S. and regularly attended the Methodist church in her town. Her religious and cultural teachings emphasized the importance of the nuclear family and the roles of women and men as parents. Ellen has two older brothers who are very successful professionals and who seem proud of her achievements even though they teased her about not being married and being a "brainiac." Interpersonally, Ellen states that she is heterosexual and currently not involved in a romantic relationship of any kind. She admits sometimes feeling like she is a failure all around—with a career in jeopardy of never starting and being over 25 and not married with no prospects.

4. Rob, a student in high school, is the youngest in a family of two children. He prefers reading and playing games to sports and social activities. He has good relationships with several teachers, many of whom comment on his intellectual curiosity and quiet sense of humor. He reports that he has two close male friends with whom he plays games. Recently, his grades have dropped in three of his classes. He has started skipping class. This behavior is inconsistent with his previous commitment to school work. During counseling, he states that nothing is wrong that he cannot handle by himself.

5. Jill is referred to counseling/therapy by a local hospital after making a suicide attempt consisting of a bottle of Tylenol and a bottle of wine. She received medical treatment and spent 2 days in the hospital for psychiatric evaluation. She was released on the condition that she seek and continue in counseling. She reports continuing hopelessness. She has trouble believing that others care about her. However, she states that she would not make another attempt because it would cause others too much pain and she has already hurt them enough.

6. Bertha is a 40-year-old married African American woman with two children (ages 7 and 13). She has been married for 15 years. Because she has been depressed for more than months, her husband Charles insisted that she get counseling.

Four months ago, the family moved to a medium-sized city in the Southeast from the metropolitan Northeast. Six months prior to this, Bertha's husband lost his job, and relocation was necessary for him to secure employment equal to his former position. Bertha, however, has spent the past 4 months searching for a job with no success. During the life of their marriage, it has always been necessary for both Bertha and Charles to work to maintain their middle class lifestyle. Bertha states that she has a high school education and graduated with fairly good grades. Furthermore, she completed several courses in office skills at a community college in the Northeast. She has worked as a receptionist, a secretary, and an administrative assistant. She thought that given her good recommendations, high-level skills, and wide variety of experiences, she would have no trouble finding a job after the move. This has not been the case.

She tells her counselor that all she does now is sit around all day, wait for the children to come home from school, and worry about the bills. Bertha admits to being fearful of returning to the poverty she experienced as a child. She does not wish this for her children. She cannot understand why she cannot get a job. She wonders aloud if it might be race related.

7. Latisha and Kareem come to you requesting couples counseling. They have dated for 3 years and have been engaged for the past 6 months. Prior to last week, they had lived together for 4 months. Kareem is now staying with a friend. Both are young professionals; Kareem just finished dental school, and Latisha is an account manager for regional sales corporation. Their stated joint goal for counseling is to communicate better. They state that they do not wish to end the relationship.

Latisha states that Kareem does not take their relationship seriously. She views it as an exclusive relationship and that, as his fiancée, she has certain rights regarding his other relationships. Kareem states that Latisha does not understand his responsibilities and stresses as the junior member of his office and that she does not understand that he has to go out and "relax" with his friends without her. Latisha's states that most of Kareem's friends are women and that this makes her feel insecure. In addition, she feels that he is somehow embarrassed by her and does not want her to be around his friends.

Currently, Latisha is better paid for her work and expresses being happy in her chosen profession and her job. Although Kareem is a dentist, he consistently expressed doubts about his career goals while in dental school and often struggled with his studies. Kareem is the middle child from a middle-class suburban family. Both his parents are teachers; however, he is the first one in his family to obtain an advanced professional degree. Latisha is an only child. Prior to college, she spent most her life in a large urban environment. Her mother did not go to college but holds a good job in city government.

Table 11.1	Format for Discussion of Case Studies

1. How would a *feminist therapist/counselor* approach this case?

   a. What are the major issues this client is facing? How will they be addressed in counseling/therapy?
   b. What would be the goal(s) for this client?
   c. What would the relationship be like? How would this be achieved?
   d. What diversity issues should be considered? Where and how do these manifest themselves?

2. What additional information would you need from this client?

   a. How is your knowing this information going to help the client?
   b. How does this information fit into a *feminist framework?*

3. Briefly discuss the following factors in this client's life and how they might be impacting the client's current life situations and problems:

   a. Gender role
      • How does U.S. culture define this person's role as a woman or a man? What are the expectations for action?
      • How does this role influence relationships with others and their gender roles?
   b. Socioeconomic status
   c. Class and racial/ethnic background
   d. Family issues (and how gender might be important in a family)

4. What areas of strength would you draw on in work with this client?

5. In what areas does the client need further empowerment?

6. What techniques and skills, compatible with feminist therapy/counseling, would you use when working with this client/couple?

YOUR OWN CASE STUDY

Who is the person seeking help?

_____

_____

_____

_____

_____

Why is s/he seeking help at this particular point in her/his life?

_____

_____

_____

_____

_____

What is the problem?

_____

_____

_____

_____

_____

What is the context of the problem? (cultural/social/environmental/family concerns, etc.)

_____

_____

_____

_____

_____

REFERENCE

Feminist Therapy Institute. (1999). *Feminist therapy code of ethics* (revised). Retrieved November 13, 2009, from www.feminist-therapy-institute.org

NAME INDEX

SUBJECT INDEX

ABOUT THE AUTHORS

Kathy M. Evans is an associate professor at the University of South Carolina. She is currently serving as the Program Coordinator of the Counselor Education program. After 7 years as a Master's level counselor in New York and Maryland, Dr. Evans returned to Pennsylvania, discovered feminist therapy, and received her doctorate in counseling psychology from The Pennsylvania State University. The week after graduating she began her career as a counselor educator—a career that she has enjoyed for 21 years. Kathy is a National Certified Counselor and has been licensed as a Licensed Professional Counselor and as a licensed psychologist. She teaches for both the entry-level and doctoral-level counseling degree programs, where she emphasizes the acquisition of social justice skills, multicultural competence in counseling and supervision, and feminist process. Dr. Evans's research interests and publications focus on multicultural, career, and feminist issues. She has made hundreds of presentations on those topics internationally, nationally, and locally. Dr. Evans has been President of the Southern Association for Counselor Education and Supervision and Secretary of Chi Sigma Iota Honor Society International. She thoroughly enjoys advocating for and mentoring women in the academy. She receives greatest satisfaction when fulfilling her cultural obligation to "give back" by mentoring African American women like herself. Personally, Kathy likes to work hard and play hard. When she isn't teaching, writing, or doing research, she is involved in competitive dog sports with her poodles, reading mystery and adventure novels, walking her standard poodle, doing cycling classes, or traveling.

Elizabeth Ann Kincade is a feminist therapist who has counseled and taught in counseling and psychology for more than 20 years. She has taught online and face to face. Classes taught include "Psychology of Women" and various group counseling theory and practice courses. She is an associate professor at Indiana University of Pennsylvania, where she is a clinician and faculty member in the Counseling Center. She has run an ongoing women's group for the past 18 years, has served as a feminist supervisor for numerous trainees, and has served as Chair of her union's Gender Issues Committee. In the Counseling Center, she has served as Chair of the Department, Coordinator of Outreach and Consultation, and Coordinator of Group Programs. Her research interests are in feminist therapy and process, social justice perspectives, ethical concerns, and group dynamics. With her presentation partners, Drs. Evans and Seem, she has presented numerous times on the theory and practice of feminist therapy. With her writing partners, Drs. Evans, Seem, and Marbley, she has published the article "Feminist Therapy: Lessons From the Past and Hope for the Future." Dr. Kincade is a licensed psychologist. She received her Ph.D. in counseling psychology from The Pennsylvania State University in 1989. On a personal level, she is originally from the Boston area, and although she has lived in western Pennsylvania for 20 years, she still considers the Northshore of Massachusetts home. She currently lives with her male significant other and a large, vocal, black cat in a small house in the woods.

Susan Rachael Seem is currently a counselor educator and has practiced as a counselor in community and mental health agencies and college counseling centers for 13 years. Feminism informs her work as an educator and counselor. She is a professor at The College at Brockport, The State University of New York. Currently, she is Assistant to the Provost for Graduate Education and Scholarship. Feminism influences her teaching and clinical supervision. She has taught courses such as counseling theories, group practice, practicum, supervision, and internship and has provided feminist supervision since 1994. She has been a leader for several professional organizations, most notably, Chair of the Council for Accreditation of Counseling and Related Educational Programs (CACREP). She has also served as a member of the American Counseling Association's Human Rights Committee, and as a board trustee and CACREP representative for The Association for Lesbian, Gay, Bisexual and Transgendered Issues in Counseling. Her research interests are in feminist therapy, gender bias in clinical judgment, feminist diagnosis, and addressing marginalized group concerns in counseling in terms of both individual and social change. With Drs. Evans and Kincade and her colleague Dr. Tom Hernandez, she has presented numerous times and has authored publications on feminist therapy and theory. Dr. Seem is a licensed mental health counselor, a national certified counselor, and an approved clinical supervisor. She received her Ph.D. in counseling psychology from The Pennsylvania State University in 1991. She has one grandson, Kayden, and enjoys the fall, walking, and quilting.

Supporting researchers for more than 40 years

Research methods have always been at the core of SAGE's publishing program. Founder Sara Miller McCune published SAGE's first methods book, *Public Policy Evaluation*, in 1970. Soon after, she launched the *Quantitative Applications in the Social Sciences* series—affectionately known as the "little green books."

Always at the forefront of developing and supporting new approaches in methods, SAGE published early groundbreaking texts and journals in the fields of qualitative methods and evaluation.

Today, more than 40 years and two million little green books later, SAGE continues to push the boundaries with a growing list of more than 1,200 research methods books, journals, and reference works across the social, behavioral, and health sciences. Its imprints—Pine Forge Press, home of innovative textbooks in sociology, and Corwin, publisher of PreK–12 resources for teachers and administrators—broaden SAGE's range of offerings in methods. SAGE further extended its impact in 2008 when it acquired CQ Press and its best-selling and highly respected political science research methods list.

From qualitative, quantitative, and mixed methods to evaluation, SAGE is the essential resource for academics and practitioners looking for the latest methods by leading scholars.

For more information, visit **www.sagepub.com**.